Additional Praise for

Firebrands
Building Brand Loyalty in the Internet Age

"Michael Moon is one of the most important visionaries of the e-era. He has a unique ability to put a useful structure onto seemingly endless digital noise. His charts and diagrams will help the CIO convince the CEO and CFO to actively invest in eBusiness."
— Mitch Krayton, President, Digital Resources, Valencia, CA

"*Firebrands* provides a clear, concise definition of branding, combined with a firebrand positioning model. This is serious, invaluable reading for marketing professionals responsible for creating and building brands in the new, trust network-centric digital world."
— Todd Garrett, Senior VP and Chief Information Officer (Retired), Procter & Gamble

"Moon delivers heavy ammunition for my e-business planning; powerful ideas, clear and well supported practices."
— Lisa Z. Wellman, President and CEO, DeepCanyon.com, Seattle, WA

"Michael Moon provides a clear, well-lit path into the future of branding and trust networks. It shows how to drive your business brand into the e-world. Throw the other books away; this is the one."
— Phil Stewart, CEO, CD Factory, Kansas City

D0200975

Steve,

, Gut success!

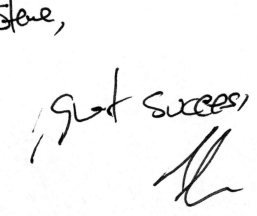

Firebrands
Building Brand Loyalty in the Internet Age

Firebrands

Building Brand Loyalty in the Internet Age

Michael Moon
with Doug Millison

Osborne/**McGraw-Hill**

Berkeley ▶ New York ▶ St. Louis ▶ San Francisco ▶ Auckland ▶ Bogotá
Hamburg ▶ London ▶ Madrid ▶ Mexico City ▶ Milan ▶ Montreal ▶ New Delhi
Panama City ▶ Paris ▶ São Paulo ▶ Singapore ▶ Sydney ▶ Tokyo ▶ Toronto

Firebrands: Building Brand Loyalty in the Internet Age
by Michael Moon with Doug Millison

Osborne/**McGraw-Hill**
2600 Tenth Street
Berkeley, California 94710
U.S.A.

For information on translations or book distributors outside the U.S.A., or
to arrange bulk purchase discounts for sales promotions, premiums, or
fund-raisers, please contact Osborne/**McGraw-Hill** at the above address.

Printed in the United States of America

34567890DOC DOC0987654

ISBN: 0-07-212449-0

Contents

Acknowledgments

I want to thank the many individuals who provided help and support in the writing of this book.

As much of this book evolves from my work with GISTICS Inc., I acknowledge company co-founder James L. Byram for his steadfast persistence in asking the right, essential questions and for teaching me how to "listen with data."

I thank Jeff Martin, now executive vice president at Beatnik, Inc., for his penetrating insights into brands and their fundamental role in the Networked Economy, as well as for his generous support and encouragement.

Charles Caldwell, vice president of GISTICS took over many of the company's operational responsibilities, enabling me to take the time to write this book.

Garry Hare, Ph.D., executive vice president of IntoNet.com, gave me a graceful and well-timed nudge to "get on with it" and stop talking about this book.

Laurie Milburn provided generous personal support and inspiration as well as the pivotal introduction to my publisher and, coincidentally, neighbor, Brandon Nordin of Osborne/McGraw-Hill.

David Dunning, who has worked with GISTICS for the past two years as a long-term contractor through Aquent Partners, provided invaluable assistance in making the graphic illustrations crisp, succinct communications, thus earning his title, "Director, Cheese Abatement."

Tony Barrett, Director, Sales, Apple Computer, encouraged me to soar with eagles and let the crows squawk all they want.

The 241 members of the Beta Test Pilots Association who downloaded, read, and critiqued the draft in its making, including Diane Tedesco, Phil Stewart, Alexander Felsenberg, Matina Koronis, and Mike Castle.

My writing partnership with Doug Millison began early in 1993 when we collaborated on the development of the seminal magazine for interactive multimedia developers and designers that he co-founded and edited, *Morph's Outpost on the Digital Frontier*. Over the years, Doug has helped write and edit many GISTICS publications, including the above-mentioned *Strategies for Building Digital Brands*, and our current *Media Asset Management Market Report*

1999. Doug helped to develop the original outline for this book, and he played a key role earlier this year in re-shaping the outline to meet the requirements of the current publisher and the market. As co-writer, he has helped me not only to structure this complicated mass of material for the general reader, but also has excelled at parsing those ideas into simple, straightforward prose.

—Michael Moon
July 2000

Preface

Why I Wrote This Book and Why You Should Read It

What do Jeff Bezos of Amazon.com, Pierre Omidyar of eBay, Steve Case of AOL, John Chambers of Cisco Systems, Peihong Chen of BroadVision, and Steve Jobs of Apple Computer know about how to succeed in the Networked Economy that your competitors will soon use against you, if they haven't done so already?

They know the power of trust networks and have deployed information technology to harness this power to build their brands. In the process, they have created hundreds of billions of dollars in new shareholder wealth.

Companies have committed themselves to the pursuit of eBusiness and all things Internet-related. They move forward at breakneck speed (and spend money at a similar clip), as if through a dark tunnel with no horizon or guideposts to mark their progress. They assume that their traditional notions of business and brands will lead them to the success they desire. Some have begun to envision how they might succeed through a dot.com strategy. Others already derive revenues or reduce costs or streamline operations with an online presence—a light at the end of the tunnel.

I hope this book will convince you that the light at the end of the tunnel comes from a bullet train speeding towards you at 200 miles per hour.

This bullet train represents the power of a new economic and political force in the Networked Economy: trust networks. Customers, investors, trade partners, staff, and the public at large, organized and mobilized through the Internet, now compel all institutions, including businesses, to do the right thing in order to earn and keep their trust.

The emergence of trust networks mean that businesses must re-engineer the core processes that they use to find and serve customers. In the past, companies could address brands and brand building as a set of communications activities that paralleled the real work of the firm—designing, making, and delivering products and services. In the Networked Economy, these parallel tracks converge. Value creation and storytelling merge in *firebranding*, our term for brand building in the Networked Economy.

This book explains what happens to the relationship between buyer and seller in the Networked Economy (the businesses that find and serve customers using the Internet and an array of related information technologies) and the impact these changes have on brands and brand building.

Why I Wrote This Book

This book lets me pull together three strands of my work and personal interests over the past 30 years: the impact that information technology has on individuals and the organizations that employ them; the dynamics of individual psychological development and interpersonal relationships; and how businesses in a free-market society can act as powerful agents for positive change and social justice.

In 1979, I put myself at the epicenter of an earthquake that would, over the next few years, shake the foundations of business and society. That year, Bill Lohse of Imsai Manufacturing hired me to sell a new, low-cost microcomputer to a burgeoning network of dealers with funny names like Byte Shoppe, Computer Factory, and Bits 'n' Bytes. On my first day of work I met founder, president, and CEO, Bill Millard who had only recently founded a sister company, Computerland—the first international chain of computer retail stores that later became Vanstar.

Just down the hall, I met vice president of marketing, Seymour Rubenstein, who left a few months later to launch a software company, Micro Pro International, later renamed after its flagship word processing software application, WordStar. Later, I would meet Gordon Stitt, one of Imsai's hot-shot engineers who went on to create high-speed modems and other telecommunications and network technology companies. Buried in one of the tiny offices, I came across Mitch Waite, who would eventually develop a technical book publishing empire, The Waite Group, now part of Macmillan USA.

Over the next couple of years, on sales calls and at trade shows and user group meetings, I met most of the people responsible for putting personal computers on desktops everywhere. I met Bill Gates back when he sold his products on paper tape, audiocassettes, and eight-inch floppy disks. I met Allen Cooper and David Carlick of a software company called Structured Systems. Cooper went on to become a user interface guru, while Carlick set trends in high tech and dot.com branding. I met Scott McNealy, a freshly minted MBA out of Stanford University, who at the time was struggling to sell multiuser microcomputer systems at Onyx Microsystems, and would later go on to launch Sun Microsystems.

In the early 1980s, while working at two prominent Silicon Valley advertising and marketing firms—Regis McKenna and Lutat & Battey Advertising—I met more industry pioneers: Steve Jobs and Mike Markulla of Apple; Gordon Moore, Andy Grove, and Dave House of Intel; Allen Shugart, Finis Connor, and Syed Iftikar of Seagate; Dave Jackson and Ron Conway of Altos Computers; and many more.

I had the unique opportunity to study two endlessly fascinating developments: how entrepreneurs use new technologies to create new markets, and how branding, marketing, and storytelling created demand for these new technologies. More importantly, when I moved on to work in market research (first with a small but prominent publisher of technical reports, Electronic Trend Publications, and later, in 1987, co-founding my present firm, GISTICS Inc., with James L. Byram), I had a chance to study customer responses to the introduction of successive waves of computer hardware and software.

Since 1987, I have conducted over 50 primary research projects, collated over 30,000 surveys, and personally interviewed more than 3,000 end users in virtually every technology market. My career as a researcher has taught me several important lessons.

First, the systematic collection of quantitative and qualitative data—the facts of an individual's experience—has proved to me that customers do not know why, really, they purchase certain products or services, nor do they *know* that they don't know. This means that opinion and awareness research has marginal value at best for predicting behavior and understanding historical market behaviors. Customers make decisions based on non-rational impulses—"I want that!"—and then feel compelled to generate a litany of rationalizations to explain why they want what they want, why they deserve it, and why they must have it.

Second, I've learned that understanding why customers behave the way they do requires a comprehensive study of the environment that shapes their social identity and economic role, including the various demographic and economic factors.

Third, asking customers to recount in step-by-step detail their buying and using experience of a product or service, spanning months or years, represents the best way to understand their true motivations, as measured by behavior. Only by studying their behavior—what worked, what didn't work, who helped them, who got in the way, what frustrations emerged, etc.—can marketing managers determine what part of their solution and brand storytelling actually worked.

Fourth, I've found that an individual buyer almost always represents a group of people, what we call the "decision influence team." This group exerts a significant influence on the actual purchase decision and subsequent deployment or successful use of a product or service. Unfortunately, most marketing programs we have studied target a specific individual and overlook the larger group dynamic that influences the buyer.

Fifth, systematic research has revealed some of the essential questions both customers and the decision influence team ask at each step of the buying, using, and disposing experience—something we define later in this book as the "satisfaction lifecycle." In other words, questions, not answers, motivate customers.

Sixth, studying the most successful, satisfied, and productive customers, then reverse-engineering their buying and using experience, provides the most powerful insights into how to grow a brand. By studying exemplars of excellence, one can quickly identify structural faults and shortcomings in the customer-making (brand-building) process.

While I learned these lessons in the marketplace, I found one could also apply them to a much more human concern: intimate relationships. My partners and I applied this research strategy—studying behavior then reverse-engineering the lessons of a lifecycle—to understand why we choose particular romantic partners and mates, how relationships evolve (or don't) over time, and how to re-create the best practices as modeled from research of individuals with extraordinarily successful relationships. It surprised me to learn that we choose brands, friends, and mates using the same strategies; the persistent issues that marriage counselors see in struggling couples mirror those in problematic relationships between buyers and sellers. And so, too, will the solutions be mirrored. I also discovered that the realms of intimate relationships and brands share another deep feature: daunting complexity. In both realms, I learned to develop models and "metamodels" (models for building models) that identify and illuminate essential elements and their relationships to each other.

In the late 1980s and early 1990s, I began to research online information systems and interactive multimedia. Despite omnipresent industry messages about the power of technology, our research showed that people really want technology to enhance their relationships, both in their private lives and in the workplace. Information itself has no power, only people in relationship.

In 1995, Jeff Martin, then senior director of marketing for Apple Computer's professional design and publishing market, challenged me to pull together these two strands—research on technology adoption and relationships—in a paper called *Strategies for Building Digital Brands*. In this paper, we (James L. Byram, Stephen M. H. Braitman, Doug Millison, and I) set forth a broad technological and marketing framework for building brands in what we later called the Networked Economy.

As the Internet and World Wide Web burst into mass conscious-
ness, our research showed that information technology, Web sites,
and related eServices would play a profound role in how traditional
brands find and serve customers. Most notably, we observed the
principal effect of the Internet: to facilitate the formation of communities of like-minded individuals who interact through e-mail,
online discussions, and chat rooms, and compare notes about their
buying and using experience regarding all the products and services
important to their lives and work. In other words, we identified trust
networks as the organizing principle for this new era heralded by the
emergence of the Networked Economy.

At this point, another facet of my life came into play. In 1975, I
graduated from the University of California, Santa Cruz with a self-
directed, interdisciplinary degree in religious studies. This entailed
not only studying the major religious traditions, but also studying
their underlying spiritual and mystical traditions. The work of Max
Weber, the great German scholar and the father of modern sociology, showed me the critical relationship between religion, econom-
ics, and the social life of modern culture (most specifically in his
seminal book, *The Protestant Ethic and the Spirit of Capitalism*
(Scribners, 1958)). His teachings reveal how religious traditions,
specifically those of Europe and North America, bring a special
dynamism to capitalism and market-oriented economies.

I used Weber's theoretical framework to think about brands as a
mechanism of culture in the service of a higher good, especially in the
context of the rapidly evolving Networked Economy that now spans
cultures, languages, and religious traditions worldwide. Reading *Communication, Culture, and Hegemony: From the Media to Meditations* by
Jesus Martin-Barbero (SAGE Publications, 1993) showed me how
trust networks, supported by interactive technologies, would emerge
as an economic and political force with unprecedented impact on
businesses and other social institutions. Martin-Barbero's theoretical
framework—which he applied to celebrities, popular artists, and
movie stars—helped me see how brands close the loop between development by storytellers and consumption by an audience.

Brands, I realized, evolve by way of collaboration between the
brand-producing firm and the customers who buy and use the brand.
This book constitutes the first volume of a proposed series that will
present a broad theoretical and practical framework to be used in
branding as a discipline.

Who Should Read This Book and Why

I wrote this book to serve as a manifesto to unite executives and staff in how they can engage and succeed in the Networked Economy. For many firms, this means undergoing a transformation that entails gaining the whole-hearted cooperation and support of all key personnel. To do this, employees need to understand what makes the changes necessary, who makes the changes happen, and what should happen during each step of a successful firebranding program.

Figure 1 shows who must read this book in order to ensure the consensus needed before deployment of a successful firebranding strategy. We urge you to distribute multiple copies of this book to these primary and secondary readers, then to begin a process of group discussions about how to apply these general principles and practices to your firm and its customers.

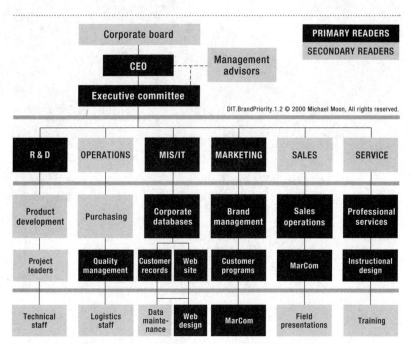

Figure 1 This book serves as a manifesto for corporate executives and staff alike in developing a branding strategy for the Networked Economy

Contact your local bookseller or Osborne/McGraw-Hill corporate sales at 800-722-4726 for volume purchase discounts. You will also find related courseware at www.Firebrands.com to help you in the education, consensus building, and deployment phases.

Chapter 1

Firebrands and the New Brand eState

Why do we need a new book on brands today? Clearly, the Internet has begun to change everything. It provides a radically different context for how we live, work, and play. Even established, proven practices and activities take on a new meaning in this new context, a new orientation. In this chapter, we examine the radical changes that necessitate a new definition of brands and a new approach to building brands.

The Emergence of Trust Networks and Their Implications for Branding

What does the Internet mean for brand managers and executives? How has the process of finding and serving customers changed?

The answers to these questions lie in an examination of the principle effects that the Internet has on commerce, society, and the individual. Let's begin with the profound insight of management guru, economist, and theorist, Peter Drucker. He divides modern economic history into five eras.

As illustrated in Figure 1-1, Drucker defines each era in terms of a single organizing principle—how the successful commercial enterprises of that era organize work and productivity, where productivity connotes the systematic application of knowledge to work.

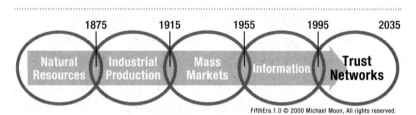

FifthEra.1.0 © 2000 Michael Moon, All rights reserved.

Figure 1-1 According to Peter Drucker, we entered the fifth era of modern economic history in 1995. We call this the era of trust networks

During the first era, companies set up operations on or near plentiful natural resources, including harbors, lakes, rivers, mines, and forests. Their competitive advantage came from knowing how to exploit these natural resources—usually by staking claims before anyone else could, protecting those claims from encroachment by others, and employing tremendous amounts of manual labor to reap the prized resources.

In the *industrial production* era, success came through access to labor pools, technical knowledge of manufacturing, and convenient, low cost transportation for raw materials and finished goods. Recently, the Nobel Committee awarded its economic prize to the economist who showed that the United States pulled ahead of Europe in the Industrial Revolution because its network of rivers and canals ensured steady supplies of raw materials and ways to move finished goods to markets both local and abroad.

The era of *mass markets* arose with the emergence of an interstate rail and highway system along with the development of newspapers, magazines, radio, film, and television. Trains and trucks provided highly efficient ways of moving inexpensive, mass-produced goods throughout a national market stimulated by advertising and promotion. Competitive advantage derived from mastering the logistics of nationwide transportation systems (designing products for shipment and distribution through an expanding network of retailers and field sales organizations), and from advertising, publicity, and promotion (novel sources of entertainment at that time, welcomed by consumers hungry for news and cultural developments beyond the parochial scope of their towns and neighborhoods).

Drucker marks the beginning of the *information era* in 1955, when enterprises began to organize work and productivity in terms of the creation and use of information. He coined the term "knowledge worker" to characterize a new form of labor: a worker who produces and consumes information as the principle focus of the job. Competitive advantage derived from information technology (IT) infrastructure (in particular, specialized computer software) and the quality of the data that knowledge workers could transform into business intelligence and answers. Because these information systems undergird the means of production, distribution, and customer interactions, better-trained knowledge workers and superior IT systems conferred great advantages to the firms that mastered these two elements.

Drucker argues that each age lasts about 40 years, and that each provides a meaningful context for understanding the previous age. He notes that while immersed in the current era, people have a hard time understanding the organizing principal of that era. Like water to a fish or air to a bird, the operating principle of the current era remains hidden behind the veil of tranquilized obviousness.

Drucker wryly notes that, following this timeline, the information era ended in 1995. He says that we now find ourselves in a new era with a fundamentally new organizing principle for work and productivity. He laments that he can smell and taste but not name this new organizing principle. He nonetheless asserts that the new organizing principle should have sufficient explanatory power to quantify the economic value of information—something that remained impossible while we stayed immersed in the information era.

We note that in 1995 the World Wide Web burst on the scene to force the Internet out of its arcane academic/military R&D closet and thrust it into the world's living rooms, offices, factory floors, and boardrooms. But, the Internet does not constitute the organizing principle of the new economic era, any more than electricity served as the organizing principle for the information era. While electricity enabled the new era, information provided the organizing principle.

We submit that *trust networks* represent the organizing principle for work and productivity in the era that began in 1995 and which will end, according to Drucker's theory, around 2035.

As illustrated in Figure 1-2, each technical advance—more transistors on each chip, higher speed networks, a broadening array of telecommunication services, etc.—drives increased consumption of personalized information, skills development simulations, and immersive entertainment.

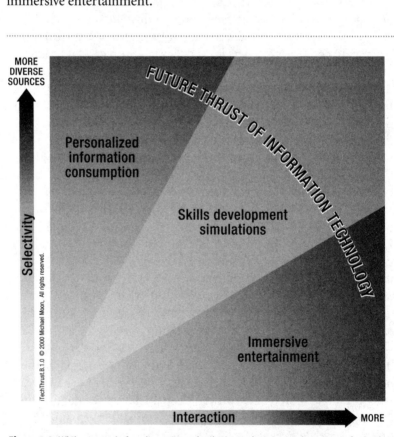

Figure 1-2 While new and often disruptive technologies push society and commerce forward, they develop along two dimensions: ever-increasing interactivity and selectivity

First with mainframes, then with minicomputers, personal computers, video games, television remote controls, and now with the Internet, we gain increasing levels of direct interaction with information, education, and entertainment sources. Higher levels of interactivity produce more and more lifelike behaviors and interactions between individuals and immersive multimedia environments.

At the same time, we get to choose from an ever-increasing inventory of information, education, and entertainment sources. Most important to this new era, individuals *themselves* become significant new sources of information and entertainment when inter-relating on the Web. E-mail, Internet discussion groups, and chat rooms now successfully compete with prime time television and publications for audience attention and participation.

As society moves along these vectors, businesses and other institutions have responded to the increasing appetite for online, interactive sources and selectivity by deploying a new infrastructure and an array of services that, in aggregate, constitutes the Networked Economy. The Networked Economy represents the wide range of businesses that use the Internet, and related infrastructure, to find and serve customers.

Figure 1-3 shows how the traditional business designs and processes of bricks-and-mortar firms, as well as new clicks-only and hybrid clicks-and-mortar firms have begun to proliferate ingenious new ways of exploiting eBusiness opportunities, thereby finding and serving customers in the Networked Economy. We'll discuss these new eBusiness models in detail later in the book.

These businesses may compete on price, or present new offerings delivered through an increasingly interactive IT infrastructure, but at the heart of each successful eBusiness lies a trust network: a group of individuals who trust each other, perhaps even more than they trust the companies that serve them. They log on to the Internet, exchange e-mail, join discussion groups, share tips, techniques, recommendations, and warnings about companies and products to patronize or avoid. They form what we call communities of practice and concern, and nominate (or acquiesce to) the leadership of a *community captain* (C-captain)—a person who moderates e-mail or chat room discussions, coalesces the community with a Web site or an in-person meeting, and mobilizes political or economic action by carrying complaints and requests from customers to a brand producing firm. C-captains act as self-appointed spokespeople for their communities and often become the point of primary contact between a community and a brand-producing firm.

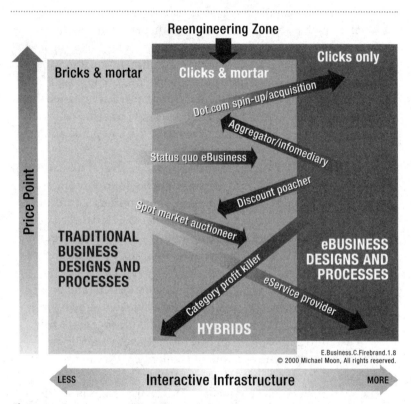

Figure 1-3 Every business will become an eBusiness of some sort, using new and ever-more ingenious ways of finding and serving customers

Figure 1-4 shows that these networks include a broad spectrum of stakeholders from the community, trade, industry, and marketplace. Trust networks include the groups that have traditionally affiliated with a brand—key customers, suppliers, distributors, and others who have a stake in the success and survival of a brand. In the Net-worked Economy, a new group emerges to lead the trust, exerting, through their online, interactive relationships with the brand and with other members of the trust network, unprecedented influence on the brand.

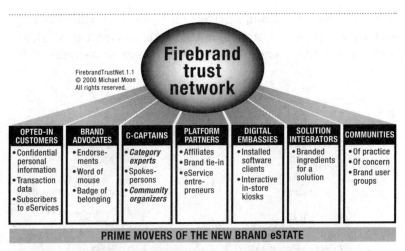

Figure 1-4 A new group of stakeholders emerges and drives the Networked Economy; each group has an online, interactive relationship with the brand and with each other

These prime movers serve as leaders of the new social class that we call the Brand eState, the power base of the Networked Economy. We discuss these prime movers, and how to marshal their activities in successful branding operations, later in this book.

The term Brand eState updates a model espoused by Cardinal Richelieu in seventeenth century France. He described society in terms of six *estates*: the king and the aristocracy; the church; the military; writers and journalists; merchants and tradesmen; and the peasants. Richelieu stands as one of the first political theorists to understand the power of the fourth estate (writers and journalists) to shape political will and societal acquiescence to the rule of law.

As illustrated in Figure 1-5, in the Networked Economy, the trust networks that coalesce around each brand wield the kind of influence on brand producer firms that the journalists of the fourth estate exert on governments.

Wired college students in the U.S., for example, have begun agitating for companies that produce school-branded apparel to respect the rights of workers and indigenous peoples, preserve the ecosystems of those countries, and eliminate sweatshop practices in the company's overseas manufacturing operations. Their action has had a tangible effect on the operations of Nike and other apparel manufacturers. Likewise, other brands have begun to feel the wrath of the

Brand eState over issues like lack of employment diversity (Coca-Cola), poor environmental and nutrition policies (McDonald's), as well as many others, encompassing a broad range of concerns.

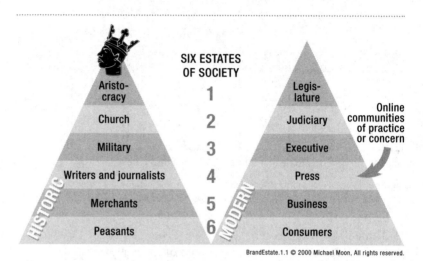

SIX ESTATES OF SOCIETY

Aristo-cracy	1	Legis-lature
Church	2	Judiciary
Military	3	Executive
Writers and journalists	4	Press
Merchants	5	Business
Peasants	6	Consumers

Online communities of practice or concern

HISTORIC   MODERN

Figure 1-5 As customers and other stakeholders interact among themselves, they will exert political and economic power comparable to that of the press

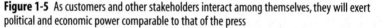

The Brand eState and its component trust networks center on the brand. A deeper understanding of the Brand eState's power leads us to suggest, in this book, a radical reinterpretation of brands and how to build them—brands that harness the organizing principle of trust networks and optimize a business for success in the Networked Economy.

As we argue in this book, brands must become firebrands. They must become collaborative expressions, with customers and other stakeholders. They must not only become fully wired, but they must also deliver new satisfactions, principally through self-service satisfactions initiated by customers and other stakeholders. This means every company must become an interactive corporation, an iCorp, and deploy a technical infrastructure uniquely adapted to the rigors of 24/7 global eBusiness processes. In so doing, we radically redefine the brand and the branding process, enlarging the scope beyond mere identity and messaging activities. The principle value that a company provides to its customers and the messaging about this value fuse—they become inseparable and indistinguishable *from the customer's point of view.*

In the chapters that follow, we outline a manifesto for revolutionizing the concept of an enterprise and its relationship with customers and other stakeholders. We take the reader beyond mere arm-waving and oracular proclamations, to prescribe concrete action: deployment of specific IT technology to address specific aspects of a comprehensive brand-building program.

Chapter 2

Brand Fundamentals

What defines a brand? In this chapter, we explain why traditional definitions of brands fail to meet the challenge of the Networked Economy. We show how buyers and sellers collaborate in the creation of a brand, and discuss why the relationship between buyer and seller has become so important. Beyond customers, we discuss several other groups who have a stake in a company's brand, and discuss why brand managers must consider their needs. We examine brands from both the sell side and the buy side, from the customer's point of view as well as the brand manager perspective. We show how a value chain model can help brand managers better understand how to work with trade partners and other intermediaries. Finally, we discuss how a brand can miss the mark and become a painful tattoo and reminder of a failed relationship.

What Characterizes a Brand?

It seems that every day we read or hear in the business press about brands, their importance to a successful company, why customers love brands, and how financial analysts and investors translate the equity of a brand into shareholder confidence and higher share prices. Because brands mean so many things to so many people, for purposes of this book, we offer a comprehensive definition and an internally consistent and logical framework to discuss brands. We will build on this definition and framework later in the book when we discuss how brands evolve into firebrands.

This book addresses a particular audience: individuals and groups tasked with the job of building brands for their companies. While many students of brands may derive great value from our discussion, for the purposes of this book we assume the reader can, will, and must take action in the near term—action that will produce measurable results of desired or unwanted consequence. To this end, we employ a prescriptive voice, using as our model a coach communicating with his quarterback or baseball pitcher. Their dialogue is action-oriented and outcome-driven, utilizing a collaborative playbook of proven tactics to implement an overall strategy.

Traditional Definitions of a Brand

Many people think of a brand as an image or an idea that customers associate with a product, service, trademark, or other image-related asset—the Shell sign, for example.

Some people think of a brand as a trusted, reliable product or service whose use brings predictable results and experiences—a *Big Mac and fries.*

Some people think of a brand as representing an idea or desired satisfaction—*Volvo cars mean safety.*

Others consider a brand a promise that a company makes to its customers—George Zimmer's Men's Wearhouse tagline, "*I guarantee it.*"

Still others believe that a brand lives in the minds and hearts of customers, taking on a life of its own—*Harley-Davidson forever.*

Some people think of a brand as an economic asset and tangible expression of what accountants call "good will," that attempts to put a dollar value on an otherwise intangible corporate possession. For instance, the bankrupt North Face was recently purchased for

$20 million on the strength of its brand name. The same reason accounts for Marlboro's multibillion-dollar price tag, according to purchaser KKR.

Each of these elements represents a single, but important facet of that multifaceted entity we call a brand.

Our Definition of a Brand

More important, these traditional definitions omit the single most significant aspect of a brand: the relationship between buyer and seller. These two actors relate to the brand in substantially different ways, employing clearly distinguished perspectives, terms, expectations, and needs. Our definition of a brand, therefore, centers on the buyer-seller relationship.

The traditional approach, however, minimizes or discounts altogether this relationship. "My customers just want toothpaste. They don't want a relationship with me or my company." The focus here lies solely on the transaction. But, as loyalty, customer retention, and lifetime customer value emerged as important metrics for brand management in the 1980s and 1990s, the relationship between buyer and seller moved to center stage. And, as we illustrate later in this book, this relationship has taken on paramount importance for brand managers who seek success in the Networked Economy.

The Four Elements of a Brand

We define a brand in terms of four interrelated elements: satisfaction, collaboration, relationship, and story.

SATISFACTION

In our definition, a brand represents the principal *satisfaction* that a customer expects and desires from the process of buying and using a product or service. This means customers buy an intangible gestalt— a thought, a feeling, a physical sensation, even, in some cases, a social interaction, which all coalesce into a pleasurable satisfaction.

Coke, for example, represents far more than colored, sugared water: as the company's slogans suggest, this drink adds a certain spice to life, representing a pause that refreshes. Between the lines, it says stop and smell the roses, revel with friends and family, enjoy your life. Decades of branding have deeply imprinted us with the notion that Coke is as much a social activity as it is a personal thirst quencher.

COLLABORATION

Hundreds if not thousands of customer interactions with a product or service, and related marketing activities, build a brand. A brand, therefore, also represents an ongoing *collaboration* between seller and buyer. While a single event may position a brand in the minds and hearts of the customer, a brand summarizes the totality of these many experiences. In a meaningful way, each positive or negative event outcome of the buying and using experience goes into the buyer's "emotional bank account." Over time this account grows and produces interest, or, through regular or catastrophic withdrawals, the balance shrinks to zero: the customer defects to another brand.

Effective collaboration means that the seller has a well-defined and effective strategy for making new deposits in the buyer's emotional bank account. It does so with the active permission of buyers. As we will show later, the branding process helps buyers understand how to translate certain experiences into deposits into the account. A brand educates new customers in how to get the satisfactions that existing, branded customers already experience. A brand passes on a set of behavioral and perceptual norms from existing customers to new customers, and from one demographic generation to the next. As such, a brand acts as a mechanism of our culture, and those brand managers who know the ins and outs of sociology and cultural anthropology will be served well. This discussion lies beyond the scope of the present volume, but can be taken up in more detail at www.Firebrands.com.

RELATIONSHIP

This collaboration produces the buyer/seller *relationship*. Most companies and marketing managers do not yet understand what it means to have a relationship with a customer. If they did, they simply would not treat them the way they so often do. Generally, service firms—professional or retail—tend to have a broader understanding and therefore do a better job of relating to customers.

One of this book's co-authors, Doug, buys his automobile tires at Big O and has no intention of switching to another company any time soon. When he walks into the shop, they treat him like a friend—even the staffers he hasn't met yet. They type his phone number into the computer and pull up a complete record of his business with the company—no warranty certificates or receipts necessary to know what he's purchased in the past. He paid a little more for his last set of tires than he might have at the local warehouse club, but Big O has replaced one of them, at no charge, three times now after Doug, on a string of unbelievable bad luck, had each of them go flat thanks to nails and other debris.

This demonstrates excellent management of the buyer-seller relationship that lies at the heart of the Big O brand, which is based on the anticipation of customer problems and, through the use of technology, solving them with the idea of a long-term relationship in mind. Later, we'll discuss in detail the key role that information technology plays in fostering brand relationships.

In other words, a relationship has no brand value until management supports it with specific policies, training, and technical infrastructure. A happy face doesn't cut it without results, and you don't get results without painstaking preparation and ongoing development that's organized to create, foster, and enhance a relationship over time.

STORY

Developmental psychology and brand management both deal with the way that human beings grow and form lifelong relationships anchored by a core social identity. As children begin to become aware of others, they must develop social skills. They must learn how to play nice. Psychologists familiar with this critical socialization process indicate that children socialize through storytelling. As a young boy, I recall playing "build a fort" and was particularly pleased when I could get other boys to join me in its construction, all of us making up a storyline for it as we went along. Occasionally, young girls would convince me to play "house" with them, wherein I took on the role of Daddy, Baby, or other domestic character. Suffice to say, at a very early age we learn that stories provide social context, pleasurable engagements, and reciprocity: I'll play in your story if you'll play in mine.

Brands operate in an identical fashion. Every brand tells a story. Some stories speak to a broader set of desires and needs than others. In all cases, the *story* gives meaning to the relationship and its evolution over time. Ultimately, the best stories transcend the buyer-seller relationship. Not for a minute do we forget that transactions make the world go around. But the context of those transactions—the brand story—can uplift the transaction into a lifelong, heartfelt affiliation. Some of these brand stories become "our" stories. They define our core identify, serve as badges of belonging and currencies of value that we share with other people, where the mere act of referral becomes an expression of love or concern. The most beloved brands in the world do the heart's work, serving as currencies of affiliation, love, and caring. But, whether beloved or simply respected, a great brand tells its story in ways that evoke deep, visceral responses from people who subsequently come back for more and advocate brand use to family and friends.

Where Do Brands Come From?

Brands recapitulate the long history of the strategic use of symbol and imagery as a conveyance of power, prestige, and goodness. Brands work on the human psyche the same way as religious symbols, totems, fetishes, and a host of other symbolic communications that include the heraldry of kings and the icons of liveries, bakers, and other craftspeople.

In Table 2-1, we highlight the most significant developments in the evolution of brands. We base our timeline in part on "Brand New History," a January 2000 article in *Red Herring* magazine as well as Adrian Room's "History of Branding" in *Brands: The New Wealth Creators* (New York University Press, 1998).

Table 2-1 Brands span most of recorded history, documenting our relationship to commerce, society, and culture. These dates mark the milestones of brand history and their gradual emergence as an apotheosis of mass culture

2000 BC	Egyptians mark livestock with brands.
600 BC	Babylonian merchants hang signs outside their shops to describe their activities and distinguish themselves from competitors.
560 BC	King Croesus of Lydia (now part of Turkey) mints and stamps gold coins with his insignia.
300 BC	Roman merchants identify the manufacturer or seller of products with symbols.
100	Christians choose the sign of the fish to indicate their clandestine faith at a time when authorities outlawed and persecuted Christianity.
1200-1600	European abbeys and monasteries use brands to identify beers and liquors.
1400s	"Brand" appears as an English word, denoting the burning of an animal's flesh to claim ownership.

Table 2-1 Brands span most of recorded history, documenting our relationship to commerce, society, and culture. These dates mark the milestones of brand history and their gradual emergence as an apotheosis of mass culture (*continued*)

1600s	Commerce flourishes with visual symbols widely used to identify products and commercial activities (liveries, inns, bakers, etc.) for a largely illiterate populace.
1760	Josiah Wedgwood creates the first brand-oriented commercial enterprise.
1848	Paris Commune, the first political act of mass culture from which all modern commercial brands arise.
1870	Texas rancher Samuel A. Maverick refuses to brand his cattle; his name enters English as a synonym for "Think Different."
1886	Coca-Cola trademarks its brand.
1910s	Modern advertising pioneer Claude Hopkins champions brand image, saying "People don't buy from clowns!"
1922	"Brand name" enters the English language.
1949	Leo Burnett "gets it" about TV. He buys a television set for each of his executives and orders them to watch all three hours of available programming each night.
1950s	Madison Avenue repositions notion of "brands" and "brand identity" as a critical marketing aim to justify huge client expenditures in the risky new medium, television.
1954	Peter Drucker publishes *The Practice of Management*, framing management as a discipline with a community of practitioners, the scientific basis for branding.
1969	Jack Trout and Al Ries publish *Positioning: The Battle for Your Mind*, revolutionizing the idea of brands and the goal of marketing: to establish a positioning in the minds of customers.
1984	Apple's "1984" Macintosh TV commercial airs only once, a shot heard 'round the world, demonstrating how a commercial brand reached the level of mythic storytelling and became an overnight cultural icon.
1993	*Wired* magazine canonizes digital culture and codifies the sensibilities of the interactive age.
1994	Netscape Navigator, the first firebrand of the Networked Economy, makes a commercial Web, with graphical brand images, possible.
1995	Yahoo! establishes the first deep gravity well supersite.
1999	WTO Seattle protests parallel the Paris Commune, this time representing the first political act of the Networked Economy.

From Digital Files to Cultural Icons

Against the backdrop of brand history, the information revolution continues to transform everything that technology touches, including brands. Just as brands have evolved through history, so each individual brand goes through its own developmental lifecycle in the Networked Economy.

While brand managers may think only in terms of slogans, campaigns, and other discrete elements of cultural detritus, great brands arise from those striving to transcend commercial culture and speak directly to deep human concerns and aspirations.

What made Apple's "1984" television commercial effective? By using George Orwell's dystopian novel as a starting point, Apple tapped the same taboo fear of all modern societies (one which George Lucas fully developed into an epic mythology in his *Star Wars* trilogy): our collective fear that human beings are mere machines with no spiritual life or legacy beyond the material world—we're just a fancy computer.

When they succeed in thus taking their cues from the great works of art that define human civilization, brand managers infuse their brands with a larger-than-life dimension that speaks directly to the human heart and our highest aspirations. They don't make brands, they create cultural icons.

But no matter where they end up in the brand evolution landscape, now, in the Networked Economy, they all start as digital files. This carries profound implications for the design and management of these files. As digital files take on a central role in brand creation and management, they also take on a specific, and significant, economic value.

Let's discuss this evolution, as illustrated in Figure 2-1.

Digital files represent units of work of craft media professionals who use highly specialized graphic design and publishing software tools and practices. As such, each file encapsulates the knowledge of the craft media professional, an investment of her time, and a branding or communication intent. At the level of a digital file, however, individuals indifferent or hostile to brand management may treat these files as mere "content"—a mass of RGB data that carries no more intrinsic value than fish wrap.

Media assets represent that portion of digital files that management and craft media professionals have specifically engineered for systematic reuse and re-expression. This means with higher reuse, the user or owner of the media asset accumulates additional economic value. This usually takes the form of reduced costs, faster cycle times, fewer defects and re-works, and, possibly, licensing revenue.

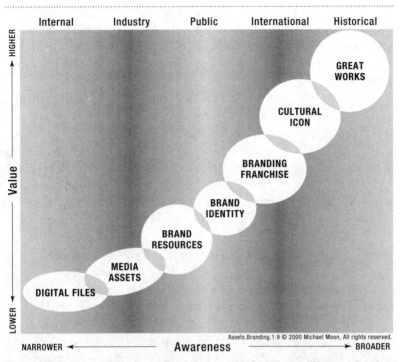

Internal   Industry   Public   International   Historical

HIGHER

GREAT
WORKS

CULTURAL
ICON

BRANDING
FRANCHISE

BRAND
IDENTITY

BRAND
RESOURCES

MEDIA
ASSETS

DIGITAL FILES

Value

LOWER

NARROWER ◄————————— Awareness —————————► BROADER

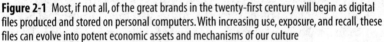

Figure 2-1 Most, if not all, of the great brands in the twenty-first century will begin as digital files produced and stored on personal computers. With increasing use, exposure, and recall, these files can evolve into potent economic assets and mechanisms of our culture

Brand resources represent the deployment of media assets that specifically link a customer or other stakeholder to the brand. Brand resources also include any form of technology (business IT application, in-store kiosk, catalog) that touches the customer experience and helps shape their experience of quality, satisfaction, and value.

Brand identity describes those brand resources that the customer most singularly identifies with the satisfaction and the positioning of the brand in a competitive market. While most brand identities remain static, customer satisfaction and referral bring this static entity to life. Thus, a brand identity acquires a "voice"—a rich, emotional resonance that reflects the singular satisfaction experienced by all or most customers.

Branding franchise represents the concerted work of three or more successful brand identities. McDonald's, Disney, and Microsoft have all established branding franchises. When any of these companies introduce a new product or service, customers try them out immediately. A branding franchise pre-positions a product or service in such a way that a customer who has never used it will quickly understand it and what it offers—a major hurdle that all new brands must overcome.

Cultural icons represent brands that transcend mere commercial activity. As a mechanism of culture, the cultural icon transmits a set of values, perceptions, and behaviors to current and future generations. Cultural icons become currencies of affection or caring among family and friends, and mark pivotal moments in the development of an individual's social identity. Consider a New York Yankees fan taking his son to the ball park for the first time, or teaching his son how to shave with his favorite razor, the mother who passes on a set of treasured china, or a young woman who accepts a piece of diamond jewelry that signifies, thanks to the ubiquitous DeBeers' "diamonds are forever" campaign, a pledge of eternal love.

Great works describe the crowning achievements of human culture. They include religious icons and artifacts, the great books of literature and science, and the technological or social innovations that have transformed how we live, work, and play (such as the printing press and textbook). While some cultural anthropologists and other scholars will continue to argue whether commercial activity produces works of this stature, consider Shakespeare, who clearly created his plays at least in part to satisfy an immediate commercial purpose, whose canon clearly stands among the great works, and who continues to represent a potent brand in the theater business. Closer to our time, and perhaps less of a stretch than Shakespeare, Andy Warhol succeeded in elevating artifacts of commercial culture to the status of high art; it remains to be seen if succeeding generations will call them great works. Likewise, many songs now considered classic and sung throughout the world as anthems of the human condition began as little more than exercises in creating another hit record.

In this context, we can discuss how culture and commerce converge in the creation of digital brands and their most potent incarnations, firebrands. As we discuss later in this book, firebrands start as digital files stored on a hard disk drive. With systematic application of these files through a storytelling process, the brand becomes a firebrand.

Where Do Brands Live?

Simply put, brands live in the minds of customers, organized in a map that we call *brandspace*.

Brandspace

In 1994, Jeffrey Rayport and John J. Sviokla, in the *Harvard Business Review*, formally introduced the notion of a *marketspace* to characterize how digital technology and infrastructure change the very nature and behavior of a marketplace. Following their lead, we use the term *brandspace* to convey a similar idea, taking into account the new interactive relationship that develops between buyer and seller in the Networked Economy (we discuss this in more detail later in this book).

Brandspace represents a mental map that customers use to organize brands in a marketspace, and thus deal with the 7,000-plus brand messages that they experience each and every day, incorporating their ability to reach out and touch the source of these brand messages through the Web and other new infrastructures that have emerged.

This concept of the customer organization of brandspace runs contrary to the traditional view that vendors shape customers and create brands. But, in fact, customers have always run the show. We hold that the brand lives in the mind and heart of a customer—without their participation and active collaboration, brands would never come to life. That brands have a vital presence in the customer's psychology firmly places brandspace in a subjective, personal realm.

Brand managers who fail to understand this critical distinction will invariably violate the psychological boundaries and sensitivities of their customers. As we will show, in the brandspace of the Networked Economy, where customers talk to each other 24/7, these failures take on global dimensions and significance.

Figure 2-2 shows how brandspace works in terms of an individual's sense of social identity.

Some brands speak to a person's *core identity*. Harley-Davidson customers defy mainstream convention and identify themselves, to some degree, as outlaws or members in good standing of a counterculture. Dilbert expresses the frustrations of corporate mushrooms—in the dark, covered with manure—speaking to the isolation of workers from meaningful work and expressing a subtle but caustic satire of middle management, and by extension, the corporate executives and corporate culture that fosters such stupidity.

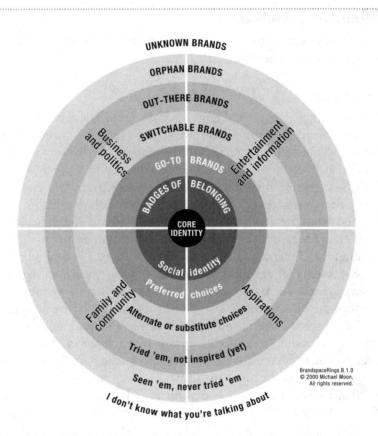

UNKNOWN BRANDS

ORPHAN BRANDS

OUT-THERE BRANDS

SWITCHABLE BRANDS

Business and politics

GO-TO BRANDS

Entertainment and information

BADGES OF BELONGING

CORE IDENTITY

Social identity

Preferred choices

Family and community

Alternate or substitute choices

Aspirations

Tried 'em, not inspired (yet)

Seen 'em, never tried 'em

I don't know what you're talking about

Figure 2-2 Brands live in the hearts and minds of customers in *brandspace*, initially entering as unproven guests who must earn the right to stay and who must ultimately come to echo the customer's aspirations and concerns

Some brands become *badges of belonging* and signify membership in a community of brand users. Harley-Davidson outlaws band together, proudly displaying the Harley-Davidson logo to instantly signify membership in this select group. Tommy Hilfiger activewear lets geeky suburban teens join the inner city hip-hop tribe—illustrating how Levi's missed a historic opportunity to build its brand with a new crop of 14-year-olds, how Levi's brand managers failed to understand the way black inner-city culture drives mainstream U.S. popular youth culture trends, and how music builds tribes of individuals who also use clothes and accessories to signal membership in the tribe.

Moving farther away from the customer's heart and self-identity we find *go-to brands*—representing the preferred functional satisfactions associated with particular brands: Crest toothpaste, the Toyota Camry, Banana Republic white T-shirts. These go-to brands tend to attract the largest shares of market and, once established, tend to maintain their position as market leaders for decades. Consumer research reveals that go-to brands also achieve top of mind recall when researchers ask a customer to identify the leading brands of a market category.

Switchable brands represent a host of substitutes and alternatives that replace go-to brands in a pinch: Old Navy Khakis vs. Dockers, for example, or an in-house grocery or drug store brand that a customer selects when she feels the need to save money or when she can't find the go-to brand. Smart brand managers can transform switchable brands into go-to brands if they successfully re-position the brand in a newly-created category, usually a sub-category of a larger category, or if they get to the new, unbranded customers as they first enter the categories—for instance, teenagers and young adults first establishing their social identity in terms of brands. Linking the brand to a currency of affection among family and friends can elevate the switchable brand to go-to, badge-of-belonging, or even core identity status in brandspace.

"Out-there" brands include an even larger group of products and services that consumers have tried, but which, for a variety of reasons, have left them cold and unmotivated to try the brands again. Think of all the bathroom soap brands found on supermarket shelves. In the course of visiting friends and family, we will probably have used all or most of these brands at least once, but continue to choose our go-to brand or switchable substitute. Perhaps the out-there brand soap has too much perfume, an unpleasant graphic design on the packaging, a price point too high, or a displeasing association from first-hand or second-hand sources. Brand managers with out-there brands must take dramatic steps to re-ignite consumer interest, taking bold steps beyond the "new and improved" route.

Orphan brands represent products or services about which the consumer has no knowledge and therefore no preference or desire. Most new brands fall in this category. To succeed and better their location in brandspace, they must bring wholly new satisfactions to the market (usually a function of a new technology), aggressively re-position leading brands as uncool or politically incorrect, or become an identifier of a new, powerful, high-prestige group to which others want to belong (Ray Bans, for instance, in *Men in Black*). A powerful new musical group can instantly lift an orphan brand to badge-of-belonging status for fans and groupies if the band uses the branded item as part of their grand spectacle.

Unknown brands live in the netherworld of scary products or services about which you know nothing nor care to know. Occasionally, something from this space bursts into brandspace—the MITS Altair and Imsai 8080 microcomputer kits that got Bill Gates and the personal computer revolution started in the late 1970s, for example.

What Functions Do Brands Serve?

Brands serve two major functions. They bring buyers and sellers into a relationship, and along the way serve a similar function for other stakeholders in the company, including employees, trade partners, and members of the press.

Brands Bring Buyers and Sellers into a Relationship

We've defined a brand in terms of four components: satisfaction, collaboration, relationship, and story. We focus on the relationship component here because it changes most dramatically as brands move into the Networked Economy and become firebrands. As illustrated in Figure 2-3, a variety of brand functions foster this relationship.

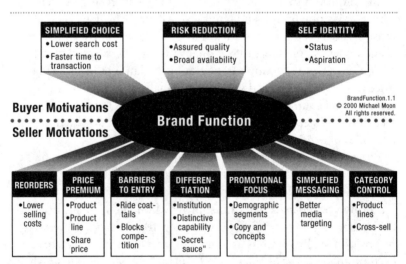

Figure 2-3 Brands help *buyers* make simple, safe purchase decisions that reflect their self-identity. Brands help *sellers* serve customers more effectively, reduce costs, and defend against competitive inroads

Nothing happens unless a customer buys something. This simple fact can elude even the most seasoned of executives, even those who have titles such as Marketing VP or Brand Management VP. Brands must sell products or services or we don't call them brands. Brands induce customers to buy.

With this reality firmly in mind, we can explore how brands help customers enter into a relationship, buy a product or service, use and consume it, and come back for more.

Buyer functions emphasize a desire for a simplified choice, risk reduction, and a reaffirmation of self-identity.

In his book, *Laws of Choice* (The Free Press, 1997), Eric Marder, who has conducted consumer choice research for 30 years, authoritatively asserts that, for consumer products, packaging, price point, and pitch (naming and descriptive language) induce customers to try a product. These elements help a customer quickly understand options within a category and direct impulse purchase behavior to the featured brand.

Marder reports that customers face too many choices and seek ways to reduce choice, including ongoing experimentation to decide if "This is the one that works for me," after which the brand moves from orphan to go-to status. For more complex decisions, especially in business-to-business markets, a brand lowers the costs of researching, evaluating, negotiating, purchasing, and re-ordering a solution. Brands reduce the time to transaction.

In addition, a brand reduces the risk associated with the buying and using experience, by telegraphing assured quality. Leading brands have the additional benefit of broad availability in a market; this translates into convenience for the buyer.

Even industrial brands—products or services—will reflect the social status and self-identity. A newer, higher-speed personal computer from a particular vendor—Compaq or Dell—may communicate higher prestige in a corporate environment, for example, than an off brand or no-name clone cobbled together with gray market parts and previous-generation microprocessors.

Seller functions emphasize price premium, differentiation, promotional focus, simplified messaging, category control, lower cost of sales, higher assurance of future sales, barriers to entry, and an overall efficiency in finding and keeping customers. These functions represent what most executives associate with brand management—what a brand does for me as a marketing manager, for example. While each of these constitutes an important function of the brand for the seller, over-emphasizing them tends to blind a brand manager to what truly motivates customers and builds loyal relationships with the brand.

Re-orders from an existing customer carry lower selling costs—an average of five times lower, according to research of leading management consultancies. Strong brands let a vendor charge price premiums, and erect barriers to entry to block competitors. High margins and protected markets can bolster investor confidence and justify higher share prices or company valuations.

Brands also create differentiation for the company, the markets it serves, and the products that lead those markets. This differentiation not only reflects a unique satisfaction experienced by customers, but also a distinctive capability ("secret sauce") not easily replicated by a competitor.

Strong, vibrant brands help marketing teams sharpen their promotional focus, simplify messaging, and exert greater control over their category. How? Great brands resonate with a crisply defined demographic customer profile that a creative team uses to focus and test the copy and concepts of a promotional campaign. Media choices become simpler, allowing marketing managers to concentrate media deployments for maximum effect—meaning a ubiquitous if not commanding presence in selected publications, TV shows, and other branding channels.

Brands give their managers better ability to negotiate more favorable terms, strategic placements on retail shelves, or at other points of market presence, more category control. Category control permits profitability of the brand firm and its most loyal and cooperative channel partners. In the mortars-and-bricks space, this amounts to a very real barrier to entry, but, as we discuss later in the book, this changes in the eMediaspace of the Networked Economy.

Brands Serve a Variety of Stakeholders

Closer examination reveals that, in addition to buyers and sellers, a brand serves many other masters. As shown in Figure 2-4, we have identified eight stakeholder groups served by the brand. Each stakeholder group associates several qualities, which we call *currencies* of the brand, with the brand relationship. Later in this book we expand the stakeholder circle to include new groups that firebrands serve, but here we focus on the stakeholders served by traditional, offline brands.

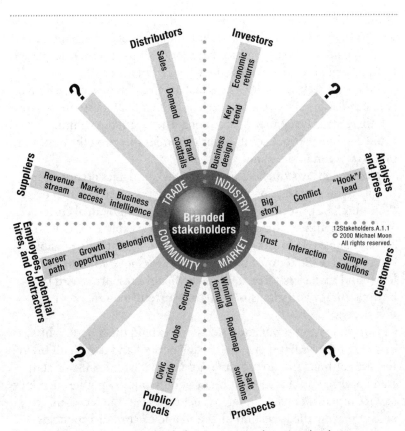

Figure 2-4 Brand managers must consider how important a role parties other than customers play in building brand equity. Here we illustrate these stakeholder groups and the "currencies" they seek in their relationship with the brand. The question marks indicate spokes to be filled by new stakeholder groups

So far in our discussion, we've mentioned buyers many times. Now let's make them more distinct by dividing buyers into two stakeholder groups, customers and prospects, calling attention to the unique currencies of their relationship to a brand. We discuss these currencies in general terms, but in practice they will differ according to the brand offering: product or service, local or global, etc.

Prospects include potential customers who can buy a product or service in the next 18 months, and who should buy something (yours or a competitive offering) because they have three defining qualities demonstrated: need, available budget, and a commitment to act. Prospects represent the *attainable universe* of future customers for a particular brand. Brand managers must focus their efforts on prospects, not the larger superset of suspects—individuals who lack one of the three criteria mentioned above. In Chapter 5, we'll explain how to use interactive relationships and Internet-based techniques to quickly winnow the wheat from the chaff.

Prospects seek safe solutions. This often requires road maps that they can use to retrace the steps taken by successful customers—we call these steps *best practice trademaps*. They want the winning formula, the bullet-proof solution for dummies that even the boss and boss's boss can understand.

Customers buy stuff. Surprisingly, most companies do not use particularly effective ways of profiling customers, the factors that drive their purchases, profitability to the company of individual customers, and their lifetime value. Later in this book, we explain exactly how an interactive relationship makes such profiling not only possible but profitable. Better profiling—the kind we show you how to do—lets brand managers focus their most effective resources with laserbeam accuracy and intensity to maximize return on marketing investments.

Customers seek simple solutions that extend the functionality or capability of what they have already bought and used. This often requires offline (and now, online) interaction with front-line staff, trade partners, affiliated solution providers, and corporate customer service organizations. Ultimately, customers want to feel comfortable in placing their trust in the brand and the brand-producing organization. We cannot overemphasize this simple-sounding, but revolutionary idea: customers want to trust companies, they want a relationship, they want a future that includes your brand and the satisfaction it brings them. Unfortunately, few companies operate with this as an organizing principle for their branding activities. Instead, they assume a position of suspicion and mistrust, or, perhaps worse, apathy regarding the customer. These companies will find it impossible to succeed in the Networked Economy; later in this book we explain why.

Analysts and press play an important role in building, or eroding, shareholder confidence, customer and prospect confidence, and the confidence of suppliers and distributors (which may translate into favorable terms of business).

Analysts work either at market research firms or in the investment community for institutional investment firms, brokerage houses, investment bankers, and venture capital funds. They write reports or articles—stories—on industry trends, a company's strategic position with regard to an industry and its trends, and forecast the future performance of industries and companies. Their opinions can have significant positive or negative effects on company valuations and share price.

Working press professionals conduct research (also called reporting) and write for publications offline and online. They strive for a measure of independence and balanced treatment of a subject, and they position themselves as storytellers who explain the key events that shape our lives and businesses and who try to make potentially scary new developments (technology for instance) approachable and understandable.

Analysts and press seek big stories that will appeal to their particular audiences and as such they often seek to identify conflicts that define story arcs that sweep readers through the story. As storytellers, they seek to identify a "hook" to pull readers into the story that neatly frames the conflict—young upstart versus market leaders, etc.

Most companies do not practice effective ways of meeting the needs of journalists. For succinct guidance on this, we recommend that you visit Doug's Web site, www.Online-Journalist.com for links to resources that explain the best practices when it comes to the care and feeding of the press. Here we offer three important prescriptives. First, send the right story to the right journalist and analyst. This often requires a press relations professional to make the connection. Second, whenever possible, build trusted relationships with key journalists and analysts—the ones with the most impact on your business. Third, master damage and crisis control techniques.

Investors expect the companies in which they invest to produce wealth—economic returns—that equal, if not exceed other possible investments. They view economic returns through the lens of key trends: how will this firm exploit that trend or expected discontinuity (falling birth rates in developed countries, for example). Beyond this fundamental expectation of economic return, they invest in particular firms for a variety of reasons. Retail investors may make an emotional investment, usually in a company whose product or service has produced some satisfaction for them personally. Others simply play the market and look for profit only. Suppliers, distributors, and other partners may invest to cement a relationship with a company.

Investors look for a business design—a plan that specifies what satisfactions the company brings to market and how it captures value—that indicates a unique competitive advantage. Later in this book, we explain the key role that business designs play for successful firebrands in the Networked Economy.

Distributors form partnerships with brand producers for one purpose: to distribute branded products and services. They select brand producers based on demonstrated or potential demand in the market. They look for long lines of buying customers, shortages of products to buy, integrated brand management programs that have successfully driven current demand and will continue to do so in the future, and, finally, exclusive deals. Above all, a distributor wants to ride the coat-tails of killer brands that bring added prestige, thus positioning the distributor with sales channels that will more readily pick up the distributor's other offerings.

Suppliers seek ongoing revenue streams from generated sales of their materials and services to brand producers. They see brands as stars to which they can hitch their wagons, ascending with them. Suppliers who become especially strategic to a particular brand will want more than just revenue, however. They will want feedback and other forms of business intelligence. Everything from data on the end-use customer, to information from the chain of suppliers and distributors linked to the brand producer. This feedback will give them the ability to spot emerging shifts in market demand as well as quickly exploit short-lived opportunities. Brand firms can often trade business intelligence for more favorable terms from their suppliers, thus cementing a long-term strategic relationship.

Employees, potential new hires, and contractors seek more than mere employment. They want security and a career path that promises a better lifestyle and growing expertise that an employer can productively harness. New employees and prospective new hires often choose a company solely on the basis of how a particular job and career path may shape their future. Once they join, however, the experience of belonging becomes a strong motivation: the firm's culture represents an "internal" brand that not only keeps employees coming back but ultimately spills over into the public brand. Whether a contractor, a new hire, or employee of long standing, they all seek growth opportunities that, especially among knowledge workers, provide some measure of personal fulfillment and a sense of serving a larger purpose. This altruistic component will represent a key element of every successful firebrand, explaining why online communities sometimes form to advocate the brand to others.

Their families also play a powerful role in employee productivity and loyalty. In many cases an employee's spouse—and cousins, nephews, uncles, the whole clan—also represent prospects, customers, and people who advocate (or don't advocate) a brand. In fact, the extended families of a brand firm's employees represent a far-reaching, global network of potential brand advocates, referral generators, and qualified prospects. Brand managers should consider instituting programs that tap these powerful networks. Later, we will show how employee family members become instrumental in forming the online communities that support successful firebrands.

Public/locals represent local communities, their politicians, government officials, and civic leaders. They encourage commercial development because it creates jobs and a tax base that pays for schools, police, and other public services and works. They will champion local brands and companies, exuding pride in those citizens who have created this wonderful satisfaction in customers worldwide. Castroville, California—"World Artichoke Capital"—lies just a few miles down the road, for example. Strong brands produced locally also provide a sense of security for local merchants, and, in some cases, even a sense of epic historic drama: consider the local merchants of Redmond, Washington, who have watched Microsoft grow over the years and spread the wealth.

We introduce this circle of stakeholders to call attention to the fact that brand managers must create effective, trusted relationships with more than just buyers. In fact, these branded stakeholders can supercharge a company's overall branding program, taking the firm into markets not now currently served, erecting barriers of entry to competitors, bolstering the trust and confidence of potentially "switchable" customers, and, ultimately, increasing the business valuation or share price. In the most fundamental economic sense, stakeholders directly help create, enhance, and protect shareholder wealth. For this reason, brand management becomes more than just a delegated marketing activity; it stands shoulder to shoulder with a CEO's other fiduciary responsibilities, mainly treasury and operations.

Value Chains

Now, let's place a brand firm, two key stakeholder groups—suppliers and distributors—and their competitors into another trademap by which to visualize how these relationships create and support a brand. For this, we draw on an economic model from the Harvard Business

School professor, Michael Porter, and his book, *Competitive Strategy.* He uses the term *value chain* to characterize groups of firms that line up in a chain-like structure to contribute the constituent products or services that ultimately constitute the satisfactions that end-use customers buy and use.

Figure 2-5 illustrates the simplified value chain of companies in the personal computer market. Each entity of the chain may include dozens or even hundreds of competing vendors. Each company sells goods or services to the entity downstream, directly to its right along the chain. Thus, value flows downstream. Payments flow upstream. Figure 2-6 illustrates that not all members of the value chain earn the same levels of profit, nor do they capture equal shares of overall industry sector revenues.

Figure 2-5 Every brand producer participates in at least two *value chains.* The one above depicts the chain of manufacturers, suppliers, and distributors of goods and services in the personal computer industry

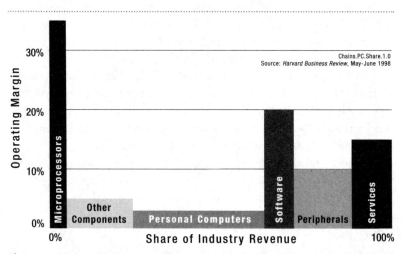

Figure 2-6 Analysis of the gross operating margins of the leading vendors of each entity in a value chain (in this case, for the personal computer industry) reveals *profit pools* and suggests sources of funds for co-branding, likely partners, and competitors

Business intelligence (who bought what and why, and if not, why not) also flows upstream. While upstream flows of information remain spotty and problematic in the old economy, in the Networked Economy business intelligence becomes as important as the money that changes hands.

High operating margins and large shares of industry revenue will highlight the source of funds for aggressive branding programs. Brand managers need to understand the value chain and profit pools of the industry in which their firms compete. This will help them identify branding partners, potential competitors, and help to explain new alliances that suppliers, distributors, and competitors may form in the future.

Brand managers must use the dynamics of a value chain to orchestrate the collective brand resources of suppliers and distributors for the satisfaction of ultimate end-use customers (and other stakeholders) and the storytelling that builds the brand around that satisfaction.

Value chains also give brand managers a powerful tool to plan and prioritize their Networked Economy strategies. Value chains highlight strategic technologies that brand managers must exploit in their quest to build trusted interactive relationships with buyers and other stakeholders.

If the brand does not deliver a satisfaction, no amount of branding and related storytelling will prevent failure. If you deliver a satisfaction but tell the wrong story, customers get confused and subsequently wander to safer harbors, seeking out crisply focused brands that offer simple, safe, understandable choices which reinforce the social and self-identity of buyers. Figure 2-7 illustrates that not all brand associations strike the consumer in a positive or desired way.

Branded or Tattooed?

Worse than confusing customers, some brand programs actively antagonize them. McDonald's tried to bring a new burger to market, targeted to adults. The marketing campaign conjured up the delights of pre-fast food drive-ins and soda fountains. While the burger, the Arch Deluxe, may have represented a great-tasting sandwich, the advertising campaign relied heavily on irony and satire—two of the most potentially toxic storytelling elements. The ads featured contemporary teenagers who derided the Arch Deluxe as too grown-up and unhip, with the assumption, apparently, that their parents would

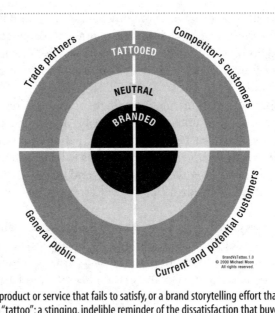

Figure 2-7 A product or service that fails to satisfy, or a brand storytelling effort that misses the mark, creates a "tattoo": a stinging, indelible reminder of the dissatisfaction that buyers now associate with the brand

gravitate to the new sandwich as an anti-teen badge of belonging. Unwittingly, McDonald's and its soon-to-be-fired advertising agency "tattooed" their target customers.

In cases like this, a strong brand may "tattoo" the consumer, leaving a stinging reminder and an indelible mark that serves to permanently disaffiliate the customer from the brand. This distinction between brand and tattoo becomes very important as brands move into the Networked Economy where increasing numbers of customers talk to each other via e-mail and compare their buying and using experiences of particular brands.

Conclusion

In this chapter, we've argued that customers buy satisfactions. They tolerate products and services as the means to get the satisfactions they desire and expect. Brands provide a variety of satisfactions to a variety of stakeholders—but satisfaction constitutes only one of four constituent elements of a brand: satisfaction, collaboration, relationship, story. Now, let's examine the techniques brand managers use to tell stories that build relationships and heighten the level of collaboration and interaction with customers.

Chapter 3

Building Brands Offline— the Branding Tradition

In this chapter, we discuss how organizations build brands. What's the relationship between a product or service and its brand? We look at the pivotal role that business designs play in brand building. We show why some brands come from Mars, others from Venus, and still others from Mercury. This accentuates the need to create a crisp, focused positioning for the brand. However, brand managers must understand the effect that corporate lifecycles exert on brands. Ultimately, branding means telling stories that customers want to hear. This highlights the need for a great story and a place to tell it—the branding theater.

Branding Defined

Branding, in the minds of most executives, amounts to a collection of marketing and sales activities organized for the purpose of creating a brand identity—an image or word that customers use as a beacon to navigate the seas of a cluttered, competitive market to find the safe harbor of a proven product or service. This definition has served more or less adequately for many years, but it falls short for several reasons.

Following this rather loose definition, these various marketing and sales activities rarely focus and build momentum around a clear positioning—the one satisfaction that customers expect and desire from a branded product or service. This focus needlessly divorces product development, service, and training—all key elements of a brand, in our view—from marketing and sales. Nor does this definition bring into play accountability for, and return on investment (ROI) from, branding activities.

We address these shortcomings by defining branding as an integrated process: *the systematic and consistent application of product or service design, storytelling, media, and technology to the buying and using experience of customers throughout a satisfaction lifecycle.* We'll explain each of these elements as we go along.

Evolutionary biologists have demonstrated how life itself evolves, not smoothly in a steady, continuous process, but instead in dramatic advances at certain points over time—perhaps Stephen Jay Gould has argued this most eloquently. We see branding in a similar context. Brands develop in leaps at pre-established points in a series of cycles that make up the branding process. In this chapter, we discuss the four most important cycles: *value creation, corporate lifecycle, brand storytelling,* and the *customer satisfaction lifecycle.*

Another way to define branding involves looking at the interplay between *brand* (what customers buy) and *value* (what sellers sell). Give and take, the pendulum swings between extremes, defines all relationships, as indicated in our choice of the yin-yang symbol from Taoist philosophy to illustrate this interplay in Figure 3-1.

This emphasizes a fundamental point: brand managers, situated within the seller firm, must work extra hard to distinguish their inherent seller perspective from the buyer's point of view. They must not ignore the buyer perspective because of their seller bias, but instead must focus steadfastly on the relationship that exists between buyer and seller—the two equal parties who interact and collaborate to create the brand.

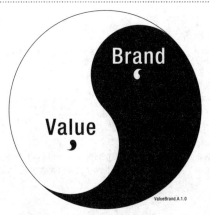

Figure 3-1 Brand managers must distinguish what they sell (value) from what customers buy (brand)—what we call the *value-brand dynamic*

If you think your company organizes around the customer point of view, please take a moment to answer these questions. How do your most loyal, profitable customers describe in emotional, heart-felt terms, what it means to have a relationship with your brand? How can you characterize this relationship with data such that you could easily go out and find more customers who match this demographic success (data) profile? How much revenue and profit will various levels of relationship produce over the next three to nine years?

In the value/brand dynamic, a company creates value that a customer then transforms into a satisfaction in the collaborative relationship that we have defined as a brand.

This transformation takes place in a complex series of cycles and interactions that we describe as *value creation* and *storytelling*, two processes that harmonize in a *satisfaction lifecycle*.

Value Creation

As illustrated in Figure 3-2, companies create the value that they offer to customers in a five-stage process that spans *offer-market development, demand creation, sales conversion, solution fulfillment,* and *strategic development.* Value creation thus integrates product development, marketing, sales, service, and training.

Figure 3-2 This model illustrates the sell-side perspective and emphasizes an inward-looking focus on business processes and value creation, how the firm relates to its market through these business processes

Offer-Market Development

In this stage, the brand firm develops a relevant offering (a product or service that meets a need) and through research identifies a market for it. The firm also develops the market infrastructure (field sales organization, repair depots, customer help desks, etc.) necessary to support the offering. This stage ends and the next stage begins when brand managers have defined a pre-emptive positioning.

We discuss positioning in detail later in this chapter. "Pre-emptive" suggests that when the brand managers bring a new satisfaction to market it reshuffles the hierarchy of desired or expected satisfactions within the customer's brandspace. When Apple Computer unveiled its iMac, for example, and positioned it as a consumer Internet appliance, home computers from Compaq and Gateway slipped down a notch in the brandspace of home computer buyers, and helped nudge Dell out of the consumer PC market.

Demand Creation

With an unserved customer need and a world-beater product and service now locked and loaded in the branding machine, brand managers must now generate demand. This generally corresponds to traditional marketing and product management activities: packaging, distribution, advertising, direct mail, publicity, point of purchase merchandising, and training of support staff, field operations, and distribution partners. But, the principal task remains development of the unique selling proposition, at which point brand managers exit this stage.

A unique selling proposition cogently frames a problem, concern, or desire not adequately filled by alternate product or service offerings, and proposes a satisfaction, benefit, or end result that customers instantly recognize as both desirable and different from other offerings. For some offerings, this proposition conveys a quality that we call *wow*—a crisp, engaging story or pitch that frames the proposition as, at least in part, an entertainment experience: the sheer delight a prospect feels on imagining a VW Beetle parked in her driveway. The unexpected pleasure of design, the anticipated compliments of friends and passers-by: it all adds up to, "Wow!"

Sales Conversion

In this stage, the firm converts demand into sales to paying customers. Brand managers identify points of market presence (retail outlets, field sales force, channel partners, catalogs and direct mail, and other sales locations), work hard to achieve maximum visibility in each venue, and develop programs for the ongoing care and feeding of the people who staff these points of market presence. Customers then begin to buy the branded product or service—we'll examine that in detail in a minute.

Brand managers move on to the next stage when they have identified the critical success factors of customer satisfaction through research. They use these findings to produce a set of best practice prescriptives—dance steps that prospects can follow, based on proven routines of successful customers. Brand managers may also need to identify solution partners—third- and fourth-party companies that offer complimentary products or solutions (retail organizations, consultants, etc.)—to clinch the sale of their branded offering.

Satisfaction Fulfillment

In this stage, the customer transforms the offering into a satisfaction in the process of successfully buying and using it. The offering meets expectations, solves a problem, or otherwise satisfies the customer. In addition to excellent product or service design, ease of use, training, and peer group support play an important role. At this point, it becomes evident whether or not brand managers have anticipated problems that might arise and have made appropriate contingency plans: botulism in the tomato soup can, exploding lithium batteries, etc. Effectively dealing with such problems will let brand managers maximize their chances for keeping the customer satisfied.

This stage comes to a close as satisfied customers start talking to each other and form communities: kenships (ad hoc groupings of like-minded individuals), peerages (more elite groups with a hierarchy of prestige), and user groups (organizing the transmission of best practices).

Strategic Development

In this fifth stage of value creation, brand managers must evaluate the future and the brand's place in it. As Clayton Christiansen discusses in detail in his book, *The Innovator's Dilemma* (Harvard Business School Press, 1997), the greater the success a brand achieves, the more blind brand managers may become to shifts in demand and to exploiting potentially disruptive innovations.

Now, brand managers must consolidate their gains and reinforce their positioning in the minds of customers. Don't make the mistake of trying to extend the brand by simply slapping the brand on other products or services—dilution almost always results. Instead, prune, sharpen, make more definite and distinct the one satisfaction that customers associate with the brand. As depicted in Figure 3-3, this means listening closely to three groups: the most satisfied customers, the most profitable, and those customers in the share-determining market sector (customers who have yet to enter the category or bond with a particular brand in the category).

Cycle Time

The value creation process gives managers a key metric they can use to measure performance: *cycle time,* how quickly a company can bring to market products or services that customers want and buy.

Cycle time answers the question: How fast do we commercialize innovation and create loyal repeat customers, as measured by how quickly, or not, they move from stage to stage in the value creation process? Measure how long it takes to reach the end point of each stage (relevant offering, pre-emptive positioning, unique selling proposition, etc., as illustrated in Figure 3-2), tracking the number of professional days consumed by staff and partners, and costs both direct and indirect. In addition to what's contained in this book, at Firebrands.com we offer more information about this and other branding performance metrics in a section called Brandwidth.

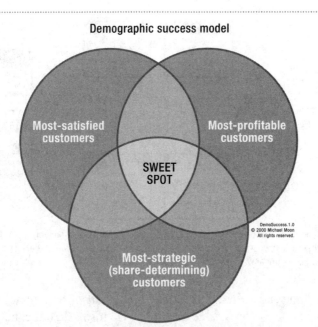

Demographic success model

Most-satisfied customers

Most-profitable customers

SWEET SPOT

Most-strategic (share-determining) customers

Figure 3-3 Successful brand managers hit the sweet spot of their markets, driving one satisfaction to a small group of customers—what we call the *demographic-success model*

Business Design

The value creation process reflects the company's internal focus and emphasizes two key ideas: *business design and model* and *corporate lifecycle.*

We start with Peter Drucker's notion of a "theory of business" (who's the customer, what satisfaction do they buy?) and Andrew Slywotzky's notions of a "business design" (what satisfaction do you bring to market and how do you capture value?) to clarify how managers must organize to create strategic positioning (how do we drive our brand to a commanding market position?) and capture value (how do we earn outrageous profits?). Figure 3-4 illustrates this.

Drucker emphasizes the importance of full alignment of executives and staff regarding their "theory of business," using formal and informal training, executive communication, and other proven management practices by which to propagate the theory of business throughout the firm. Drucker also emphasizes the need to motivate knowledge workers and to create psychic or spiritual rewards for work

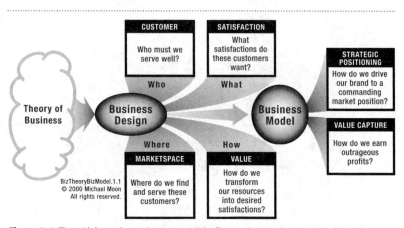

Figure 3-4 The widely used term *business model* reflects a deep understanding of why the company exists and what underlying theories of business frame its answer to the question, "Why do we exist as a company?"

worth doing and a sense of corporate mission that brings these rewards into focus. Slywotzky's value capture mechanisms describe the nature of transactions between the firm and customers and how the mechanism (software license, service contract, etc.) shapes customer perception of value and loyalty. If not well developed and slotted for a brand, the value capture mechanism of a business design may become a major impediment to customer adoption and loyalty.

Brand managers should not underestimate the power of a business design. How important is it? If you plan to eventually do business online, consider that many leading dot.com businesses, including Amazon.com, Priceline, Broadvision, and eBay have patented key aspects of their business design, in particular business processes, and hope to derive significant royalty streams from other firms for years to come.

Figure 3-5 illustrates the key elements of a business design as they relate to brand-building. In the previous chart, From Theory of Business to a Business Model, we see the role of the customer, satisfaction, marketspace, value, strategic positioning, and value capture, so we skip over those elements in Figure 3-5 and move to the next level.

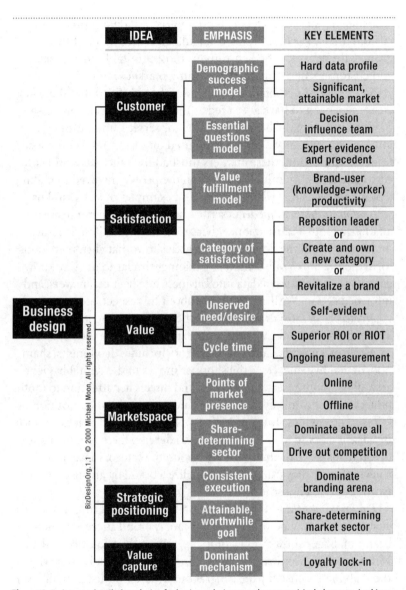

Figure 3-5 A more detailed analysis of a *business design* reveals many critical elements. Lacking any of these will cause a business to fail. Use this chart to grade your firm's successful identification and use of these key elements

Demographic-success model represents a hard data profile of the customer base sweet spot, the triangulated center point of three groups: the most satisfied customers, most profitable customers, and customers in the share-determining market sector.

An *essential-questions model* includes the questions that these key customers need to have answered as they go through the process of buying and using the branded product or service, and ultimately joining a community of practice focused on the brand. Within a customer organization, these answers must address the needs and concerns of a decision influence team (all the people involved in making a purchase decision) with evidence and examples of successful use.

A *value-fulfillment model* describes how the customer transforms an offering into a satisfaction, either an economic or lifestyle return on investment in the brand. Our research shows that customers transform a value into a satisfaction in a manner similar to the way knowledge workers transform data into business intelligence, answers, and informed action. We'll explain more about this aspect later.

A *category of satisfaction* describes the customer's mental map that locates particular brands in more generic categories: in the personal care aisle of a grocery store (metacategory includes deodorants, shampoo, dental hygiene, etc.), the shopper moves to the dental hygiene area (floss, mouthwash, toothpaste), and directs her attention to toothpaste, where she quickly associates brand names with their positionings (Crest = no cavities; Tom's of Maine = all natural), and makes a choice. Because it takes so long for customers to develop these mental maps, brand managers can attempt to reposition the category leader, creating a new category they can own, or revitalize a brand by giving customers new reasons to choose it.

Unserved need/desire calls attention to how an offering can serve a customer in a way no other offering can. A brand succeeds when the brand manager showcases a complete, self-evident solution—the Netscape Navigator browser which, in 1995, made it obvious why the Web made sense for the general public and not just a small, technically savvy in-group.

Cycle time measures the efficacy of value creation, how quickly the enterprise creates an offering and a market, creating a superior return on investment or its lifestyle equivalent: returned investment of time (RIOT).

Points of market presence describe where in a marketspace a firm converts prospects into customers, highlighting traditional offline venues and emerging online venues (which we discuss in detail later in this book).

Share-determining sector describes the small, generally overlooked portion hidden in every market comprised of customers not yet branded for the category or particular brand within the category. Lifelong brand loyalties usually start with the successful branding of teenagers and college students. Brand managers must not only target this sector, they must also aggressively dominate it, driving out competitors with superior value and storytelling.

Consistent execution means that brand managers must tell one crisply focused story to one customer segment with brilliance and consistency, never straying from the one chord—the satisfaction— that resonates most deeply with the buyer.

Attainable, worthwhile goal describes how a company drives its brand into an unassailable, dominant positioning in the share- determining market sector. In this context, worthwhile means that you have targeted a market with sufficient profit potential to more than offset the cost of market entry.

Dominant mechanism represents the way you get paid and how buyers perceive all the currencies of exchange as fair and equitable. In addition to money, these currencies include the hassle factor, demands on attention and detail, etc. Ultimately, the brand's value capture mechanism characterizes the essential transaction between buyer and seller: what satisfactions must we give you so that you will form lifelong loyalty with the brand, thus accepting a loyalty lock-in. Choose your handcuffs.

The Nature of the Offering

Why do successful brands so often fail in an attempt to launch a new brand or extension of the brand? Not understanding the nature of the offering ranks as the most significant reason.

Products Come from Mars, Services Come from Venus, New Hybrids Come from Mercury

Figure 3-6 describes the three broad categories of offerings. We borrow this approach from the very entertaining but nonetheless insightful relationship guru, John Gray, and his successful series of books, *Men are from Mars, Women are from Venus.* Since brands constitute a relationship between buyer and seller, much of Gray's work can find productive application in branding.

	Mars	**Mercury**	**Venus**
OFFERING	Products	Self-service results	Services
MARKETPLACE	Store or office	Tailored logistics space	Trust network
ACTIVITY FOCUS	Selling	Self-service satisfaction	Consulting
BRANDING EMPHASIS	Persuasion	Tools to customize	Storytelling
PROCESS INTENT	Reorders	Loyalty lock in	Long-term engagements
VALUE CAPTURE MECHANISM	Markups and commissions	Transaction, license, and aggregation fees	Fees and prestigous referrals

Figure 3-6 John Gray's series of books, *Men are from Mars, Women are from Venus,* help us understand that some branded offerings have a distinctly Martian character, while others feel Venusian. Many dot.com brands will blend the two in a Mercury hybrid

With Mars, we characterize products, sold in retail stores or in office calls, with an activity focus on selling, a branding emphasis on persuasion, a process intent of capturing reorders, and a value capture mechanism of markups and commissions. Mars represents an outgoing, goal-seeking intent for creating relationships that usually emphasizes accumulation of power through dominance: for instance, Microsoft or Oracle who says "It's not enough to win, everybody else must lose."

With Venus, we characterize personal or professional services sold through a trust network (referral and word-of-mouth), with an activity focus on consulting or helping, a branding emphasis on relating and storytelling, a process intent of long-term engagements, and a value capture mechanism of fees and prestigious referral. Venus represents a receptive, accommodating, safety-seeking intent for creating relationships emphasizing the accumulation of power through calling attention to oneself—the Elizabeth Taylor school of branding: Big Five accounting firms, banks, and movies.

With Mercury we characterize self-service results, sold in a tailored logistics space (Home Depot; Ikea; Costco), with an activity focus on self-service satisfaction, a branding emphasis on customization tools, a process intent on loyalty lock-ins, and value capture mechanisms of membership, transaction, license, and aggregation fees. Mercury represents a playful interaction among members of a community of practice with an intent to enlarge the community, emphasizing the distribution of power among brand advocates and other leaders of the brand-using community. As we show later, Mercury presents the best model for successful online offerings.

How Quickly (or not) Customers Buy the Offering

Figure 3-7 shows how customers relate to various types of offerings. Do they buy on impulse (video game), or after great deliberation (enterprise-level customer relationship software)? This relates to the customer's need for information or extensive education prior to purchase, as well as the degree of involvement of a decision influence team, the relevant maturity of the market category (how many buyers understand the category?), and the degree to which the brand's satisfactions strike buyers as self-evident. Brand managers must learn through research where customers put their brands on these axes in order to maintain customer confidence and, especially, before launching new brands. An 89¢ McDonald's burger represents a quick-turn impulse purchase, while a $4,995 cruise with Ronald McDonald would represent a purchase requiring far longer deliberation.

Positioning

We define *positioning* to mean a fully developed satisfaction uniquely associated with one seller: the more distinct, unambiguous, and experiential the positioning, the greater its power to move markets and create loyal, repeat customers.

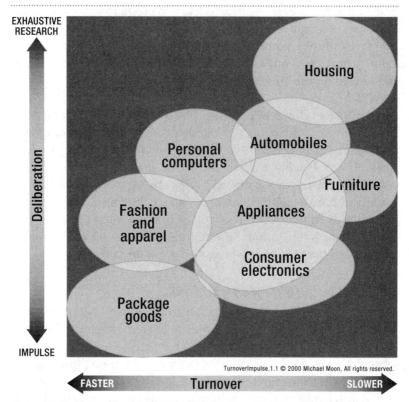

Figure 3-7 Important differences exist among various types of offerings. Customers buy some offerings every week (perishable foodstuffs). They may buy other offerings every couple of years (new car) or once in a decade (new house). Against the baseline of faster or slower turnover, deliberation of a purchase moves from impulse to exhaustive research

Figure 3-8 illustrates the key elements of a positioning strategy. *Defining idea* means the one word that captures the essence of the satisfaction. Brand managers use this word to create a pitch (BMW's "Drives like a sports car with the luxury of a Mercedes and the safety of a Volvo") or slogan (BMW as the "ultimate driving machine").

Market category. In our earlier business design discussion in this category, we defined a market category using the toothpaste/Crest example. Crest uses the credentialed authority of the American Dental Association to endorse its use of stannous fluoride and establish its category leadership.

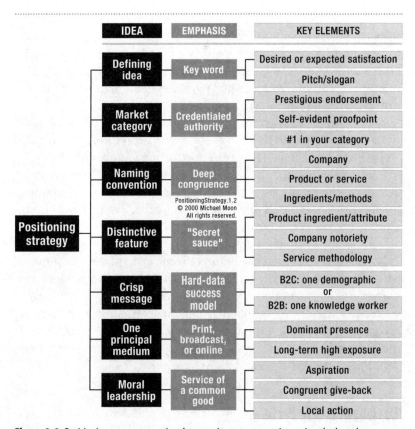

IDEA	EMPHASIS	KEY ELEMENTS
Defining idea	Key word	Desired or expected satisfaction
		Pitch/slogan
Market category	Credentialed authority	Prestigious endorsement
		Self-evident proofpoint
		#1 in your category
Naming convention	Deep congruence	Company
		Product or service
		Ingredients/methods
Distinctive feature	"Secret sauce"	Product ingredient/attribute
		Company notoriety
		Service methodology
Crisp message	Hard-data success model	B2C: one demographic or B2B: one knowledge worker
One principal medium	Print, broadcast, or online	Dominant presence
		Long-term high exposure
Moral leadership	Service of a common good	Aspiration
		Congruent give-back
		Local action

Positioning strategy

PositioningStrategy.1.2
© 2000 Michael Moon
All rights reserved.

Figure 3-8 Positioning strategy remains the most important creative action the brand manager takes. It brings together many factors of market dynamics, customer expectations, and marketing communications

Naming convention emphasizes a brand name and names of ingredients associated with the brand. These names must all resonate with the company name, the category, and the brand satisfaction. For example, Clif Bar Inc. has positioned a new health bar for women, sold under the Luna brand with the slogan, "The Whole Nutrition Bar for Women." The package shows women dancing beneath a crescent moon.

Distinctive feature communicates the "secret sauce"—in the case of Treetop brand apple juice, "A perfect blend of fresh Red Delicious, Golden Delicious and a little Granny Smith."

Crisp message means that you address what one customer group wants to hear, de-emphasizing or excluding what other groups want to hear. Outside of design and publishing markets where it sells high-end systems, for example, Apple no longer positions itself as a seller of business computers, focusing low-end systems on home and education use. As a result, Apple's market share has doubled.

One principal medium means that brand managers limit promotional, marketing, and branding activity to one branding channel (we explain those in detail later in this chapter). Why one? This forces brand managers to focus resources and punch through the clutter and noise of a particular medium (the one or two magazines most prospects and customers read: Absolut vodka on *Wired* magazine's back cover, for example) instead of spreading resources thin and never achieving critical mass.

Moral leadership links the brand to some form of service of the common good, addressing the aspirations and social conscience of customers. This won't work without authenticity. The Body Shoppe successfully brands its use of environmentally friendly ingredients (acquired in ways that promote economic self-sufficiency from the indigenous people who supply them) and its programs to help these suppliers with medicines and other necessities.

Corporate Lifecycle

How a company approaches value creation and the rest of the branding process depends on where the company finds itself in a corporate lifecycle. Young brash, entrepreneurial firms demonstrate markedly different value creation, branding processes, and customer relationships than older, mature firms. The corporate lifecycle explains the wide diversity of branding messages that consumers encounter, from fresh, new, young ideas to sturdy, old, cantankerous campaigns. Corporate lifecycles also explain why great creative ideas sometimes get killed by corporate culture.

Figure 3-9, based on the pioneering work of Ichak Adizes, *Managing Corporate Lifecycles* (Prentice Hall Press, 1999), shows the overall contour of infancy, adolescence, prime, and senescence. Figure 3-10 relates these lifecycle stages to the distribution of authority and responsibility for branding within the company.

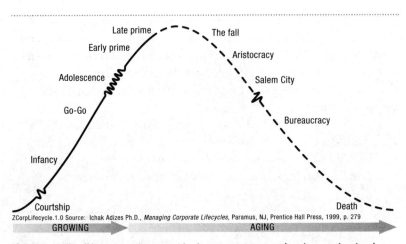

ZCorpLifecycle.1.0 Source: Ichak Adizes Ph.D., *Managing Corporate Lifecycles*, Paramus, NJ, Prentice Hall Press, 1999, p. 279

Figure 3-9 Like all living organisms, organizations grow, mature, and expire over time in what Ichak Adizes calls a "corporate lifecycle"

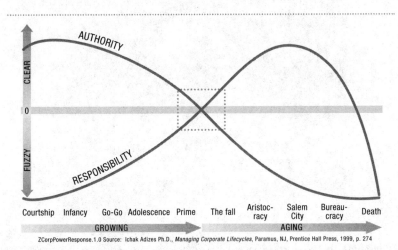

ZCorpPowerResponse.1.0 Source: Ichak Adizes Ph.D., *Managing Corporate Lifecycles*, Paramus, NJ, Prentice Hall Press, 1999, p. 274

Figure 3-10 At each stage of a corporate lifecycle, authority and responsibility will have an inverse relationship. Generally, young firms encourage individuals to exercise tremendous authority, while older firms with large, entrenched bureaucracies will have rigidly defined responsibilities

Adizes' study of thousands of corporations led him to conclude that as companies age they become more bureaucratic (where the authority and responsibility lines cross on the second graph), and will eventually die unless they become aware of this lifecycle and do something extraordinary to change it. They must fight the trend towards bureaucracy, and instead give individuals greater authority to take independent, intrapreneurial action, and dramatically decrease management control through strictly defined roles and responsibilities.

How does this apply to brand management? Figure 3-11 shows that the most consistently effective branding efforts occur under CEO-led branding teams, generally early in the corporate lifecycle: Amazon.com under Jeff Bezos, and Nike under Phil Knight.

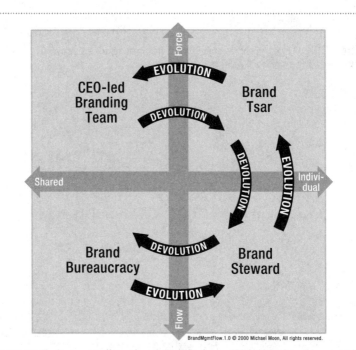

BrandMgmtFlow.1.0 © 2000 Michael Moon, All rights reserved.

Figure 3-11 The best, most efficient branding results from a CEO-led branding. This can quickly devolve into the tyranny of a brand tsar, the political compromises of a brand steward, or the calcification of the brand bureaucracy

If the CEO falls asleep at the branding wheel as a company ages, a *brand tsar* will emerge: a highly regarded co-founder or an ambitious vice president who, through the force of personality, takes control of branding as a personal mission. Sergio Zyman at Coke and

Bob Herbold at Microsoft represent brand tsars who have achieved considerable success. But, compared to a CEO-led branding team, they pale because they control only the storytelling part of the branding process, and not the larger value creation process that brings whole new categories of satisfaction to market.

A *brand steward*, generally a highly regarded mid-level marketing executive, has influence but no control over the way other marketing managers spend branding dollars. This generally results in branding by committee, a recipe for muddled, fuzzy positioning, impotent branding, and loss of market share.

Senescent companies, where branding has fallen off top management's radar screen, relegate branding to a *brand bureaucracy*, a near-clerical task of applying slogans to mature products and services.

A new CEO can reverse this devolution by taking charge of an aggressive branding team and effort. Instead of delegating the branding activity, she incorporates branding into the basic business planning process. Carly Fiorina has begun this process at Hewlett-Packard. Steve Jobs' revitalization of Apple Computer with the iMac for home and education users, the iBook for students, and the G4 for publishing and graphics professionals represents one of the most extraordinary examples of a CEO achieving success after taking over from a weak brand tsar.

What do brand managers do? What actions do they take to build a brand? They tell stories that customers want to hear.

Branding Intent

The branding process demonstrates an intent, a motive for creating a relationship between buyer and seller. This intent reflects many factors, including the corporate lifecycle, the branding authority, a positioning strategy, the nature of the offering, and the business design.

Figure 3-12 shows four major branding intentions and the kinds of relationships that emerge from their interaction.

Some branding intentions reflect the advertising campaign's *creative vision*—Bennetton, Coke, and The Gap, to name a few. The advertising serves as the point of differentiation for an otherwise undifferentiated product or service.

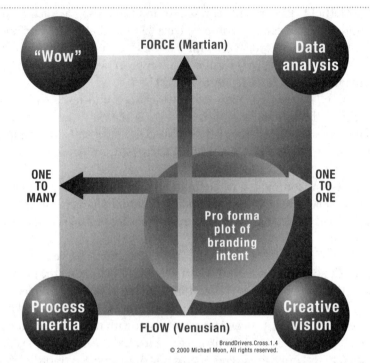

Figure 3-12 The intention to build a brand will reflect several factors, the most important of which will entail the focus of the relationship and its Martian or Venusian nature

The branding process can also reflect the ruthless insight of rigorous *data analysis*—who bought what, why, and how can we get more customers just like them? On a more strategic level this may entail development of an econometric data model, an extensive data analysis by which brand managers target individual accounts or groups of accounts. IBM, Andersen Consulting, and Merck provide examples of this approach.

Another branding intent entails the forceful insertion of a shocking delight—*Wow*—into a market of relatively undifferentiated competitors. Here the product or service sells itself—customers fall in love with it at first sight, reflecting industrial design, packaging, or grand spectacle. The 1964 Ford Mustang, the new VW Beetle, and the Sony Walkman stand as good examples.

Finally, some branding intentions reflect bureaucratic or institutional status quo—*process inertia*. Leveraging a historical legacy and prestige, some firms simply represent themselves as the destination without peer in the market. Examples include Harvard University, Northwestern Life, and New York's Plaza Hotel.

These four intentions fuel a branding effort and will shape the kind of relationship that buyer and seller will form. Generally, Wow and process inertial branding intentions will emphasize a *one-to-many* relationship—the buyer will see herself as a member of a group and through this group they have a relationship with a brand: sports teams, amusement parks. Likewise, data analysis and creative vision will emphasize a more personal, *one-to-one* relationship between a buyer and the brand, holding the seller accountable to understanding the needs and desires of the individual buyer.

Branding intentions characterized by Wow and data analysis tend to get into the buyer's face, displaying *force*, a Martian approach. Intentions characterized by process and inertia and creative vision emphasize *flow*; they pull people into a story or intrigue, a Venusian approach.

Use this branding intention model to help understand not only your firm's branding efforts, but also how to intelligently compare them to other firms—competitors in your market category, suppliers, and other firms that may influence your customer's purchase decisions.

Brand Storytelling

Customers respond to the company's value creation process in a series of stages we call the *storytelling process*, as illustrated in Figure 3-13.

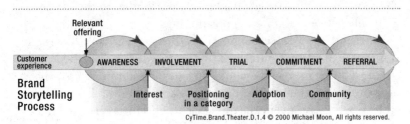

Figure 3-13 Companies build their brands through stories that explain to the customer the buying and using experience. These stories, if created and told well, build communities and referrals—the source of short-cycle, high-margin repeat purchases

Why do we call it storytelling? Brand managers must tell potential and existing customers about the buying and using experience. They must connect the various branding events—moments of truth—into a coherent, meaningful narrative of what it means to use the brand and enjoy its satisfactions. Brand managers succeed when they link brand use to a customer's social or professional identity. Customers must put themselves in this story, envisioning themselves as an actor "wearing" the brand as a badge of belonging in a larger-than-life drama: part of the whole human family drinking Coke and singing together, for example. Shortly, we'll discuss brand storytelling in terms of classic story structure, but first let's look at the brand storytelling process from a wider perspective.

In the brand storytelling process, customers move from a state of ignorance regarding a brand, all the way to acting as an enthusiastic advocate for the brand, in five stages: *awareness, involvement, trial, commitment,* and *referral.* These stages mirror the five stages of the brand firm's value creation process, emphasizing the buyer's experience and the deepening of trust and reciprocity in the relationship the buyer forms with the brand and its producer.

During the *awareness* stage, the buyer encounters a relevant offering for which she may or may not currently have an in-the-moment need. She may tuck away in her mind, "If I ever encounter *this,* I might need *Brand X.*" She exits the awareness stage when the brand has piqued her interest, linking the offer to a real need or desire.

During the *involvement* stage, the buyer may scrutinize advertisements, talk with friends, read magazine articles, or otherwise demonstrate an increased appetite for information related to the category and the particular brands within it. The buyer exits this stage when she can accurately associate the brand positionings in the category—generally no more than seven positionings.

During the *trial* stage, the buyer test-drives cars, visits showrooms, or makes exploratory purchases (in the case of low-cost goods and services). She can write off a meal in a new restaurant, but she balks at spending the time and trouble necessary to uninstall a $50 software program. A buyer exits this stage when she has adopted the category—this stuff works for me—and begins to form a preference for a particular brand.

Repeated buying, using, and disposal experiences lead either to bonding with a brand in the *commitment* stage, or to a move back to the trial stage with other brands. Here the customer begins to form emotional allegiances with the brand. In terms of the customer's brandspace, the brand becomes a go-to brand. If the brand evolves into a badge of belonging, the customer enters a community of like-minded brand users and enters the next stage.

In the *referral* stage, the brand becomes a currency of exchange among members of the community and the customer becomes a brand advocate who seeks to expand this group of happy campers. I have many friends with Palm Pilots, for example, who keep trying to convince me to buy one.

Brand managers should use this brand storytelling model to prioritize their investments and explain their allocations to higher executives.

Brand Identity

Advertising agencies and brand consultants speak of a brand identity. We've defined a brand as a satisfaction that customers buy, the collaboration of buyer and seller that evolves into an ongoing relationship, and the story that explains the buying and using experience. So what do we mean by brand identity?

Figure 3-14 defines brand identity in terms of buyer effects and seller activities. Buyers formulate an understanding of a brand identity as a result of their constant exposure to a seller's consistent execution of branding activities. Brand identity thus represents a *gestalt* or system of images and ideas that a buyer associates with the brand or service and the company behind it. In other words, brand identity constitutes what most people call a brand.

Buyer Effects

A brand identity strikes the buyer as instantly *recognized* in its market category (Crest toothpaste in dental hygiene category, for example). A brand identity stimulates the memory of past satisfactions (*recall*) and reinforces reasons to buy again (*preference*). Some brand consultants believe that a brand identity makes a promise, but it does not. The category of satisfaction conveys a promise that an individual brand fulfills (or not). For this reason, management of a category becomes paramount for most brand managers.

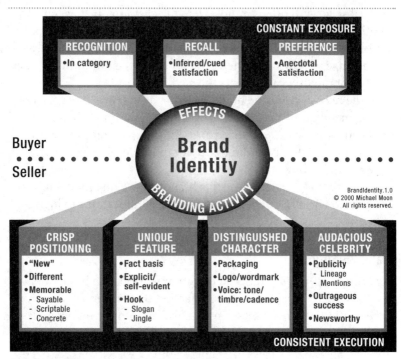

Figure 3-14 Through constant exposure, a brand identity produces recognition, recall, and preference in buyers. This requires consistent execution of branding activities: crisp positioning, unique feature, distinguished character, and audacious celebrity

Seller Activities

Seller activities emphasize the creation of a *crisp positioning*—something that strikes the customer as new, better, different, and memorable. Sellers reinforce their positioning by calling attention to a *unique feature* or attribute—a proof point—that validates the brand's distinction. *Distinguished character* means that all brand identity notes (packaging, logos, "voice") sing together to strike one deep chord. Great brands break away from the pack if they add *audacious celebrity*—a "wow" satisfaction that draws media attention (VW Beetle or iMac, for example), or a brand story that captivates the media, as in the case of the Champagne Growers of California's Romance Council, established to position champagne as a currency of exchange between romantic couples.

Brand Expressions

As brand managers begin to tell their stories they will employ a variety of modes of expression. Figure 3-15 illustrates their range.

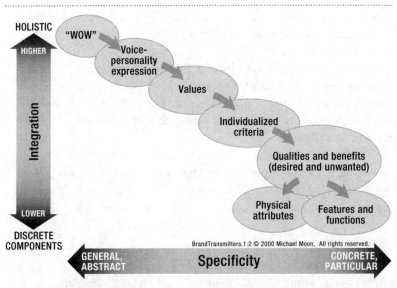

Figure 3-15 Each brand tells a story, using different modes of expression. The most effective mode creates an immersive gestalt—a wow!—that conveys on multiple simultaneous levels the story of the brand

Some brand managers will focus on expressions such as features and functions while others will focus on physical attributes. Bernd Schmitt, in his book *Experiential Marketing*, calls this an ineffective method because it fails to achieve lasting recognition, recall, and preference, requiring massive expenditures to compensate.

The most effective brand expression conveys in a single, stunning gestalt, a *wow!* that overwhelms and immerses the customer in a nuanced, multilevel experience of the brand. We've mentioned the iMac and the VW Beetle in this category. Hit video games (*Mortal Kombat* and many others) and movies (*Titanic*, the *Star Wars* trilogy, and many others) perfectly express wow! They need no explanation; upon first encounter, buyers "get it." As we explain shortly, Hal Riney started at the top of the brand expression curve, somewhere between voice-personality and wow!, in his award-winning series of television advertisements that introduced the Saturn automobile company.

Brands with *voice-personality expression* have the same kind of distinct, recognizable boundaries and characteristics that earn worldwide recognition for distinguished people: appearance (FedEx's orange and purple, for example); behaviors (FedEx's overnight delivery); emotional presence in the mind of customers (FedEx's "Did you FedEx it?" question of heartfelt concern); social identity and shared recognition in the community (When I say "FedEx it" you know exactly what to do and who to call).

Lacking a voice-personality expression, brand managers often highlight *values* of the brand. Campbell's *Simply Home* premium soup line focuses on the broad appeal of the values of homemade soups like grandma made, with nostalgic graphics and type, sold in a home-canning-style jar.

Individualized criteria work like values, but narrow the focus to a more specific taste or personality type. Just about everybody thinks fondly of Grandma's soup, but not everybody wants to be a snooty English gentleman who insists on Grey Poupon mustard.

From Brand Expression to Branding Theater

How do brand expressions develop? Figure 3-16 shows how they evolve from *metaphors*, taking on *facets of brand personality*, and developing into a rich *voice* that echoes and amplifies customer input and satisfactions. As a brand expression evolves, each successive development level incorporates the previous level, in a cumulative, and, we hope, synergistic fashion.

Metaphors describe the intent to communicate a new and often complex idea in simple, direct terms, by comparing a known entity, with many attributes and qualities, to an unknown entity. Office automation vendors use file cabinets to talk about mass storage systems, for example.

Wells Fargo's television advertisements play like a Western movie, featuring the familiar stage coach and horses roaring into town, safely delivering people and valued cargo. This conveys the pioneer spirit and tradition of service symbolized by the stagecoach.

Metaphors provide a good starting point for a brand expression, but can't stand alone. Scratch them and they fall apart; a metaphor conveys only image and no substantive information.

Brand managers can build on a metaphor, however, by introducing various *facets of brand personality*, using associated images, moods, ideas, qualities, facts, and keywords. In a recent newspaper

Figure 3-16 Most brand identities evolve from a simple metaphor that attempts to convey the intangible satisfaction offered to the customer. As brand managers make this identity more relevant and suitable to the customers, the brand identity begins to associate various facets (images, facts, qualities, keywords, etc.), and soon finds its voice in the satisfactions of customers

advertisement, Wells Fargo shrank the stagecoach and superimposed a laptop computer screen (as in DVD movie playback) and the wells-fargo.com URL across a western panorama. In subsequent brochures, they build on this to show the user interface and online services they offer to small business owners.

The *voice of the brand* expresses the contents of the emotional bank account a customer accrues through a series of buying and using experiences. These contents include the functional attributes of the product or service ("it opens cans"), the brand metaphor, and facets of personality. What makes it a voice? Brand managers have identified, through customer feedback, the essence of the satisfaction they have found in the brand. Brand managers then express these satisfactions in a coherent, unified fashion across all branding media (TV, point-of-purchase, etc.), using the language and emotional qualities that satisfied customers use. In this way, the voice of the satisfied customer becomes the voice of the brand.

Hal Riney's Saturn television campaign provides a classic example. Saturn's extensive research of car buyers showed a tremendous dissatisfaction with the car-buying experience, a lack of warmth or human connection with "Detroit" or "Japan, Inc.," the lack of pride Americans feel with respect to U.S.-made cars in contrast with their Japanese counterparts, and a suspicion that assembly lines strip the autoworker of pride in craftsmanship and thus contribute to low-quality cars.

Riney's ads reflected the process that Saturn created in response, proclaiming that Saturn does not merely represent a new car but a whole new company and, by inference, a whole new buying and using experience for customers. He re-positioned Saturn as a type of product that made America great, in which the craftsman's spirit remains vital and alive, evoking the experience of dealing with a trusted small-town merchant who earns an honest dollar in exchange for an honest product (fixed-price, no-haggle buying process). In an avuncular voice-over narration that evoked Walter Cronkite or Charles Kuralt, Riney told the Saturn story in a series of award-winning commercials that used American car customers' own words and experiences to create the voice of the Saturn brand. It represented a story that American car buyers desperately wanted to hear, and they bought Saturn cars by the millions.

The *branding theater* represents the ultimate evolution of brand expression. At their most successful, the branding theater production becomes a global media event acted out on a world stage. Microsoft's Windows 95 launch provides perhaps the best example.

Long-delayed but ballyhooed by the technical, trade, and business press as the next great leap forward in computing, Windows 95 would make its triumphal entry with all the pomp and circumstance of a Shakespearean king returning from an epic battle.

Microsoft enlisted a host of skillful actors—captains of industry and the newly appointed king of late-night television comedy, Jay Leno. The company paid a reported $5 million dollars for the launch soundtrack, the Rolling Stones' hit, *Start Me Up*, alluding to the Windows 95 start button. Microsoft set up a global satellite television broadcast to which the company invited virtually everybody who was anybody.

In a long run-up to the launch event, Microsoft leaked a carefully orchestrated series of tidbits to reporters who scurried to publish stories about the upcoming event. They granted interviews with otherwise unavailable key executives to top broadcasters, such as NBC's Tom Brokaw, which, in turn, stimulated additional television coverage that asked the PR professional's dream question, "What makes

Windows 95 so significant?" and let Microsoft experts provide the answer. This created a feeding frenzy that drew in even such conservative media actors as *The New York Times* and *Washington Post* which then covered not only the launch but the hype around the launch. The launch itself followed a script put together by Microsoft executives and their PR and advertising partners. Even people who didn't own PCs found themselves swept into this dramatic story, while customers waited in line to buy Windows 95 when it appeared in stores at midnight on the appointed day. To their shocking delight, customers found that Windows 95 did represent a significant advance over Windows 3.*x* and MS-DOS. Microsoft provided an encore, demonstrating its mastery of the branding theater and global media events, with its launch of the Internet Explorer Web browser.

Theater of Brand Storytelling

As we've seen, every branding theater production needs a story.

What kinds of stories can a company use to express a brand identity? Story arcs have remained unchanged since Aristotle wrote his *Poetics* in the fourth century BC. Every story moves from a setup through the build to the pay-off. *Gravity's Rainbow* does it in 760 pages; Nike's television commercials do it in 15 seconds.

Brand storytellers can use one of four basic plots (they can also mix elements to produce hybrid genres): romance, comedy, tragedy, and satire. For a brilliant, in-depth treatment of the rhetoric of storytelling, see *Metahistory—The Historical Imagination in Nineteenth-Century Europe* by Hayden White (The Johns Hopkins University Press, 1973); we'll post a detailed discussion of White's work as it relates to brand storytelling at Firebrands.com because space won't permit it here.

In brand storytelling, the romance plot emphasizes the branded product or service sweeps the customer into a larger-than-life pleasure: BMW's romance of the road, DeBeer's "diamonds are forever," or the Taster's Choice soap opera of neighbors falling in love.

Tragedy triggers fears of the consequences that follow a bad choice: choose *this* brand (FedEx) and avoid *that* tragedy (humiliation among peers as a result of not FedExing that important package).

Comedy conveys a sense of fun, play, and liberation from the strictures of society, but liberation as a function of personal choice: the brand symbolizes the realization of freedom. Examples include the FedEx mile-a-minute talker, the Michael Jordan and Tweety Bird ads for MCI, MetLife's Snoopy stories, E-Trade's Super Bowl 2000 commercial, "He's got money up the wazoo!" and Budweiser's talking animals.

Satire pokes fun at the stupidity, greed, or other sins of the power elite. Satire, however, has one big problem: it often expresses a mean, heartless spirit that can polarize people into an in-crowd and out-crowd. Taco Bell's Chihuahua has produced a short-term success but will, we predict, ultimately fail because it steps over the line of comedy into hard-edged satire.

Use these classic plot genres carefully because they quickly go flat with today's story-drenched media-savvy audiences.

Using our plot genres metaphorically to explain the process of brand building , we can say that most brand stories begin as romance; a promise of satisfaction. Rude competitors and stormy seas threaten— the tragedy of markets. The brand manager must provide proof that the brand's satisfaction will endure. When the brand begins to reflect a community of practice (satisfied customers), the story may take on qualities of fun and eccentricity: comedy. The story twists into satire if these brand-user communities erect hierarchies—of power, taste, etiquette—that reflect the socioeconomic and class distinctions of society. The real tragedy happens when brand managers don't submit their rosy, romantic strategies to the reality of markets, customers, and data by which to validate lasting and authentic satisfactions.

Who Wants to Hear a Brand Story?

Previously, we said that brand managers must target their brand stories to an audience that represents the intersection of three groups: the company's most profitable customers, most satisfied customers, and the share-determining market sector. Now, let's further define this audience to help brand managers achieve greater success in their brand storytelling.

The master storyteller, Walt Disney, early in his career bet his fledgling company on the success of his first full-length feature animated movie, *Snow White and the Seven Dwarves*. From his earliest filmmaking years he had believed fervently in testing works in progress with their intended audience—children.

He used testing first in the story development process. He began with traditional stories—the kind we just discussed, that meet

Aristotle's model. Disney used the screenplays as bedtime stories for his nephew, and made changes based on the nephew's feedback thus tailoring them for a perfect representative of his target audience.

About halfway through production of *Snow White*, Disney began test-screening the film. He wanted to identify the effectiveness of plot structure, character development, musical scoring, and myriad other aspects of the production. The kids loved it. But Walt noticed something potentially disturbing: many of the children had urinated in their seats, apparently in response to the scary Witch. Part of the creative team argued for softening the Witch if not taking her out altogether or moving her off screen. Disney refused, arguing that the removal of this vibrant villain would destroy the story.

Someone came up with the idea to wire the seats with saline moisture detectors linked to a display board in the projection booth that would light up when the kids let loose. The Witch came and went; no lights flashed. Instead, later in the movie, the lights went off all at once when the dwarves came to Snow White's rescue. Not fear of the Witch, but delight at the heroine's rescue triggered the tangible expression of their emotions. Disney thus closed the loop with hard data feedback and could proceed confident that his offering would satisfy his audience: the movie told a story his customers wanted to hear.

Every brand manager knows that some customers respond more warmly and wholeheartedly than others to the same brand story. A particular customer's response depends on where the customer finds herself in the storytelling process we discussed earlier in this chapter. Within the audience for a brand story, a brand manager will find individuals at every point along the spectrum from awareness, to involvement, to trial, commitment, and referral. The response to the brand story also depends on the kind of customer behaviors that an individual exhibits.

Switchable Customers (or Not)

How can a new drug therapy come out of nowhere to gain tremendous market share at the expense of a deeply entrenched, proven market leader? Adrian Slywotzky explained the winning strategy a decade ago. First, identify the share-determining market sector—doctors still in their residencies and not yet in private practice. Second, use hard data to attack the principal weakness (a side effect, cost, etc.) of the market leader. Third, pursue this attack mercilessly at the expense of all other marketing programs. The result? As these doctors moved into private practice, they prescribed the upstart therapy, not the market leader.

In other words, as illustrated in Figure 3-17, brand managers get the highest return on marketing investment by targeting switchable customers already in a category. Switchable customers have begun the trial stage, buying and using various products in a category. By the time they reach the optimization phase of the commitment stage, they have already formed their largely unshakable brand allegiances.

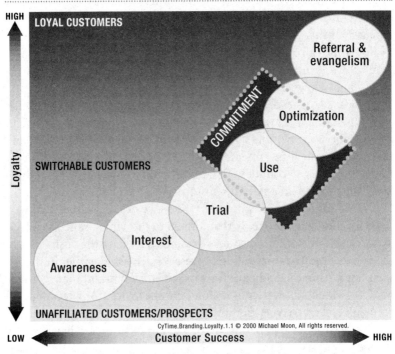

Figure 3-17 Brand managers maximize their return on marketing investment by focusing on switchable customers, buyers already educated in the category but not yet locked in to a particular brand

Market research reports often suggest that because locked-in customers buy in such large volumes, they make an attractive target, but our research shows the opposite. Trying to unhook committed customers from optimized solutions built around a competing brand proves extremely difficult and enormously expensive.

Likewise, if brand managers target customers too early, they will educate a market but may not see sales for years, and they risk watching a more nimble competitor come in and steal these educated customers. Target switchable customers first, and invest in educating ignorant customers (i.e., not yet in the category), leveraging word of mouth referral and communities of practice to help educate them.

Customer Behaviors

Branding stories must target customers based on their behavior. Figure 3-18 illustrates the four basic types: shopping, sourcing, buying, trading.

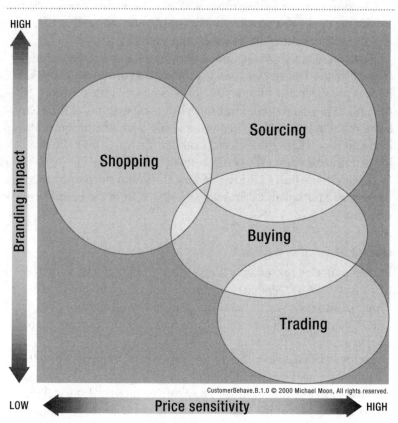

CustomerBehave.B.1.0 © 2000 Michael Moon, All rights reserved.

Figure 3-18 Buyers demonstrate different behaviors that reflect high or low price sensitivity and the high or low potential impact of effective branding. These behaviors dictate the kind of stories that customers want to hear

When *shopping*, customers want to consider lots of choices, options, and combinations. Shopping represents a kind of entertainment, and generally happens in retail venues. For customers in this mode, brand managers should use brand stories that play as romances, sweeping the customer into the experience.

Customers in the *sourcing* mode seek long-term supply contracts, a steady flow of consistently high quality products and services, from a handful of providers. Here, brand managers should tell stories that reassure customers that they will remain viable suppliers for decades to come. They will want to demonstrate financial stability and offer product or service road maps that show how new innovations will meet customer needs in the future.

Customers in the *buying* mode seek highest quality products or services at the lowest possible price, available for immediate delivery. The brand story must reflect these criteria.

Customers in the *trading* mode want to use non-monetary currencies (in kind, barter, etc.) to acquire desired products or services. Each deal reflects the unique relationship between the trading parties and the items traded. The brand story will emphasize the exclusivity of the relationship ("just you and me") and the unique nature of the items exchange ("a special deal just for you"), and, often, a limited time horizon ("I'm only in town this week").

Beyond these purchasing behaviors, the brand story must reflect the mix of Martian and Venusian values present in the brand firm's offering.

ROI or RIOT?

Martian offerings emphasize tangible economic gains, a return on investment (ROI). Venusian offerings emphasize whether the customer considers it worth her time, returned investment of time (RIOT), highlighting intangible gains that she can't express in economic terms.

Figure 3-19 illustrates the way these powerful influences pull the customer towards one or another or a mix of purchase motivations—the true source of the impulse to buy. Successful brand storytelling will center on one of the eight motivations as the primary theme; otherwise, the story will fail to punch through, grab attention, and move people to purchase action. The story may include other motivations, but only as supporting actors.

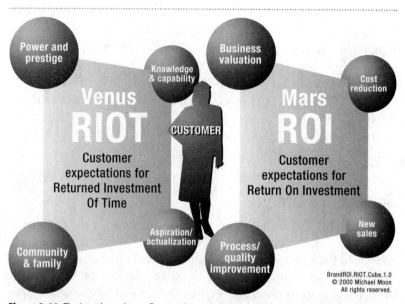

Figure 3-19 The impulse to buy reflects eight motivations that a brand manager can validate with demographic data. To express a crisp positioning, brand managers must highly emphasize only one of these eight motivations in their brand storytelling

Found most often in the business-to-business sphere, ROI motivates purchases that enable a company to win new sales, reduce costs, achieve quality or business process improvements, or increase share price and company valuation.

Even the most business-like of buyers will want to realize a more personal reward or gain from the transaction. Here, RIOT enters the picture, for both business and personal buyers. Will buying this new computer system fulfill one of my aspirations—to get a promotion based on my wise choice, or to have my own computer to surf the Web and play games at home? Will the purchase, and the knowledge and capability I gain through it, increase my office productivity, or help me get better grades this semester? Will it add to my power and prestige by putting on my desk the computer only the top employees get, or if I buy a cool iMac in order to impress my friends? Will investing in this computer allow me to take an active role in the community of professionals in my field, or let me keep up with family members through e-mail?

MasterCard's recent series of TV advertisements shows RIOT brand storytelling in a highly elegant and effective way. As an individual goes through a heartfelt moment of sharing with loved ones—a little boy going with Dad and friends to his first baseball game, a woman in her 30s discovering her roots on her first visit to Grandma in Ireland—the costs involved (baseball tickets, hot dog) appear silently on the screen. At the emotional peak, the voice-over narrator proclaims, "These memories are priceless. For everything else there's MasterCard."

Satisfaction Lifecycle

We began this chapter with a discussion of the value-brand dynamic, separating the sell-side and buy-side experience of the brand. We then examined the sell-side, using our value creation process model which emphasizes the relationship of the brand and the market. Value creation tends to focus internally on the activities and processes by which the firm brings value to market. In the brand storytelling process, we explored the buyer's relationship with the brand producer and the category. The brand storytelling model shows how customers come into a category, orient themselves to the brands the category contains, and ultimately form a lasting relationship with a brand, based on trust and an ongoing exchange of value.

Now, let's focus on the interface between these sell-side and buy-side processes, and show what happens when buyers and sellers meet, and ask the question, What happens when one customer focuses on one solution in a relationship with one brand producer?

The value creation activities of the seller and the customer's responses to brand storytelling converge in a process that we call a *satisfaction lifecycle*, illustrated in Figure 3-20 and Figure 3-21. We encourage brand managers to use this satisfaction lifecycle model as a way to analyze their promotional activities and discover where they need to add resources to fill holes, not to mention where they may be spending less money than necessary to draw customers (and other stakeholders) into trusted relationships with the brand and into communities of practice and referral.

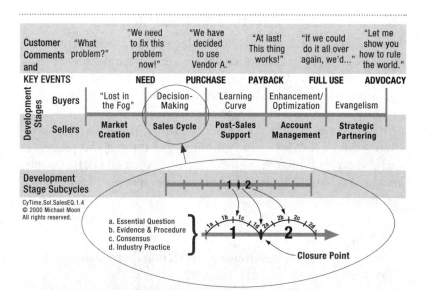

Figure 3-20 The *satisfaction lifecycle* highlights a key function of marketing and sales: the systematic framing and answering of the essential questions of buyers at each stage of their process of developing a trusted relationship with the brand

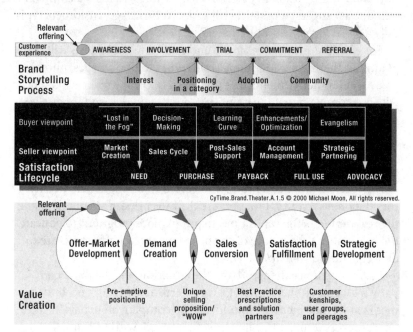

Figure 3-21 The satisfaction lifecycle serves as the area of convergence, or interface, between the value creation process of the seller firm and the customer's experience of the brand storytelling process

Seller and Buyer Aspects of the Satisfaction Lifecycle

The satisfaction lifecycle integrates seller and buyer perspectives, in terms of development stages, customer comments, and key events. Let's examine these development stages in greater detail, using our ongoing research of customers and vendors in the emerging market category for media asset management solutions.

We illustrate the satisfaction lifecycle with a business-to-business (B2B) example, but individual consumers go through this process as well. As you read through the following discussion and B2B example, imagine a consumer going through the process of purchasing a new automobile.

Development Stages

Sellers and buyers move through a satisfaction lifecycle in several *development stages.*

Most buyers start *lost in the fog.* They may not even know they have a problem, or to what extent the problem has grown important enough to address. They do experience symptoms and issues, typically interpreting them in psychological or fuzzy terms—a complaint that doesn't suggest a practical solution. At this stage, customers typically ask, "What's the problem here?"

For example, graphic designers and publishing specialists will complain that they spend too much time trying to find images, photographs, and other elements that they need to complete their job. They will also complain that the items they do find do not lend themselves to easy re-use—they have to spend too much time fixing or modifying them.

Enter the seller—in this example, a database company—in the market creation stage of the satisfaction lifecycle. In this stage, a vendor suspects that it has a product or service that might help this frustrated, potential buyer. But, because the buyer doesn't yet understand the real problem, the vendor has to put in place programs to educate the buyer about the nature of the problem, and an infrastructure to deliver solutions—*market creation.*

In our example, after studying the situation, the database company realizes that its technology can meet the emerging need for media asset management solutions. The company marshals its internal resources to meet this new customer need, with training for in-house and field sales, technical support, and instructions about how to respond to customer needs. The company will create brochures, presentations, customer testimonials, and other collateral pieces that orient, educate, and reassure the potential buyer that her complaints represent a legitimate business problem: the systematic creation and reuse of reusable media and the automation of workflows throughout that publishing activity.

This stage concludes when the buyer has successfully identified the underlying need and can state, "We need to fix this problem now." Brand managers must understand that this statement usually represents the consensus of a decision influence team. Using our example, the decision influence team now understands that it has a business problem (how much money and time the company wastes, and the likely dire consequence of not optimizing this vital business function) that it now must solve with a media asset management system.

Buyers now move into the *decision-making* stage where they begin to research the category. They examine potential solution scenarios, locate providers for these solutions, and conduct a more formal study of the business case, an investment analysis that justifies a purchase decision.

In the case of our media asset management (MAM) system, a task force at the buyer firm will conduct an audit of their workflow practices, often with the help of a consultant, with the intent of identifying bottlenecks and problem areas that a MAM system will address. They also develop a short list of a dozen or so vendors and issue a request for information to narrow the field to a handful of qualified companies they will invite to answer a request for proposal (RFP).

On the seller side, the solution provider enters the *sales cycle*. It marshals its field marketing and sales resources to help the customer reach a decision that, the company hopes, will specify its solution. The database company in our example will direct its media specialist team to work the customer, in all appropriate ways. The team may help the buyer firm benchmark its media asset workflow, conduct a system performance analysis and identify needs for software and hardware upgrades, and cost the MAM solution against a calendar of milestones. This stage ends when the buyer states, "We have decided to use Vendor A," and makes a purchase.

Buyers now move into a *learning curve*. They remain switchable customers—they have purchased a solution and begun to deploy it, but they will still keep their options open, examining other possible solutions as fallback strategies. The buyer firm might even discover it doesn't have the necessary focus or resources and put the whole thing off until later.

Continuing our example, the MAM solution buyer will organize a deployment team that installs the software, often for a scaled-down production pilot system (a solution for one workgroup), trains the digital librarian and end users, and fixes whatever problems arise. They want to see the pony run around the track before they buy the whole stable. They will continue to look at possible fall-back strategies—another MAM vendor, or an outsourced solution.

The seller has moved into the *post-sales support* stage. They execute the project plan, hitting their milestones. This includes addressing all of the normal start-up issues, user training and support, and reassuring managers that they have made the right choice.

This stage ends when end users and managers at the buyer firm can say, "At last! This thing works." They have begun to see payback—tangible results.

Buyers now move into the *enhancement/optimization* stage. They begin to weave the solution into the fabric of their business process. The loyalty lock-in begins and they make a commitment to this solution. In our MAM example, the company now relies on this system. It has moved tens of thousands of media asset files into the system and has meticulously indexed them using a keyword authority list. Likewise, it has re-engineered workflows to take advantage of the MAM system.

On the seller side, the solution provider moves into *account management* mode. It addresses shortcomings, fixes bugs, suggests (and sells) upgrades and add-on modules. It offers extras and special favors if the satisfied customer will provide testimonials and let the seller use them in other sales and marketing efforts.

In our MAM example, the seller has consolidated its control of the account, forming effective alliances with IT staff, business management, and end users at the buyer firm. The account manager may become a de facto process consultant and change agent, helping management at the buyer firm to optimize the overall business, in the process moving the buyer to a more complete roll-out of the MAM solution throughout the firm.

This stage ends when buyers can state, "If we could do it all over again, we'd do so in a heartbeat." The buyer firm has reached *full use* of the solution. It has received a full return on investment and begins to reap substantial dividends.

The buyer firm now moves into the *evangelism* stage. In our example, the leader of the MAM implementation team has probably received a couple of promotions and in the process has thoroughly documented the business case for the total solution that has now yielded a manifold return on investment. As she discusses her experience, her colleagues at other firms now recognize her as a subject matter expert—a maven—in the MAM category. Word gets around. Technical conferences seek her out as a keynote speaker, a role model for others to follow. She likes the attention, the opportunity to travel and meet other successful pioneers like herself, and recognizes that the exposure opens up broader and more lucrative career horizons. She becomes an evangelist for the category, and an advocate for a particular solution and a methodology (a set of best practices) that produces consistently great results.

On the sell side, the vendor enters into the *strategic partnering* stage. In the MAM category, vendors work with buyer firms to promote the solution throughout the value chain as an industry standard. Vendors and buyers work together to develop next-generation solutions.

This stage ends when buyers can say, "Let me show you how to rule the world," and *advocate* both the category and branded solution.

Earlier, we saw how brand managers can use cycle time to measure the effectiveness of the value creation process. Here, they can apply the cycle time concept to how quickly they move with buyers through the satisfaction lifecycle. Shorter cycle times produce higher sales productivity (higher revenues per sales representative), lower cost of sales (lower customer acquisition costs), and faster consolidation of category dominance. What can brand managers do to accelerate a buyer's movement through the satisfaction lifecycle?

Essential Questions

At each stage of the satisfaction lifecycle, customers ask essential questions. After receiving answers to these questions, they move on to the next stage. Let's examine this more closely, exploring how essential questions work as buyers move through the decision-making stage (the sales cycle, for sellers).

Figure 3-22 illustrates how it works. A company asks an essential question that frames a need to know and a requirement for a particular answer. Each answer characterizes a set of evidence and a procedure by which to process the evidence (quantitative data, etc.) to the satisfaction of the decision influence team, thereby creating a consensus. Often, the procedure for assessing the evidence comes from established industry practices and independent consulting and research firms that have developed models and best practice prescriptives.

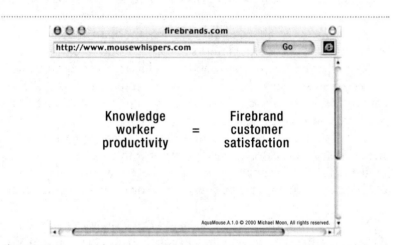

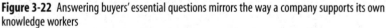

Figure 3-22 Answering buyers' essential questions mirrors the way a company supports its own knowledge workers

Sellers develop marketing materials that attempt to answer these essential questions. In the final analysis, marketing and sales amount to nothing more than framing and answering the essential questions of customers. They have no other purpose. Therefore, brand managers must undertake a systematic effort to identify, frame, and codify the essential questions related to each satisfaction (product or service) that they sell. This requires activity-based research.

SYSTEMATIC PROFILING AND RESEARCH

The best answers to buyers' essential questions derive from the systematic profiling and research of a company's most satisfied customers, or customers of similar products and services offered by competing firms. Effective brand managers correlate each branding activity and related artifact to these essential questions, asking: How does this answer my key customer's essential questions?

In the course of doing this, brand managers will discover two important things. Their key customer groups—as characterized by the demographic success model—uniformly ask the same essential questions and require, uniformly, the same answers, evidence, procedure, and industry validations. Second, brand managers discover that if buyers ask essential questions that successful customers do not ordinarily ask, they will have encountered a customer they should not serve (one who won't succeed with this particular branded solution) or that they have discovered an entirely new market category.

INFORMATION PREFERENDA: THE QUEST FOR ANSWERS

We borrow the term *preferenda* from biology, where it refers to a preferred choice within a continuum available to a motile organism. In our context, we use it to connote all of the types of information and experiences that an individual might prefer out of the choices available to them. Customers want, need, and demand more than just answers. They want answers that solve their particular problems, or at least what they perceive as their particular problems. This means they need a flow of answers that will also educate them as to the nature of their problem so they can ask better questions.

In our research of 3,700 software programmers over a three and a half year period, examining what information products most contribute to programmer productivity, software quality, time to market, and lower demand for expensive technical support interventions, we discovered that information comes in seven different food groups. Depending on the nature of the question and the cognitive capacity of the person asking the question, an offered answer may or may not satisfy or produce the desired result.

Figure 3-23 diagrams these seven groups in terms of *pacing* (how fast one can assimilate an answer) and *structure* (requirement for prior knowledge or experience in order to digest the answer).

Business theory represents subtle distinctions within a tradition or discipline of practitioners. More often than not, these distinctions serve as a context or realm in which one can think about and analyze current or future scenarios. This requires a considerable amount of time to reflect on and assimilate these distinctions, plus a schooling in the grand theories of business for comparison.

Business models and designs characterize the intellectual capital of a firm, how it finds and serves customers, and captures value in return. This intellectual capital comes from a variety of sources, including the management team, acquisition of patents and licenses, strategic partners and consultants, and other sources as noted in the chart.

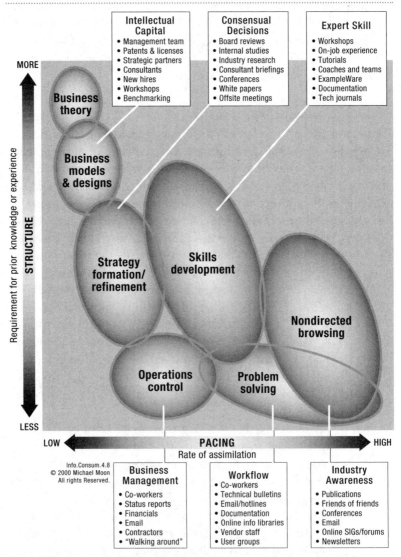

Figure 3-23 Our research of 3,700 software programmers revealed a diverse appetite for information and sources in what we call an *information preferenda model.* Buyers of your products or services will have similarly diverse appetites

Strategy formation and refinement describes how a company arrives at consensual decisions. This may include board reviews, internal studies, purchase of industry research, consultant briefings, and other vehicles.

Skills development entails the production of expert skill through workshops, on-the-job experience, tutorials, and other educational and professional materials and tools.

Operations control represents the information needed for business management. This includes verbal feedback from co-workers, status reports, financial statements, and other sources of information about the daily operations of a firm.

Problem solving focuses on workflow providing the raw materials (including knowledge, information, and media assets) that workers need to do their jobs. These sources include informal conversations with co-workers, technical bulletins, documentation, and other sources of technical or professional "how-to" answers.

Nondirected browsing covers a variety of activities that in a business to business context generally translate into industry awareness. This may also include entertainment and "digital coffee breaks" that, in the big picture, add to overall productivity but which may show no immediate payback.

We offer this model to illustrate how a brand manager can analyze the kinds of answers that buyers and other stakeholders may have. In this case, our client used this model to identify unserved information needs among their software developers, as well as how to validate the best medium (offline or online) for delivering particular kinds of answers.

As brand managers research the information needs of their buyers, they must work hard to distinguish what kinds of answers will most accelerate a customer's progress through the satisfaction lifecycle. The mere provisioning of answers will likely fail if the buyer or stakeholder does not possess the cognitive capacity to assimilate them. They may need more training, remedial education, peer-to-peer consultation, and coaching.

As we will show later, in Chapter 5, the process of identifying and answering the questions of a particular customer will parallel how the company supports its front-line knowledge workers—a key concept in the creation and implementation of a successful firebranding strategy.

Where Does Branding Take Place?

Earlier, we argued that brands live in the minds of consumers, as a result of their buying and using experience plus their responses to the seller's storytelling. Now, we exploit another sense of "theater" and expand the metaphor to describe where the buying experience and storytelling take place: in the branding theater of operations, as illustrated in Figure 3-24.

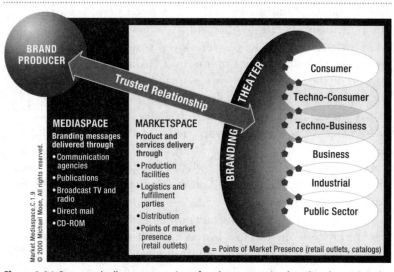

Figure 3-24 Buyers and sellers meet at points of market presence in a branding theater. Brand managers must take care to coordinate the flow of brand messages through the mediaspace. Otherwise demand may not match supply

Mediaspace/Marketspace

Mediaspace describes the various ways by which a brand producer communicates with and builds trusted relationships with buyers, including broadcast, print, and offline digital media such as CD-ROM or DVD.

Marketspace describes the area in which buyers meet *points of market presence* (retail venues, catalogs, field sales calls, workshops or seminars, trade shows, etc.), where buyers take possession of goods and services. A marketspace also includes the value chain of companies or functions that serve the purpose of logistics and fulfillment of goods and services, including warehouses, call centers, shipping companies, and repair depots.

Brand managers have always grappled with coordinating the messages they send through mediaspace with the movement of goods and services to the points of market presence in the marketspace. A serious problem arises if they drive brand messages to market and do not have sufficient inventory for sale. This produces unhappy customers and opportunistic sales for competitors. Unless you have an exclusive good or service that customers cannot substitute ("I've got to have Pokemon"), failure to coordinate activity in supply chain logistics and the mediaspace leads to disaster.

Prior to the Networked Economy, the mediaspace and marketspace constituted two separate and relatively independent domains. As we begin to discuss in the next chapter, mediaspace and marketspace now converge, collapsing into what we call eMediaspace— where brand storytelling and transactions occur simultaneously. In the Networked Economy, tightly synchronizing the cycle time (the flow of brand storytelling and the flow of digital goods and services) becomes critical to the success of the brand—we explain how to do this, in detail, in the next part of this book.

Mediaspace Value Chains

Because mediaspace plays such an important role in brand storytelling, it warrants a closer look. Figure 3-25 illustrates how a brand message must traverse multiple business entities and media formats before reaching customers and other stakeholders.

Here, a unified messaging strategy plays a critical role. We cannot overstate the importance of such a strategy for the integrity of the brand. Everyone who touches (with media) the customer's experience must quite literally sing from the same songbook. They must consistently use keywords, pitches, slogans and their visual equivalents—all brand resources—to reinforce the story that explains and enhances the buying and using experience of customers. Brand managers who have mastered the brand storytelling process fastidiously pursue consistency of messaging to the nth degree, including consistent representation of color across broadcast, print, and online media, the use of logos and other design elements, a comprehensive architecture that coordinates the look and feel of business forms, signage, packaging, marketing collateral, interior design, etc. The more unified and internally consistent the brand identity, the more quickly and efficiently you can move the brand storytelling through a cluttered and chaotic mediaspace, giving the brand story a greater ability to resonate deeply with customers.

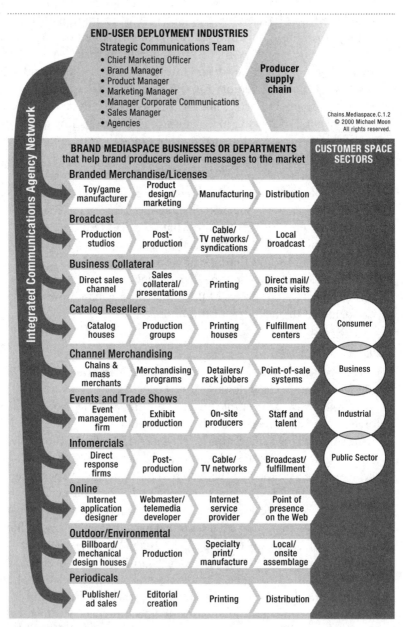

Figure 3-25 Brand managers must optimize their brand storytelling for the various *value chains of their mediaspace*. Each business entity or department indicated above requires a unique media format (broadcast video, print collateral, presentations)

Each value chain (broadcast, periodicals, etc.) has its own lag times and unique requirements for media assets and brand resources. The integrated communications agency (or network of agencies) must create media assets and brand resources tailored to the media deployment format required by each mediaspace value chain. This places a tremendous emphasis on creating agile, multipurposed media assets explicitly engineered for rapid optimization in each deployment. This represents a critical success factor in reducing cycle time and costs for offline branding, and becomes even more important—as we discuss in the next part of this book—in the Networked Economy.

Sadly, most companies do not realize the extent of waste and cycle time inefficiencies of their brand storytelling and the way they move these stories through their mediaspace value chains. A detailed discussion of this topic lies beyond the scope of this book. At Firebrands.com, you will find information about our *Media Asset Management Market Report*, a thorough, definitive analysis of these issues.

Principal Branding Channels

We've discussed the importance of a crisp, focused positioning and a business design that can drive this positioning to an unassailable market dominance, supported by active evangelists and customer advocates who generate high-margin, repeat purchase orders in record volumes, referrals of new customers to the brand, and the conversion of switchable customers into loyal locked-in customers.

What mix of branding channels best supports such positioning and business design? We advocate a radically simplified, power media mix. When a company starts telling brand stories, it must choose one principal medium and dominate that medium with the brand story. Otherwise, the story gets lost in a clutter of media and branding channels.

In our discussion of the nature of offerings, we described them in general terms as Martian products, Venusian services, and Mercurial hybrids. Which branding channels work most effectively for each? While we cannot say which branding channel will work best with *your* Martian product or Venusian service, we do say that one best way, one branding channel, will best serve your product or service. Figure 3-26 illustrates your menu of options and some of the attributes and entailments of each. Choose well; you may not get a second chance.

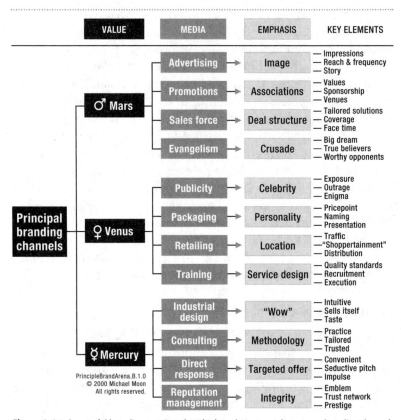

Figure 3-26 Successful branding requires that the brand manager choose one *branding channel* and dominate it, subordinating other channels to a secondary role if not ignoring them altogether. Failure to dominate one branding channel will cause the most brilliant brand story to become lost in the clutter and chaos of ruthless, competitive markets

Mars

As a branding channel, *advertising* best conveys an image or mood through repeated impressions across a large audience. Masters of this channel routinely tell the short-short story in 15 seconds.

Promotions emphasize sponsorship of special events and venues, often with the intent of linking a company to the lifestyle or demography of spectators or participants—association.

Many firms use their *sales force* as the principal branding channel for tailored solutions in face-to-face interactions with customers. Here, the deal structure (terms and conditions of the specific engagement) also play an important, if not pivotal role, in branding.

Evangelism comes out of an old American tradition where inspired individuals take up a personal crusade to change the world, or at least try to, through direct persuasion of other individuals. We find best practice examples in direct marketing programs such as Amway and Mary Kay Cosmetics, which focus on true believers in a big dream.

Venus

Venusian strategies emphasize attracting attention to the brand, in contrast to the Martian strategy of going on and aggressively pursuing the business.

Publicity represents the clever manipulation of mass media with the goal of creating celebrity through consistent exposure, outrage, and enigma.

Packaging attempts to create a vibrant, engaging personality on the shelf, in the showroom, or on the street. Here, price point, naming conventions, and presentation venues play an important role.

Retailing has always emphasized location, location, location, which translates into traffic. Once in a store, shoppertainment and well-stocked shelves (distribution) convert visits into sales.

Training, the backbone of McDonald's, Nordstrom's, and other high-touch service firms, creates a brand through an effective service design—a recipe by which positive branding events occur in the mundane interactions of sales clerk and customer. This emphasizes consistent, high-quality standards, a super-effective recruitment and selection process, and brilliant execution deriving from effective management.

Mercury

Mercurial branding channels combine elements of Venus and Mars, and emphasize a self-service mode of interaction with a potential buyer.

Industrial design strives to create a product or service presentation that wows the prospective buyer into wanting it now, speaking in the intuitive language of desire and aspiration. Quite literally, the product sells itself, often using the taste sensibilities of a particular demographic cohort as its distinguishing character.

While *consulting* firms don't exactly fit the self-service characterization, they use mercurial branding channels because of the high level of customer interaction and involvement necessary prior to the engagement. Clients buy the methodology—the system of knowledge—that gives the consultant the ability to produce results. Consulting firms highlight the professional rigor of their practice, their ability to tailor a general approach to specific needs, and to do so with the utmost of confidence and trust.

Direct response dynamically presents a compelling offer to a prospective customer who must then in turn fill out an order form or engage a teleservice representative—a form of self-service satisfaction. This branding channel emphasizes convenience, impulse purchase, and acceptance of a seductive pitch.

Often, the chairman or CEO of a firm must build a personal brand that comes to represent the vibrancy and integrity of the firm as a whole—Jack Welch is GE, Bill Gates is Microsoft. Here, *reputation management* highlights the integrity of the brand firm's leader as the emblem, the source of the brand satisfaction, and the central figure of prestige in the trust network that ensures customer satisfaction, a network that may include trade partners and various third- and fourth-parties.

Trusted Relationship Between Brand Producer and Consumers

In this chapter, we have summarized the key principles of offline branding, looking forward to the ways this branding process must change for success in the Networked Economy. This inch-deep survey mines nuggets of insight from a vast library of books by branding experts. We encourage you to visit Firebrands.com for pointers to these grand masters of branding, and for information on specific branding practices.

Having surveyed the basics of branding and traditional offline brand building, let's explore what stays the same and what must change as brands evolve into firebrands of the Networked Economy, where the trusted relationship between a brand and its stakeholders takes on even more importance.

Chapter 4

Firebrands

What makes a firebrand? In this chapter, we show which resources, eServices, and self-service satisfactions create a firebrand and make it sizzle. We explain where firebrands live, how they work, and who they serve. We suggest ways to use a firebrand to put dot.com mojo on your company's valuation, including how to use loyalty lock-ins and value-based pricing to multiply firebrand equity.

Firebrands Defined

From the dawn of recorded history, fire has played a central role in the formation of groups, families, and clans. In the movie *Quest for Fire*, humanity takes the first steps up from the animal kingdom, when people learn how to kindle fire. From pottery to blast furnaces, fire enabled industry.

Fire set the stage for our earliest stories. Without these stories, we would have no culture or civilization to speak of—a way by which we transfer our collective from one generation to the next. Storytelling, reflecting our deepest concerns and issues, remains as central and as vital to us today as it did 30,000 years ago.

Stories, and our ability to understand their subtleties, have become more sophisticated—and we have harnessed them for commercial purposes. As we discussed in the previous chapter, brand building puts storytelling at the service of industry and commerce—the agents of mass culture that now vie for dominance with other agents of high and popular culture.

In the Networked Economy, the television and computer have converged, replacing the hearth and community campfire. Around this digital fire, a new form of storytelling has emerged. Where we once sat around the campfire listening to our elders recount what it means to be a tribe, we now use interactive media to actively participate in the creation and telling of stories among ourselves. The self-service satisfactions of the Networked Economy radically transform storytelling from a passive, one-way transmission into a collaborative process based on trust, fair exchange of value, and reciprocity.

When a brand fires a community to action, it becomes a firebrand. When communities of practice or concern organize around a self-service satisfaction provided by a vendor and other members of the community, that satisfaction becomes a firebrand. When the collective stories of other members of the community create as much or more value for an individual member of the community as the product or service itself, that product or service becomes a firebrand.

If you plan to compete in the Networked Economy you must master the art and science of building a community of digital storytellers around your digital hearth, your firebrand platform. Before we can explain how to do this (which we do in the next chapter), let's take a closer look at the firebrand platform—the digital equivalent of logs, tinder, kindling, spark, and environmental conditions—that makes it possible.

In practical terms, we define a firebrand in terms of its major elements: the *satisfactions* that *consumers and other stakeholders* experience as they interact with a producer's *digital brand resources*. These interactions create and maintain a *trusted relationship* between consumers (and other stakeholders) and producers. But first, let's talk a little bit about the distinction between a brand and a firebrand, and how firebrands have evolved from video games, computer application software, and online services—the original "firebrands" and progenitors of the Networked Economy.

From Traditional Brand to Firebrand

Pure-Internet-play companies—dot.coms such as Yahoo! and Amazon.com—enjoy the luxury of beginning as a firebrand. For offline brands, however, a firebrand will constitute a new category of satisfactions alongside the principal satisfactions that define the offline brands.

Whether you're dealing with a start-from-scratch firebrand or trying to put dot.com mojo on an existing offline brand, we cannot overstate the importance of correctly positioning your firebrand. The rules of positioning still apply to your firebrand. This means that your key customer group will associate one word (your firebrand) with one idea (a satisfaction) and with one interaction (a self-service experience).

Case Study: How BMW Drives Its Brand in Cyberspace

Let's illustrate how positioning with one word, one idea, and one interaction might work, using a distinction BMW might make between its offline brand positioning and its emerging firebrand positioning.

Offline, BMW sells "ultimate driving machines," the experience of high-performance luxury cars. In a recent campaign introducing the BMW sports utility vehicle, the company raised *experiential marketing* (as discussed by Bernd H. Schmitt in his book of the same name) to an exquisite pitch. In TV spots, the company associates the quiet splendor and elegance of a woman skiing in fresh powder to the driving experience of the new SUV. BMW's storytelling here becomes even more aesthetic and visceral, using a subtle but powerful soundtrack and stunning imagery to extend a 15-year positioning legacy.

Should BMW merely transfer this experiential motif to the Web and use it to build its firebrand positioning?

Simply transferring the offline "ultimate driving experience" positioning to cyberspace fails for several reasons. First, the Web's low-resolution sensory capabilities cannot adequately translate the visual and auditory components of BMW's rich print and broadcast campaigns—maybe in a few years, with broadband delivery, but that remains to be seen.

More important, these one-way, broadcast, mass-media modes do not invite the personalization, sharing, and community-building that distinguishes a firebrand from a traditional offline brand.

Finally, people come to BMW.com motivated by a completely different set of needs, and bring with them a wholly different and distinct context for relating to the brand, as compared with magazine readers and television viewers—consumers in a passive "entertain me" context, where the consumer places the responsibility for the experience on the storyteller.

By contrast, the proactive, self-serving BMW.com visitor has specific outcomes in mind and holds him or herself at least partially responsible for producing those outcomes. Self-directed customers want the tools and power to customize the design and delivery of satisfactions to their particular needs. They don't want more entertainment (a URL in an entertaining television or magazine advertisement brought them to the site). Once they have "crossed the Rubicon" and entered into the BMW.com site, they want results. They may wish to see these results as the byproduct of a fun and entertaining self-service experience, but in the end the results remain paramount.

Instead, the law of firebrand positioning dictates that BMW should distill the essence of an ultimate driving experience to one self-service satisfaction. But for whom: existing customers or new prospects? Should BMW position this self-service satisfaction for existing customers, using it to build loyalty, or target it to a new customer group?

Firebrands build loyalty: non-switchable customers throughout a satisfaction lifecycle. BMW will continue to spend marketing dollars to bring tire-kickers into their showrooms. Online, they must dedicate themselves to serving the most important group in their customer base: the share-determining sector and source of future profits. For example, the 35-year-old who purchases the low-end BMW model now and who in the future will move up the product line.

BMW brand managers must ask the essential questions: "What do we do to annoy, disappoint, or disaffiliate 35-year-old first-time buyers?" "How can we create an eService that proactively solves this branding problem?" It may come as a surprise to these brand managers that the problem may not relate to the product itself, but instead to financing, or to finding time in their busy lives to get a car serviced.

On a recent trip to Germany, a colleague met me at a Munich airport gate. We walked to the rental car parking lot there and drove away the late-model Porsche he owned. I figured he must have an inside connection: Who did he know at Avis to let him park in their rental lot? In fact, Porsche reached an agreement with Avis to let all Porsche owners park free of charge at convenient Avis airport parking lots. Porsche proactively eliminated a common dissatisfaction of its proud, frequent-flyer owners: leaving their prized automobiles vulnerable to vandals and blockheads in crowded airport parking lots.

In positioning its firebrand, BMW could learn a lesson from Porsche. BMWUSA.com should position the firebrand to enhance and complement the principal satisfaction of driving their automobiles. BMW's firebrand would consist of a set of eServices and interactions that make owning and driving the ultimate driving machine a more meaningful and more beloved experience. Why? Because they will use BMW's Web site to facilitate maintenance, to customize the car with accessories, interact with designers and expert service technicians, as well as other BMW owners. The more knowledge a consumer has about the buying and using experience, the greater the consumer's appreciation. This adds to the sense of personal vindication that they have made the right choice.

We haven't conducted a thorough analysis of BMW's brand and key customer segments, but the law of firebrands dictates that BMW has an opportunity to own one eService/self-service satisfaction for one customer group. If they get that right, everything else will fall into place.

A Thumbnail History of Firebrands

Firebrands arise from the imprint of digital culture. As consumers we have learned to interact with digital media in our use of computer application software, video games, and commercial online services. In the process, we have formed our basic expectations and developed the preliminary skills and habits we can now apply to firebrands. This opportunity emerged definitely when the Internet and World Wide Web reached critical mass—after years of quiet development and relatively restricted use—in the early 1990s.

Brand managers who want to build firebrands can profit from the hard-won lessons of the digital brand pioneers illustrated in Figure 4-1. These pioneers learned that the most effective and memorable aspect of a digital brand—whether delivered in application software, video games, CD-ROM titles, online services, or the Internet—comes from the elegance, simplicity, and power of the user interface.

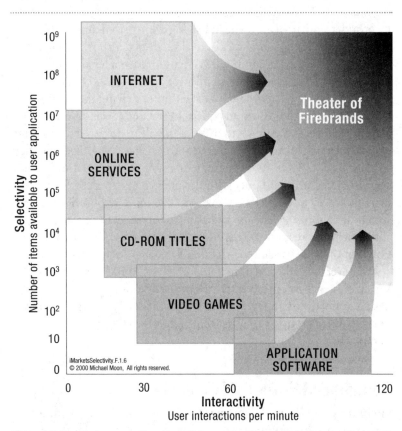

Figure 4-1 Firebrands emerged from the digital precursors shown here. Each, in a particular way, emphasized the importance of the user interface as an alignment of the two important dimensions, interactivity and selectivity

We analyze the user interface in terms of two technical dimensions, interactivity and selectivity. Interactivity characterizes the number of interactions possible in a given unit of time. Selectivity indicates the number of items or subjects with which a user can interact. Traditional application software provides extraordinary levels of interactivity with relatively few items for user selection. At the top of the scale, the Internet offers relatively low interactivity with a corresponding increase in selectivity: lots of Web pages, but not a lot of interaction with those Web pages. The history of digital brands to date relates how bleeding edge pioneers have through trial and error perfected the balance of interactivity and selectivity to best serve customers with available delivery media.

Quicken offers a textbook case. Intuit founder and president and former Proctor & Gamble marketing executive Scott Cook once said that the company started with a remarkably new innovation for a software company: they conducted comprehensive research, both qualitative and quantitative, of customers and their relationship with their personal finances. What problems did they experience and what user interface metaphor would customers most warmly embrace? Intuit found that most consumers could not relate to a geeky computer user interface with the abstract terms and unfamiliar procedures that characterized the PC software programmer approach. Instead, armed with usability research to justify the move, Cook and his team delivered powerful personal finance software with a user interface that everybody understood: first and foremost, the personal checkbook, which entailed automating the tedious, unpleasant chores of balance calculation and reconciliation, along the way adding new capabilities previously practiced only by the most motivated professionals—expense categorization for tax and business reimbursements, and graphic visualizations of financial trends.

Following the user interface metaphor, Intuit answered customer requests by investing in the business of offering pre-printed checks and business forms to work with their software. (This now constitutes a significant portion of the company's revenues and a huge percentage of profits. Shortly, we'll show how this represents another important firebrand trait: loyalty lock-ins.)

Moving through the early 1990s, Quicken moved into a multimedia format on CD-ROM, addressing sorely needed education and remedial coaching on the basics of personal finance and record keeping—increasing user selectivity, adding rich media and interactive tutorials. Unwittingly, Intuit invoked another law of firebrands: training and

skills development associated with brand use stimulates the formation of a community of practice and a compelling reason to stay
engaged with the brand. By the mid-1990s, Intuit moved this community of practice to the Web and extended its basic product with an
array of online information and services related to personal finance.
With great foresight, the company named its Web community destination Quicken.com, distinguishing it from the professional product,
QuickBooks, and its income-tax preparation product, TurboTax.

While we applaud Scott Cook and his team for pioneering new
eServices such as automatic bill paying, banking, mortgage, and
other services, the company violated one of the laws of firebrands
we now understand thanks to the virtue of hindsight: they lost focus.
They failed to identify the unique single self-service satisfaction that
the Quicken.com firebrand brought to the Web branding channel;
instead, they simply deluged and diluted the Quicken offline brand
with a hodgepodge of online offerings.

They could have made Quicken.com a distance-learning portal
for the ongoing support of Quicken users. They could have built,
nurtured, and fed a community of Quicken entrepreneurs—local
solution providers that use the consumer versions of Quicken as a
platform for delivering simple bookkeeping and other value-added
personal finance services. This would have made Quicken a tool for
a network of platform partners and a referral service for these service affiliates. Quicken.com could have become a deep repository of
advanced Quicken techniques for these platform partners as well as
setting them up as sales affiliates who would in turn sell Quicken
into their markets. This alternate channel would have dramatically
expanded Quicken's points of market presence, created new incremental revenue, and established a more effective loyalty lock-in
among the leaders in the Quicken community of practice.

In 1995, we researched the customer registration and installed-base
marketing programs of 85 software and CD-ROM companies, including Intuit. Our research showed that every profiled customer—a complete database record—for a $99 software product produced $37 in
additional annual revenue, through the sale of upgrades, cross-sells,
and accessories. While Intuit scored on the upper end of customer
registration rates, six out of 10 customers failed to register and thus
give the company the opportunity to build that database record.
Armed with this hard data, Intuit could have pulled out all the stops to
use the Web as a customer registration facility. Here, a field of enrolled
Quicken "agents" (third- and fourth-party aftermarket and service

providers) could induce their clients, Quicken users, to immediately register, and thus gain access to important additional eServices.

But we're getting ahead of ourselves here. We'll explain the mechanisms that make this possible in our discussion of firebrand components and we'll describe these firebranding techniques in detail in the next chapter. Just be glad you can learn from Scott Cook and his intrepid pioneers.

We could repeat case studies from all the digital brand pioneers. We could detail how Amazon.com proved the power of affiliate marketing. We could explain how AOL made the transition from proprietary online service to Web site with the crisp positioning of "You've got mail," the now 40,000+ online communities that suck in and hold participants, and their massive offline direct mail drop of billions of floppy disks and CD-ROMs that give new customers a free sample and easy startup. We could describe how the lovable characters of video game hits like Mario, Donkey Kong, Jr., and the multiplayer game interplay set the stage for the Web gaming interface which has since become standard in the online branding experience. Myst, for instance, became the first "storydwelling" and entertainment-oriented deep gravity well in which people spent days and weeks. On a similar note, Doom smartly teased players by letting them download free game segments that would inevitably lead them to purchase more of the addictive episodes. Such a history lies beyond the scope of the present volume, but brand managers in the Networked Economy will find that a study of these developments will repay itself many times over. (Readers who want more on this can let us know at www.Firebrands.com.)

The Anatomy of a Firebrand

Just as tribal elders wove a rich tapestry of story around evening campfires, transmitting core values and beliefs to future generations, so brand managers tell stories that explain and personalize the buying and using experience of customers. A firebrand exploits the luminosity of a "digital campfire"—a computer screen—to bring into focus the stories that help create the brand.

Firebrand managers use a variety of digital resources to tell their stories. As we have discussed, these resources come into a crisp, focused positioning—one self-service satisfaction for a single customer group, around which a community of practice springs, igniting the firebrand. Once ignited, you can add more fuel to the fire. You can add additional resources and eServices to fan the flames into a bonfire that attracts people from miles around; lured by their curiosity, they stay for the warmth, community, and kenship.

As illustrated in Figure 4-2, we describe a firebrand most generally in terms of *customer satisfactions* generated by interactions with the *firebrand platform*. The firebrand platform organizes a variety of brand resources in categories of eServices focused to customers through the user interface. Use the firebrand platform as a way to organize more detail-oriented discussions about those resources and eServices that will make the biggest difference for your key customers.

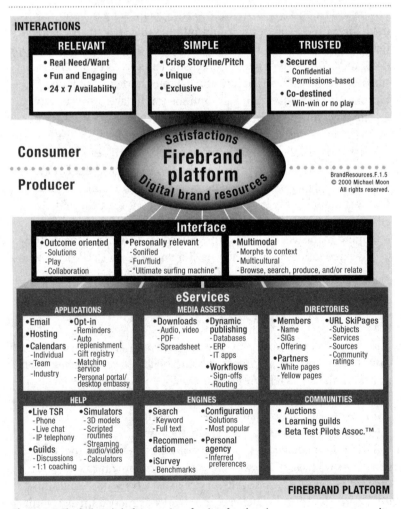

Figure 4-2 The firebrand platform consists of an *interface* that gives consumers access to a suite of *eServices*

eServices

An eService encapsulates a self-evident proposition—*an intuitive, needs-no-explanation offer of a discrete satisfaction for a particular customer.* As such, each eService requires no explanation as it solves or eliminates a problem or empowers a stakeholder to solve a problem with a new capability.

For business-to-consumer (B2C) consumer firebrands, eServices fall into one of four categories of satisfaction: enjoying a pleasurable entertainment experience (temporarily redirecting the consumer's attention from life's problems), solving a problem by doing more with less (time, money, hassle, brainpower), learning something (preemptively solving future problems), and self-actualization (generally enhancing self-esteem, social standing, and creative expression).

For B2B business firebrands, eServices fall into one of four categories of satisfaction, here ranked in order of ascending value: *process improvement* (less hassle), *cost reduction, increased revenue,* or enhanced *business valuation* (usually a combination of the previous three).

A firebrand carries the torch for one and only one category of satisfaction. The customer will associate her satisfaction with one of the four B2B or four B2C categories of satisfaction. Warning: do not attempt to build a firebrand with more than one category of satisfaction. You will almost certainly fail to achieve critical mass and fail to ignite a community of practice or community of concern around the one pivotal satisfaction defined and shaped by its category of satisfaction (entertainment, cost reduction, et. al.).

This constitutes another law of firebrands: *you can only brand one satisfaction within one category of satisfaction.* In the do-more-with-less category of satisfaction, for example, Quicken emerged as the must-have solution for eliminating the hassle of personal financial record keeping. Spanning categories—which Quicken did when it failed to identify a killer eService and instead offered an unfocused series of brand extensions—diluted the positioning and undermined the formation of a community of practice or concern. As we will show later, Intuit should have used community captains and platform partners (third- and fourth-parties) to ignite their firebrands around a new and uniquely differentiated self-service satisfaction.

In practical terms, eServices include applications such as e-mail, calendars, and reminders; directories; help and training facilities; search, configuration, and other engines; auctions, learning guilds, and other communities; and a broad variety of media assets. As we will examine in the next chapter, eServices also represent elements that a company will need to add to its business IT applications in order to serve customers and other stakeholders 24/7 in the Networked Economy.

Interface

More than any other digital brand resource, the interface creates the firebrand. Why? Because the satisfactions that make up the firebrand in the consumer's mind derive from interactions with digital brand resources at the interface.

A library of books and an army of specialists address interface design in far more detail than we might here. Suffice to say, your interface should reflect the individual workflows and usage patterns of each type of knowledge worker—a customer or other stakeholder from a particular market segment—you seek to serve. To achieve this level of expression and congruence, engage an interactive brand consultancy with deep knowledge in user interface theory, information engineering, multimedia storytelling, intelligent database queries, and the technical parameters that define Web interactions.

Our research of digital brand masters reveals three guiding principles for effective interface design.

First, good interfaces focus on specific outcomes and must give users meaningful results in the fewest possible mouse clicks. Visitors come to a Web site seeking a satisfaction; make it easy. Make it fun, too. Some of the best user interfaces have come from video game and multimedia CD-ROM designers who understand that a large portion of the satisfaction derives from the engaging and intriguing process of reaching the desired result. One tip: if you require a customer or stakeholder to complete a series of tasks (configure and buy a product, for example), always provide a visual map of "you are here" all the way through the sequence of steps. Offer collaboration facilities that include live chat and coaching from the firm's call center or inside sales group, and use push technologies that enable a teleservice representative to present recommended accessories and complementary products to go along with a customer's first choice.

Second, successful interfaces feel personally relevant. They speak to individuals in a familiar voice and with a comforting tone and timbre. They reflect a visual hierarchy of items that the target customer considers important. Use solution tracks to structure the interface and follow-on pages, using the results of research that uncovers the essential questions this particular customer group most often asks and the problems associated with these concerns. Offer a power search function with menu selections that enable a customer or other stakeholder to quickly characterize status ("existing customer"), size and type of firm ("large business," "financial services"), level of engagement ("researching a possible solution"), scope of responsibility ("technical advisor"), time frame for action ("active search leading to purchase in less than 30 days"), and relevant demographic or economic profiling factors. This power search function will let you brand your site as the "ultimate surf machine"—providing rapid, fun, self-revealing interactions that produce immediate and personally relevant results.

Finally, effective interfaces provide a multimodal relationship with the eServices and resources of the Web site. As customers and other stakeholders reveal themselves (via power search functions and opt-in subscription forms), the site dynamically assembles and prioritizes its digital assets to reflect the needs and behaviors of the economic actor revealed in this profile. The enabling technology must accommodate the multiple "personalities" that any individual stakeholder might display: an existing customer may seek technical support in the morning and, as an investor, pose a question about a stock holding in the afternoon.

Consumer Satisfactions

Careful research of consumers and other stakeholders will reveal what kinds of interactions with the producer's firebrand platform will produce satisfactions desired by particular stakeholders. Producing these satisfactions creates and maintains a trusted relationship between consumer and producer.

In the previous chapter, we discussed brand functions from the buyer perspective and saw that buyers seek simplified choice, risk reduction, and confirmation of self-identity. With regard to a firebrand, consumers seek these same qualities, but their expectations, shaped by experience with personal computer software, video games, and other elements of digital culture, shift to emphasize relevant, simple, and trusted interactions. We can't prescribe how your firebrand will express these qualities, but instead we offer a series of essential questions that will reveal such qualities to you.

Relevant

Does the producer's firebrand platform offer eServices that consumers really need and want? Do these eServices engage consumers in a fun and immersive manner? Can consumers use these eServices 24/7?

Please remember that customers rarely understand, nor can they articulate, their true wants, needs, and desires. They say one thing and often do another. Only primary research of their behavior correlated to demographic factors can safely guide you in this regard.

Simple

Does each eService make a clear, crisp, and compelling pitch for its use? Does it tell a story that consumers want to hear? Do the eServices strike a consumer as uniquely suited to her? Do the eServices meet needs that competitors don't meet? Do they reinforce the proper positioning and category in which they compete?

Trusted

Do customers accurately intuit your true motives for having an interactive relationship? Have you made your motives explicit? Do customers and other stakeholders understand what information you collect and how you use it to benefit the relationship? Do you have an explicit privacy policy and adhere to it? Do you invite consumers to help you help them by offering permissions-based eServices? Have you explained, convincingly, how the relationship can evolve to higher levels of mutual benefit? Do consumers see a big upside?

Firebrand "Heat"

Let's face it. Sitting in front of a computer screen and surfing from one silent Web page to the next pales in comparison to sitting around a campfire with a group of close friends and family. It lacks warmth. Lacking warmth, trust deflates. People become more suspicious and less inclined to share; the trusted relationship that lies at the heart of a firebrand never ignites. How can brand managers use digital technology to offset the inherently isolating and dehumanizing aspects of the Web experience?

Our research shows that brand managers who "get" the firebrand concept—how to foster relevant, simple, trusted interactions—now use multimedia assets to add warmth. They create an exciting, all-encompassing experience that we call firebrand *heat.*

Media Assets That Deliver "Heat"

Brand managers add "heat" to the Web experience through a process we call brand sonification, offering Web visitors a variety of interactive, downloaded or streaming audio, video, animation, and virtual-reality media assets. We detail these assets in Figure 4-3, and here highlight a few high-payback applications.

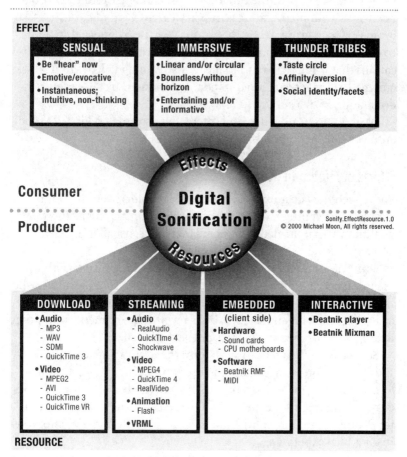

Figure 4-3 Brand managers can make a firebrand sizzle by applying a variety of multimedia brand resources. These include downloaded audio or video and streaming audio, video, animation, or VRML files

Among downloadable audio assets, MP3 has emerged as the hands-down winner for audio. In addition to music, brand managers can create MP3 files of customer testimonials, interviews and speeches of key executives—the opportunities abound. We also recommend that brand managers create downloadable video files for use in presentations by sales and marketing organizations, user documentation and training materials, and other collateral pieces, using MP3 or Quick-Time audio soundtracks.

RealAudio has emerged as the de facto standard for streaming audio. Beyond the obvious popularity of Web-based radio stations, we advocate its use for the broadcast of shareholder meetings, product debuts with presentations from key executives and customer testimonials, focus-group research sessions (for use by internal staff and trusted partners), customer service calls, and a hundred other applications that bring the brand to life. For streaming video, MPEG4 has emerged as the international standard (embraced by all leading vendors) and serves a similar function.

We'll discuss embedded and interactive assets later. First, let's look at the effects that brand sonification creates.

Effects of Firebrand "Heat"

We've seen how customers and other stakeholders seek relevant, simple, trusted interactions. Brand sonification augments these qualities with multimedia elements that add sensual, immersive, and tribal dimensions.

Sonification makes a brand sensual by invoking the warmth of the human voice, often richly inflected with emotional meaning, the rhythm of music, and the punctuation of sound effects. Audio especially, because of its transience, pulls us into the moment, as opposed to launching us into an abstract intellectual realm.

Sonification thus tends to immerse the user in a space or dimension without horizon, pulling the user into deeper, more intimate levels of involvement, overcoming the inherently alienating qualities of the computer-user experience. Our research shows that the auditory component may contribute up to 50 percent of the memorability of a Web experience.

In making us sensually stimulated and immersed, multimedia assets—especially music—pull us into tribes. Music plays a key role in the development of social identity—a set of tastes and dislikes that often stay with a person throughout a lifetime. Brand managers who want to address Baby Boomers can use rock and roll classics from the 1960s and 1970s to immediately arrest their attention and pull them into a message, while Big Band jazz attracts their parents.

But the effects of brand sonification go even deeper. In Figure 4-4 we show how firebrand "heat" helps pierce a customer's bubble of suspicion, assuaging the fear, uncertainty, and doubt that creep into the lonely, silent Web experience. These assets keep visitors on the page, interacting with the firebrand platform, setting the stage for a trusted relationship and community involvement.

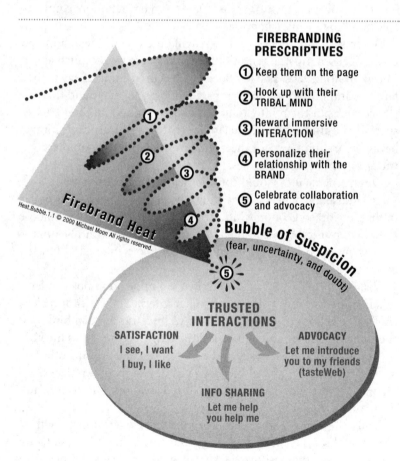

FIREBRANDING PRESCRIPTIVES

① Keep them on the page

② Hook up with their TRIBAL MIND

③ Reward immersive INTERACTION

④ Personalize their relationship with the BRAND

⑤ Celebrate collaboration and advocacy

Firebrand Heat

Heat.Bubble.1.1 © 2000 Michael Moon All rights reserved.

Bubble of Suspicion (fear, uncertainty, and doubt)

TRUSTED INTERACTIONS

SATISFACTION
I see, I want
I buy, I like

ADVOCACY
Let me introduce you to my friends (tasteWeb)

INFO SHARING
Let me help you help me

Figure 4-4 Firebrand "heat" that results from the smart use of multimedia assets induces a Web visitor to spiral into deeper cycles of interaction with the brand and its communities. This model prescribes five prescriptive practices that can turn casual visitors into brand advocates

The Sound of Music in Retail Aisles

Market researchers and retailers discovered that huge product selections in post-World War II department stores and suburban malls tended to overwhelm consumers with choices. Worse, the silence made them feel the need to suppress emotion and display Sunday-church behavior. Retailers noticed that they tended not to pick up featured merchandise, try samples, or use demo products—they didn't buy. They found that music, especially when keyed to seasonal events like Christmas or Independence Day, made people feel more comfortable. They could talk without the fear of someone overhearing them down the aisle or across the store. They felt more comfortable handling the merchandise.

For this reason, retailers began playing the toned-down, homogenized, licensed musical renditions offered by companies such as Muzak. In the 1980s, as Baby Boomers began to come of age with families and moved into higher paying jobs, retailers found that classic rock put them into a shop-and-spend mood. In the 1990s, specialty boutique store chains found that special music selections became part and parcel of their retail brand—building on the music's ability to create tribes.

Online merchants should consider using these proven brand-merchandising practices while taking advantage of the native strengths of the Networked Economy infrastructure: let Web site visitors choose their own music. We recommend the Beatnik Player from Beatnik, Inc. (www.beatnik.com) to give users a complete, interactive music experience.

Visitors to MTV's S-Track Web site see a mini-boombox displayed in a floating window. Using this familiar interface, the visitor makes musical selections (hip-hop, acid jazz, techno-trance), combining them into a looping ambient sound track that accompanies the visitor throughout the MTV site and even follows them to surf other sites. The Beatnik Player also lets the visitor re-mix up to 64 stereo channels to produce a highly personalized creation. The visitor can even e-mail these re-mixes to friends.

Thus, the visitor personalizes her interactive environment with moods and sounds most comforting and reassuring. As a result, our research shows that visitors will stay on a Web page eight times longer and will return 25 times more often than other Web visitors who have not thus personalized a site. This goes way beyond making a Web site "sticky." It induces customers and other stakeholders to take up permanent residence in your firebrand's storydwelling.

Firebrands Live in eMediaspace

In Chapter 2 we discussed how customers create a constellation of brands that orbit each individual in what we call brandspace—a personal space containing the brands that express an individual's core identity, badges of belonging, go-to solution, out-there, and orphan brands. In Chapter 3 we saw the role of a marketspace: the points of market presence where buyers and sellers meet and do business. Within a marketspace, customers engage in the four basic behaviors of shopping, buying, sourcing, and trading. We showed how brand managers engage in storytelling using various branding channels.

Firebrands also live in the hearts and minds of customers, organized in a map that we call *eMediaspace*. As illustrated in Figure 4-5, this somewhat shadowy construct represents the convergence of markets, media, and points of market presence framed by the online world (a.k.a. cyberspace). Relationships between producers, customers, and other stakeholders also change in eMediaspace. Stakeholders not only interact with brand producers, they interact with other stakeholders—a newly emboldened class of intermediaries.

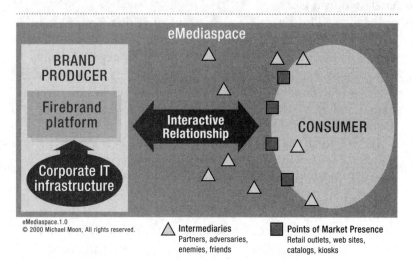

Figure 4-5 eMediaspace describes the convergence of traditional brand mediaspace, industry value chains, and interactive relationships between producers and consumers in the Networked Economy. Highlighted here is a potent new force in the brand eState: intermediaries eMediaspace denotes not only the shift in context from offline to online, but also a shift from storytelling to digital storytelling. Relationships shift from face-to-face to digitally intermediated, screen-to-screen relationships. Points of market presence shift from bricks-and-mortar retail venues and in-person business calls to 24/7 online eTail and eService outlets, some of which the brand manager can control, but many of which fall within the sphere of trade partners and their affiliates.

eMediaspace frames a fundamental challenge for every brand manager: how to build relationships based on 24/7 trusted interactions with as many as 200 million individuals, interacting with as many as 10 million of them in a single day? The very notions of communication and relationship undergo a startling transformation.

Relationships of eMediaspace

While eMediaspace constitutes the place where customers, producers, and intermediaries create relationships in the Networked Economy, unfortunately we lose the familiar feedback of face-to-face interaction. In the physical offline world, body language and tone of voice can immediately identify friend or foe and the degree to which we share common goals. We can't do this in eMediaspace, because too many interactions occur too quickly with too many faceless individuals.

Figure 4-6 illustrates the four basic relationship types—friends, partners, enemies, and adversaries—that brand managers can use to begin sorting out their interactive relationship strategies. Affinity expresses emotional involvement and warmth (the kind we normally associate with family or friends) while alignment expresses a deeper understanding and support of an individual's professional or creative endeavors.

Use this model to begin defining the data that characterize an individual relative to the spectra of alignment and affinity. Ultimately, an effective firebrand manager will have databased profiles that position each stakeholder group, customer, and intermediary someplace in this affinity-alignment matrix. Armed with this data, they can strategically allocate brand resources for each group, maximizing return on investment and minimizing erosion of brand. We describe how to do this in Chapter 5.

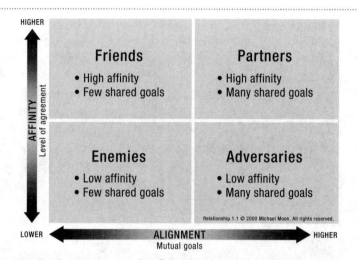

Figure 4-6 Brand managers can use this *affinity-alignment* model to quickly characterize a variety of commercial relationships

Intermediaries

In traditional offline marketspaces, the relationship between buyer and seller is buffered by magazines, trade shows, consultants, and rating services. The same holds true for eMediaspace, except that the condition is amplified many times over in the Networked Economy.

Figure 4-7 shows how eMediaspace augments these traditional intermediaries with a host of new hybrids, including consumer and community portals (Yahoo! and AOL), business-to-business exchanges (ChemDirect.com), special-interest magazines and telezines (c|net), retail sites (Amazon.com), auction sites (eBay), ratings services (Consumer Reports, ePinions), substitutors (Priceline), and consumer watchdog groups (AdBusters).

Intermediaries have the power to enhance or destroy your firebrand. Brand managers who understand how these eMediaspace relationships work will make sure to appropriately provision intermediaries with brand resources by offering multimedia assets, access to Web site resources, co-branding eServices, shared business intelligence, and other meaningful expressions of a branding partnership.

Intermediary relationships can dramatically increase the points of market presence for a firebrand. When supplied with appropriate multimedia assets to use on their Web sites, intermediaries can add "heat" to your firebrand at those points of market presence, dramatically increasing traffic to your firebrand Web site.

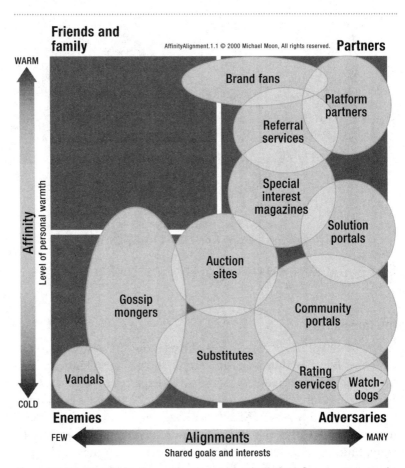

Figure 4-7 This figure depicts the most important *intermediaries* that influence customers and other stakeholders of your firm, each one wanting to earn a commission or transaction fee for the favor

Intermediaries can also tarnish a firebrand through a variety of corrosive acts, either malicious or unintentional. As unsavory as it may appear, firebrand managers may want to build a database of individuals or companies of known bad intent, and subsequently set out to counter their efforts, even by blocking their entry to the firebrand Web site if necessary. With the proliferation of "shadow" or anti-brand sites (IhateCompanyX.com, ProductYsucks.com, etc.), an increasing number of public relations consultancies can advise in appropriate responses.

Deep Gravity Well Supersites

We offer the deep gravity well model to help firebrand managers understand the nuances of drawing stakeholders into trusted relationships that move up the affinity-alignment scale, relationships that become progressively more intimate and more valuable to both parties.

In space, a gravity well corresponds to any astronomical body or mass; the more mass, the greater the gravity. Stars, planets, moons—each has a gravity well which attracts nearby objects. As a metaphor, this can help explain certain seemingly paradoxical laws of attraction for a firebrand. Nobody goes anywhere on the Web except by choice; you have to choose a destination and click the mouse. At the same time, certain sites exert a powerful influence to attract these volitional surfers.

In eMediaspace, the deep gravity well supersite represents a brightly lit, intriguing destination that draws the curious individual into closer orbit. Ultimately, the individual may land and establish a permanent presence. If the visitor experiences sufficient levels of affinity and alignment with the brand and its community, she may become a citizen, accepting the brand as a badge of belonging—part of her social identity. She becomes an active participant in the brand's community of practice and concern.

How does this work?

Five Layers of eServices

As illustrated in Figure 4-8, deep gravity well supersites pull in customers and other stakeholders with a set of progressively more intimate interactions offered in five layers of eServices.

Free Space

This portion of the firebrand Web site welcomes one and all, directing people who know what they want to their designated "cyberhoods" and solution tracks. This layer must achieve two basic goals: quickly orient a new visitor to the breadth, depth, and scope of the company and the site, and quickly direct return visitors to the areas or items that address their particular needs and desires.

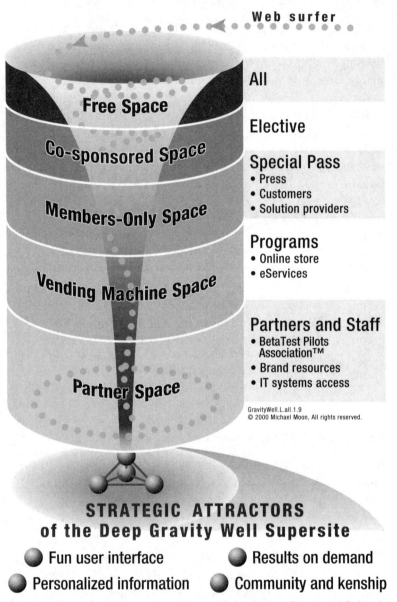

Web surfer

All

Free Space

Elective

Co-sponsored Space

Special Pass
• Press
• Customers
• Solution providers

Members-Only Space

Programs
• Online store
• eServices

Vending Machine Space

Partners and Staff
• BetaTest Pilots
  Association™
• Brand resources
• IT systems access

Partner Space

GravityWell.L.all.1.9
© 2000 Michael Moon, All rights reserved.

STRATEGIC ATTRACTORS
of the Deep Gravity Well Supersite

● Fun user interface   ● Results on demand

● Personalized information   ● Community and kenship

Figure 4-8 The interface where consumers interact with the eServices of a company's firebrand platform and business IT applications finds its most robust expression in an enhanced Web site design that we call the *deep gravity well*

Interactive brand consultancies and Web design firms continue to pioneer best practice for this layer, espousing a variety of strategies along a constantly evolving design spectrum. We do agree with David Siegel in his book, *Futurize Your Enterprise* (John Wiley & Sons, 1999), when he asserts that this zone must organize itself according to the specific needs of customers and their process of investigating, buying, and using a particular product or service. Siegel forcefully argues that a Web site and its modes of navigation should *not* reflect the company's internal organizational structure.

In all cases, make it easy for the new customer to quickly grasp the fundamentals of your business by answering the questions of a formal request for information (what you produce, the kinds of customers you serve, etc.). Make it easy for a new visitor who may be an existing customer to quickly grasp the navigational structure of the Web site. And make sure that return customers become users of the power search function. Highlight it. Promote it.

Co-sponsored

Having brought people in the front door of the free layer, where they sort themselves into specific stakeholder groups (customers, investors, trade partners, staff, and significant sub-groups), direct them to their desired cyberhoods and solution tracks here in the co-sponsored space. Co-sponsors include affiliates, platform partners, suppliers, distributors, and other third- and fourth-parties involved with the brand.

Your research of satisfied customers and other stakeholders will have revealed the essential questions that framed each critical development of their satisfaction lifecycles. Use these essential questions as signposts to point stakeholders to the right resources. For example, if your company sells industrial pumps for the petroleum industry, a customer in the final stages of formulating a request for proposal might want to know "How do maintenance cycle requirements change in the Arctic compared to temperate undersea environments?" Design links to a page that offers answers and resources for this concern, and do the same for other key stakeholder questions.

We recommend that firebrand managers aggressively partner as a way of sourcing high-cost and expensive-to-maintain eServices. For example, the firebrand firm and a number of partners might benefit from a shared industry calendar and online directory of consultants and resellers of your respective products and services. Figure 4-2, shown earlier, offers many ideas for such co-sponsored eServices.

Co-sponsors also represent a good source of editorial and media assets that can plug in at this level. Make such assets—Flash animations, Beatnik sound libraries, QuickTime VR movies, etc.—available on co-sponsors' Web sites and on their affiliates' sites. Co-sponsors can also provide experts to lead online forum discussions, expanding the database of essential questions and answers. They will also drive traffic into the deep gravity well from their own Web sites or from kiosks in their bricks-and-mortar locations.

While this level depends heavily on co-sponsor participation, resist the pressure to fill it with banner ads, whether they be co-sponsors' ads or your own. Customer research clearly indicates that banner ads now constitute a toxic branding event. They annoy customers. They clutter up valuable "answer space." We recommend the wholesale prohibition of banner ads. Focus on editorial, dialogue, and conversation instead.

Members Only

Entry to this level requires that visitors opt-in by profiling themselves as economic actors (consumer in a household, professional in an enterprise, etc.) and in terms of their areas of ongoing interest. We discuss this profiling process in detail in the next chapter. At this level, brand managers will identify members by e-mail address, full name, zip code (or other specific geographical marker), and year of birth.

Here, members can personalize the look and feel of the Web site to suit their tastes. Excite.com reports that individuals who personalize MyExcite.com return 25 times more often than those who do not. However, be careful not to make the personalization process so complex that users will abandon it. Given the value of personalization (more frequent visits), it may make sense to devote considerable resources to making this attractive and easy, perhaps including discussion boards, live interactive chat, animated demonstrations, and even live telephone help. Guide such efforts with focus groups and usability testing feedback.

Members also gain access to additional layers of eServices provided by the firebrand firm and co-sponsors willing to offer higher value to these identified and opted-in individuals. These eServices might include interactive return-on-investment calculators, 3D simulations, interactive surveys and focus groups, newsletters and other subscription-based vehicles, download libraries containing Power-point slide shows, white papers distilled into Acrobat PDFs, editable word processor documents and spreadsheets, tab-delimited database records suitable for importing to contact-management applications, self-contained run-time databases (an industry resource directory or product locator in a FileMaker Pro application, for example—a great cross-platform database with a free runtime version), live teleconfer-ences, and Webinars—use your imagination.

Communities begin to coalesce in co-sponsored space, but here in member space they bloom and begin to bear fruit. Communities create social assets and other types of value that feed existing mem-bers and attract new members by the thousands. The secret of AOL's success lies in the online forums, now approaching 50,000 in num-ber, where people regularly participate.

While some discussion forums will take place in co-sponsored space, the juicy ones happen here. Disclosed speech (where individu-als accurately identify themselves) induces people to take responsi-bility for what they say—a lesson that members of the pioneering online community, The Well, learned years ago. Anonymity breeds anti-social online behavior—flame wars and grudges. Ban anony-mous speech and let members of good standing moderate the dis-cussion so everybody feels comfortable, included, respected, and therefore willing to share at a deep level.

Members-only space also hosts press and analyst centers, accepting credential participants in press conferences, executive briefings, and other high-level events. These centers may offer ready-to-broadcast video and audio segments for mass media broadcast outlets and high-resolution multimegabyte still images and photos suitable for the highest quality four-color print publications.

Vending Machine

Whether or not the firebrand firm sells a product or service directly to a customer or not, an effective deep gravity sell supersite will nonetheless offer a transaction-processing capability that functions as a self-service vending machine.

If you already sell to end-use customers through direct channels (catalogs, field sales force, company outlets, direct mail, telemarketing, etc.), you already own and operate a vending machine within the deep gravity well supersite.

Companies that don't sell directly to end-use customers will use a 24/7 online vending machine for transactions—supplies, parts, services, etc.—with their value chain partners. This may include sales and marketing materials too expensive to give away but which a brand manager may sell to a reseller, debiting a co-op marketing fund. The vending machine can also facilitate a procurement portal where employees and trusted trade partners buy commodity products with group discount privileges from the firm's supply chain.

A fully automated vending machine, programmed to handle all kinds of credit cards, invoicing and bill presentment, or even scrip or eCred instruments, enables your platform partners to use your deep gravity well to sell their products and services. This not only creates additional traffic and brand awareness for your gravity well, but also begins to lock in a customer to your eCommerce system (ordering, product configurations, personalization profiles, manners of payment, project tracking, etc.).

Partner Space

This represents the level of deepest trust and reciprocity between the firebrand firm and its community of stakeholders; those people and organizations who in some tangible way add new value to the overall satisfaction of a customer.

Here, platform partners have access to the tools and materials that they can use to build their own nested Web sites within the firebrand firm's deep gravity well and link their Web sites to its eCommerce infrastructure.

It also serves as the development and staging area where the firebrand firm, entrepreneurial-minded employees, customers, and other stakeholders create and test new eServices. In the next chapter, we discuss in detail how to build out this entrepreneurial eServices platform.

Every firebrand manager should form a Beta Test Pilots Association and deploy it at this level of the deep gravity well supersite. This association represents a highly evolved form of what market researchers call a market panel. The association consists of pre-profiled market participants from all stakeholder groups, who have agreed in advance to participate in some form of market research study including online, telephone, and mail-back surveys, online and in-person focus groups, Web site usability tests, and "follow-me-around" observational studies.

What motivates stakeholders to dedicate this kind of time and attention? Some will do it because they love and deeply identify with the brand. The rest require compensation in more tangible form. Compensation can range from outright cash payments and honoraria, donations on a stakeholder's behalf to a charitable organization (an excellent way to reward someone whose company or affiliation prevents acceptance of cash or gifts), discount vouchers (for products and services from the firebrand firm and its trade partners), or, most desirable, free downloads of prized digital objects (products or services that have little or no logistics fulfillment costs). Such digital objects can include survey results, market research reports, music and video downloads, newsletters, or in fact anything with a high perceived value to the stakeholder.

The Beta Test Pilots Association serves as a sounding board by which brand managers can quickly assess new product features, changes in policy or practices, unserved market needs, areas and sources of customer defection, areas of exceptional service, or employees of distinction. Due to the emphasis on rigorous quantitative methods, brand managers may choose to partner with a research firm or outsource this capability to a trusted, long-term business intelligence provider.

Don't forget to have one of the most important stakeholder groups fully impaneled in the Beta Test Pilots Association: employees of the firebrand firm, especially those with job functions and demographic profiles that match key customer segments. They represent an invaluable resource.

At this level of the deep gravity well supersite, brand managers should encourage designated employees to create personal pages from which to interact with customers and other stakeholders, adding a face, name, and story to the overall firebrand.

Strategic Attractors

At each layer, the deep gravity well supersite uses strategic attractors to induce a stakeholder to form progressively more intimate, trusted relationships and to reward their contributions. These attractors include a fun user-interface, personalized information, results on demand, community and kenship, and take on a special form at each layer.

Radio station Web sites provide one of the best examples of the way these attractors can draw people into trusted relationships. Figure 4-9 illustrates the results of research by Arbitron and Edison Media Research into consumer preferences at radio station Web sites.

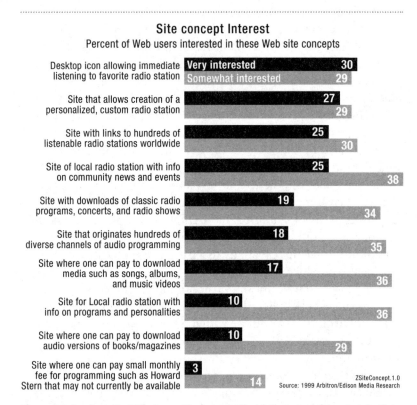

Site concept Interest
Percent of Web users interested in these Web site concepts

	Very interested	Somewhat interested
Desktop icon allowing immediate listening to favorite radio station	30	29
Site that allows creation of a personalized, custom radio station	27	29
Site with links to hundreds of listenable radio stations worldwide	25	30
Site of local radio station with info on community news and events	25	38
Site with downloads of classic radio programs, concerts, and radio shows	19	34
Site that originates hundreds of diverse channels of audio programming	18	35
Site where one can pay to download media such as songs, albums, and music videos	17	36
Site for Local radio station with info on programs and personalities	10	36
Site where one can pay to download audio versions of books/magazines	10	29
Site where one can pay small monthly fee for programming such as Howard Stern that may not currently be available	3	14

ZSiteConcept.1.0
Source: 1999 Arbitron/Edison Media Research

Figure 4-9 A radio station Web site provides an unusually rich illustration of the principles that underlie a deep gravity well supersite. Every firebrand manager should adopt and systematically study one new radio station Web site a month

We selected this radio station example because, of all the media-related properties and formats we could study, radio stations best illustrate the principles of a deep gravity well supersite. Radio stations demonstrate a firebrand fundamental: music (and other firebrand "heat" assets) creates tribes; radio stations attract cohesive communities who share tastes in music and may also share political and social concerns. As a visitor dives into a radio station deep gravity well supersite, she seeks ways to expand her entertainment or information options—concert schedules, playlists, expanded liner notes or performance descriptions, purchase of hot new CDs or concert tickets, sweepstakes drawings and contests, fan club activities, a range of discussions and forums, and other ways to more deeply involve herself.

Strategic attractors also exist offline. Figure 4-10 shows how firebrand managers can use traditional offline media, characterized by their broad reach, to transport stakeholders to the deep gravity well supersite. They can use offline media to drive traffic and use online media to create trusted, one-to-one interactive relationships as stakeholders descend through a deep gravity well supersite's layered services. You will discover that what works in the offline world almost always fails in the online, interactive world, and vice versa, reflecting the very different nature of these parallel universes in eMediaspace.

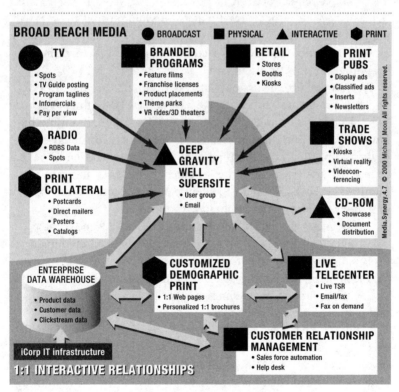

Figure 4-10 Your deep gravity well supersite straddles two parallel universes of the eMediaspace. In the offline world, broad reach media induces stakeholders to visit. Once there, their use of eServices ignites the formation of a community

Your Brandstand in eMediaspace

URLs play a key role in bringing visitors to a deep gravity well super-site, as illustrated in Figure 4-11. Firebrand managers must make sure that customers, prospects, and other interested stakeholders can find the brand through rationalized naming conventions adapted to maximize exposure on Web search engines and directory sites. Firebrand Web developers should use metatags and other specialized techniques that help search engines profile the firebrand presence in eMediaspace. Use the URLs on all company literature, advertisements, billboards—at all possible points of market presence.

For example, we have developed a companion Web site, Firebrands.com, for the purpose of creating an interactive relationship and exchange of information with readers such as you. Follow-up questions and answers related to each chapter of this book constitute the principle self-service satisfaction of Firebrands.com. We believe that asking readers for follow-up questions and posting answers will stimulate our development of future versions of the Firebrands book as well as promote our executive education programs (workshops, branding summits, and seminars).

We also practice the use of related URLs to increase the draw of our deep gravity well supersite. We have several URLs directly related to book chapters: Brandstand.com, BrandeState.com, Brandingthe-DotCom.com, BrandResources.com, DigitalAssets.com, bellwether-brands.com, goodmousekeeping.com, and over two dozen more that represent our equivalent of the "branded ingredients" indicated in Figure 4-11. Each URL links to a home page dedicated to the topic, with links to the broader Firebrand.com site itself.

We use metatags that let Web search engines quickly index these pages and their subject matter. We recommend that firebrand managers populate a set of metatags with like-sounding words (homonyms for the brand name, key ingredients, solutions, and satisfactions associated with the brand), misspellings (Firebrend, Fireburn, Firebland), and phonetic spellings (Fyrbrand, Fyrland).

Many firms have registered trademarks and service marks for which they should seek URL domain name registration. This sometimes involves negotiation or litigation with "cybersquatters"—an evolving legal practice. For each trademark, we recommend that a firm create one static HTML page whose content includes appropriate legal statements and attributions, as well as a short description of the mark and its relationship to the brand firm, its customers, markets, industry supply chains, etc.—all keywords that search engine spiders may use to index the site. Also seek URL registration for each product, including all formal and informal names, as well as former names and nicknames both positive and pejorative. If you do not wish to publicize or otherwise call undue attention to such names or nicknames, hide them in metatags. Use the names of competing companies, products, and services in metatags, too.

Register URLs and create a Web page for the formal and informal names of communities that form around the brand; we use BetaTestPilotsAssociation.com, for example. Give each of your online forums and discussion groups a name that can work as a URL and branded destination in its own right. Do the same with any specific practices and disciplines associated with the brand; we also use SonifyTheWeb.com.

We have begun to track a small group of consultancies that specialize in digital naming conventions and techniques for Web search optimization, including Danny Sullivan, publisher of the e-mail newsletter Search Engine Report. A search for Web site promotion services yields numerous resources.

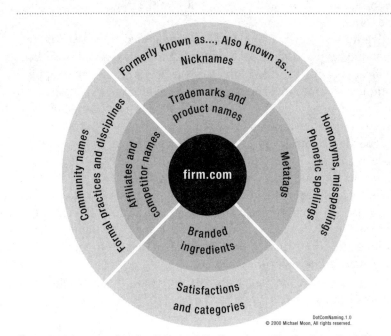

Figure 4-11 Large portals such as Yahoo! and Alta Vista, along with referral sites like AskJeeves and About.com use specialized software robots called spiders that crawl through the Web, cataloguing and indexing millions of sites

Digital Embassies

A successful deep gravity well supersite enables firebrand managers to develop the ultimate of intimate relationships with a stakeholder—a permanent presence on the stakeholder's computer desktop (or broadband TV set-top device).

Consider this: Microsoft establishes the equivalent of a digital embassy on almost every personal computer in the world as customers have accepted the terms of a software license and installed MS-DOS, Windows, Office, or Internet Explorer. This has become obvious—and a point of legal contention—as Microsoft has moved to tightly link these software products to Microsoft-controlled Web sites and eServices.

We can also see this in applications (such as Intuit's Quicken, QuickBooks, and TurboTax, Adobe InDesign, QuarkXPress, Auto-CAD, or AOL's browser) that have achieved mass acceptance and installation. We find perhaps the most powerful and suggestive example of a digital embassy in the integration of Mac OS 9 and the Sherlock search engine to a QuickTime TV network and a burgeoning array of free and paid eServices at the iMac-branded Web site series.

Figure 4-12 shows a digital embassy integrated at the level of the operating system interface. This approach can also work at the level of an application suite. In both cases, the operating system or application hard-wires its users to specific destinations in eMediaspace and specific eServices at those destinations, generally using the deep gravity well supersite as an entry point.

The digital embassy gives a firebrand a permanent point of presence at the most important location in eMediaspace: a stakeholder's equipment. Figure 4-13 shows how this firebrand resource integrates digital assets (the content of eServices), applications of a stakeholder information system (profiles and current satisfaction lifecycle status of individual stakeholders), and interactive logistics (online and offline facilities) to an eCommerce platform that the firebrand firm may operate internally or outsource.

In other words, the digital embassy represents the stakeholder's personal gateway to the firebrand's deep gravity well supersite.

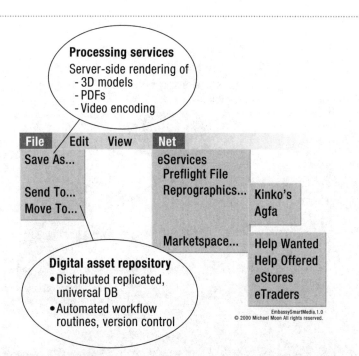

Figure 4-12 The digital embassy uses the familiar interface of a favored operating system or application to hard-wire a stakeholder to a firebrand deep gravity well supersite and eServices

The digital embassy embodies the best principles of n-tier client/server computing. More than just a browser, the stakeholder uses the embassy application for local processing—Quicken personal-finance data entry, for example—to prepare data for processing and consolidation by the deep gravity well supersite servers which then squirt results back to the Quicken digital embassy for storage and local manipulation.

If you're not Intuit or Microsoft, how do you build your own digital embassy? We highly recommend that you become a FileMaker Pro developer, using this robust, general purpose, cross-platform database to build client-side applications (ranging, for example, from simple order processing to complex bid-procurement procedures). FileMaker Pro's scripting language makes it easy for the desktop digital embassy to upload locally entered data, grab data from a variety of systems and Web pages accessed through the deep gravity well supersite, perform operations on it, then automatically squirt it back to the stakeholder embassy.

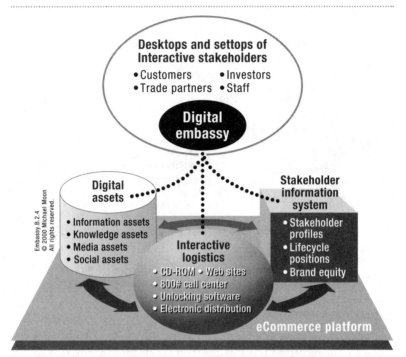

Figure 4-13 Your *digital embassy* should integrate stakeholder profiles to digital assets, interactive logistics, and the eCommerce platform that undergirds your deep gravity well supersite

What Functions Do Firebrands Serve?

Firebrands serve two primary functions. They bring consumers, producers, intermediaries, and other stakeholders together in eMediaspace and into your deep gravity well supersite. In particular, firebrands serve several new categories of stakeholders. Firebrands can also put "dot.com mojo" on any company's valuation and share price.

Firebrands Serve New Stakeholders

In our earlier discussion of the way traditional brands bring buyers and sellers together, we explained the importance of stakeholders other than buyers, and we said that new stakeholder groups emerge in the Networked Economy. Figure 4-14 shows how we add opted-in customers and other stakeholders, Community Captains, platform partners, and eService entrepreneurs to the traditional stakeholder circle.

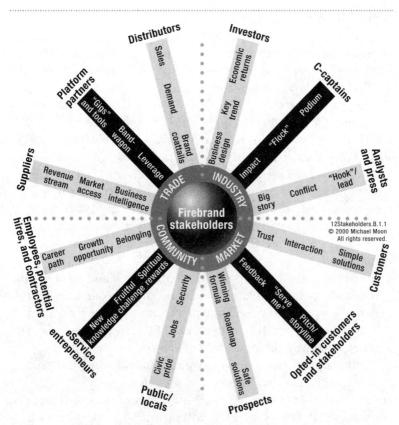

Figure 4-14 Four new *stakeholder groups* ignite a firebrand. eServices of a deep gravity well supersite create new currencies of exchange—feedback, impact, leverage, and spiritual rewards—which reward interaction in trusted relationships with the firebrand

Opted-in Customers and Other Stakeholders

These stakeholders have willingly shared—through Web site registration, for example—sensitive information with the brand producer in exchange for special privileges and access to eServices, such as free e-mail service or a free newsletter. Opting-in means that they have entrusted the firm with information in the expectation that the firm will use it to better understand and serve them. To do this you will need to give them a *pitch* or *storyline* that crisply telegraphs why they should opt-in: "register for free insider stock tips from the best Wall Street traders." In all cases, the opted-in customer says, "Serve me"—that's why she opts-in. Meaningful feedback from the opted-in stakeholder represents the currency of exchange in this transaction.

Community-Captains

Individuals in this very important group create, organize, and lead
communities of practice or concern. In practical terms, C-Captains
need a podium or "soapbox" powered by the eServices of the brand
firm's deep gravity well supersite.

They define themselves as leaders of a flock, deriving deep emotional rewards from this position of prestige and influence. A C-
Captain's self-esteem relates to the positive impact she has on her
flock. While they do influence, they cannot command; rather, they
follow a consensus. Helping them help their flock will repay many-
fold the efforts of firebrand managers. Generally, a C-Captain will
have active, direct relationships with between 15 and 150 community members. As many as 10 or 15 of those members may have
junior flocks in the making. This quickly pyramids into a huge
community.

These communities serve as the soul of a brand (and more so with
a firebrand), giving producers eyes and ears to hear and see how to
better satisfy customers. Firebrand managers must take great care in
vetting policy and practices with a panel of C-Captains who will help
identify potentially glaring acts of omission or commission.

Firebrand managers must formulate a plan for finding and moti-
vating C-Captains. They may need to provide monetary or other
concrete forms of compensation. Some communities form around a
category and its best practices (the Webmasters guild). Other communities organize around an issue (Mothers Against Drunk Driving,
Greenpeace) or special interest (PYNCHON-L email discussion group
among connoisseurs of Thomas Pynchon's books).

Following this same principle, firebrand managers should consider themselves C-Captains, and seek out other employees to jump-
start the formation of communities to support the firebrand.

Platform Partners

These stakeholders create new products or services using the digital brand resources of a deep gravity well supersite. For example,
Schwab.com or eTrade.com encourages registered financial planners
and other consultants to use online investment calculators at their
sites to serve the planners' own clientele, some of whom may not yet
invest through Schwab or E-Trade. Amazon.com's affiliate program
pioneered this concept. The company expanded on its book affiliate

program with Z-shops where retailers can set up shops using Amazon's back-end infrastructure for online sales and financial services.

As the name suggests, platform partners put food on their table by leveraging firebrand resources. They seek "gigs" and tools—paying engagements and access to the resources, eServices, and traffic of the firebrand firm's deep gravity well supersite.

What payback does the firebrand firm receive for its generosity? Platform partners increase traffic. They become, in essence, frontline technical support for the firebrand firm. The platform partner may induce a customer to personalize the firebrand firm's deep gravity well supersite to his or her preferences, perhaps even including the installation of digital embassy software. Platform partner customers may become customers of the firebrand firm. The currency of exchange with platform partners is impact.

Our research reveals that between 15 to 40 platform partners can create a global bandwagon effect that ignites your firebrand.

eService Entrepreneurs

This group represents firebrand firm employees who help develop and champion new eServices for stakeholders. We discuss the details of how they do this in the next chapter.

In all cases, employees may emerge as some of the most powerful advocates of the firebrand and may represent some of the most potent resources for involving other stakeholders with the firebrand.

For example, an individual in a customer-service or help-desk operation, if motivated and rewarded, could create an electronic newsletter containing tips and tricks of value to stakeholders outside the firm. This new knowledge (answers to essential questions) adds value to the firebrand.

An eService entrepreneur seeks an interesting and fruitful challenge for personal and career development. She may champion a new eService simply as an expression of "doing my job," or "this really adds new meaning to my job," or "I come to work to do *this* and my regular job is just an excuse for them to pay me." An eService entrepreneur may even discover that the personal and spiritual rewards of serving lead to becoming a firebrand manager of the first order.

Firebrand managers should actively scout, recruit, and motivate these eService entrepreneurs, even to the point of holding formal workshops and support groups.

Circle of 12

Great firebrands not only bring buyers and sellers together, they also express a chorus of voices from all stakeholder groups. Branding thus shifts from the high church of advertising agencies and specialists into the hands of the people: the people who really create value (stakeholders) work as active, engaged members of the firebrand team.

Senior managers must embrace a brand storytelling framework that fosters trusted relationships with all stakeholder groups. They must work hard to develop a brand story that embraces all of these stakeholder groups, all the while maintaining a crisp brand positioning with its emphasis on the principle offline and online satisfactions.

Shareholder Tracks at the Deep Gravity Well Supersite

The deep gravity well supersite should offer each stakeholder group its own home page, which in turn becomes a deep gravity well serving that community, as we illustrate in Figure 4-15. Stakeholders must find clear pointers at the deep gravity well supersite's home page directing them to the appropriate second-level stakeholder home page in the co-sponsored service layer.

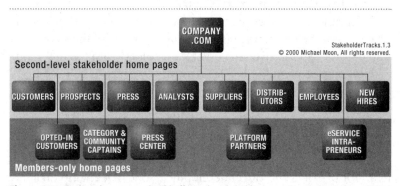

Figure 4-15 Firebrand managers should offer each stakeholder group its own home page, linked from the deep gravity well supersite's home page

Each of these secondary stakeholder home pages should reflect the group's categories of interest, solution tracks, and information consumption preferences. Analysts and press who have not yet opted-in as credentialed members in good standing, for example, will look for breaking news, corporate and financial information, current officers, lines of business, and industry data that helps position the company and its product in appropriate industry segments and markets.

In other words, each stakeholder represents a formal request for information to which the stakeholder home page should respond. To do so you will have to talk to a cross-section of representative individuals in each stakeholder group to determine what information they need, what problems they want to solve, and other essential questions and key concerns regarding the company, its products and services, the industry it serves, and how to probe deeper.

Get Your Dot.com Mojo Working

In the spirit of the rock and roll classic, firebrand managers enjoy an unprecedented opportunity to increase company valuation and shareholder value through effective firebranding.

Everybody marvels at the ever-increasing share prices and company valuations for dot.com companies like Yahoo!, BroadVision, and the latest crop of IPOs. While many factors contribute to these valuations, we highlight here how a firebrand contributes.

A firebrand can provide "dot.com mojo" through the exploitation of an interactive business design which centers on eSupply, value capture, and loyalty lock-ins.

Interactive Business Design

In the previous chapter, we discussed value creation in the context of traditional brand building. We explained that a business design described what satisfactions a firm brings to market and how it captures value. An interactive business design emphasizes digital self-service satisfactions and new, more powerful value-capture mechanisms.

Creating an interactive business design means planning or re-engineering a company specifically for the Networked Economy. As we see in the next section, a company with an interactive business design satisfies customers through the strategic use of eSupply.

eSupply

Firebrands with dot.com mojo use eSupply—a combination of digital assets and eServices—to fulfill consumer satisfactions. As we illustrate in Figure 4-16, eSupply turns the laws of supply and demand upside down.

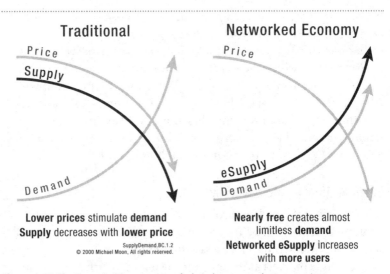

Traditional

Price

Supply

Demand

Lower prices stimulate **demand**
Supply decreases with **lower price**

SupplyDemand.BC.1.2
© 2000 Michael Moon, All rights reserved.

Networked Economy

Price

eSupply

Demand

Nearly free creates almost
limitless **demand**
Networked eSupply increases
with **more users**

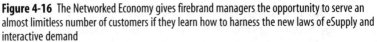

Figure 4-16 The Networked Economy gives firebrand managers the opportunity to serve an almost limitless number of customers if they learn how to harness the new laws of eSupply and interactive demand

In the traditional model, lower prices stimulate demand and increased sales deplete inventories. The eSupply model explains how a company can fulfill almost limitless demand without depleting inventory. Companies using eSupply have no practical limit to the number of customer self-service interactions they can deliver through eMedia-space. These companies not only eliminate the cost-of-goods for each digital product or services sold, they also eliminate most if not all costs associated with logistics distribution and fulfillment. This creates a "zero-gravity," intelligent, pre-emptively positioned firebrand.

eSupply works best for pure-play dot.coms. Clicks-and-mortar hybrid companies can also benefit from eSupply's dot.com mojo to drive sales of non-digital products and services by offering eServices that add new digital satisfactions.

Figure 4-17 illustrates the eSupply model. As managers seek to acquire dot.com mojo, they must investigate four resource areas.

INTERACTIVE BUSINESS DESIGN

An interactive business design helps create eSupply when it highlights self-service satisfactions, thus eliminating, to the greatest possible degree, labor costs and management hassle associated with high-touch, offline service.

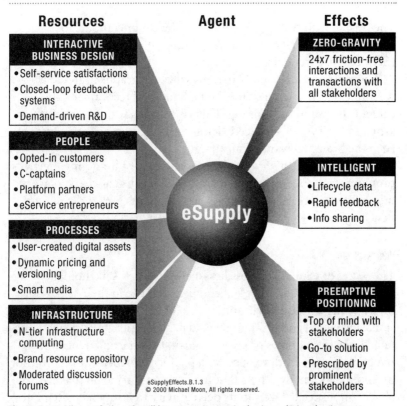

Resources

INTERACTIVE BUSINESS DESIGN
- Self-service satisfactions
- Closed-loop feedback systems
- Demand-driven R&D

PEOPLE
- Opted-in customers
- C-captains
- Platform partners
- eService entrepreneurs

PROCESSES
- User-created digital assets
- Dynamic pricing and versioning
- Smart media

INFRASTRUCTURE
- N-tier infrastructure computing
- Brand resource repository
- Moderated discussion forums

Agent

eSupply

Effects

ZERO-GRAVITY
24x7 friction-free interactions and transactions with all stakeholders

INTELLIGENT
- Lifecycle data
- Rapid feedback
- Info sharing

PREEMPTIVE POSITIONING
- Top of mind with stakeholders
- Go-to solution
- Prescribed by prominent stakeholders

eSupplyEffects.B.1.3
© 2000 Michael Moon, All rights reserved.

Figure 4-17 All great firebrands will harness an interactive business design that integrates people, processes, and infrastructure optimized for the Networked Economy. By so doing they generate a zero-gravity, intelligent, pre-emptively positioned firebrand

It also relies on a closed-loop feedback system that operates in real time, or as close as possible to real time. A large online shopping network, for example, uses a statistical model to price hot products for maximum total profit (the greatest number of sales with the highest net margin) by time of day, day of week, and season.

When applied to new product or service development, the closed-loop feedback system can fuel demand-driven research and development. A Beta Test Pilots Association, for example, can help a firebrand manager quickly determine demand for existing products, identify emerging markets, and satisfy newly identified unserved needs.

PEOPLE

The people with the biggest impact in the eSupply model include opted-in customers, community-captains, platform partners, and eService entrepreneurs.

They attract customers. Their presence telegraphs brand trustworthiness. Their word of mouth referrals and recommendations cement the brand positioning. Their infectious zeal inspires enthusiasm and their intelligent feedback stimulates firebrand managers to keep the brand relevant, vital, and growing.

These people also serve as the eyes and ears of brand intelligence, providing not only early warning of problems but also first news of unexpected successes that, when exploited, can carry the brand to new heights.

PROCESSES

The secret of eSupply success lies in empowering stakeholders to create digital assets that other stakeholders will use in their self-service interactions with the firebrand. These digital assets include discussions, formatted and pre-populated databases and spreadsheets, annotated links to resources of proven worth, training and educational materials (originally developed for a platform partner's workgroup, for example), and many others that the firebrand firm will make available at appropriate levels in its deep gravity well supersite. Remember that stakeholders contribute these digital assets at little or no real cost to the firebrand firm, feeding the eSupply model which on first inspection may seem to stand traditional economic principles on their head.

When a firebrand's self-service satisfactions derive from digital assets (of the firm's own making or generated by stakeholders), firebrand managers can quickly establish a dynamic pricing and versioning structure to maximize profits and tailor solutions to specific stakeholder requirements. Such tailored solutions command price premiums and return high margins from highly satisfied customers who, far from feeling gouged, feel well-served and catered to. Here, smart media—which we discuss in detail in the next chapter—play a key role in building digital assets that managers can quickly reconfigure and deploy in aggressive brand storytelling, especially in the creation of publications and other vehicles produced at relatively low incremental cost.

INFRASTRUCTURE

In the next chapter, we describe in detail the n-tier computing infrastructure that makes eSupply possible and makes firebrands sustainable, brightly lit destinations in eMediaspace. A key component of this infrastructure is the brand resource repository, which organizes all of the digital assets related to the firebrand and makes them broadly available to all of the people and organizations involved in building the firebrand. This repository contains the moderated discussion forums, surveys, and all other materials used in sales, marketing, training, and support.

EFFECTS OF ESUPPLY

We've said that eSupply produces a zero-gravity, intelligent, pre-emptively positioned firebrand. What does that mean?

Zero gravity means that any stakeholder can engage in a transaction or interaction 24 hours a day, seven days a week, avoiding the "friction" of having to go to a store or office, finding somebody to take a phone call, or other interaction involving the care, knowledge, and attention of another live human being.

In this context, intelligent means that firebrand managers have linked the value creation and storytelling processes directly to market feedback. They use satisfaction lifecycle data to tune the delivery of eServices to stakeholders for maximum effect. Ongoing cycles of rapid feedback not only keep everybody on the same page about their respective needs and intentions, but also constitute an ongoing information sharing, the substance of a trusted relationship. Not only do managers learn about customers and other stakeholders, those stakeholders learn more about, and involve themselves more closely with, the firebrand and the company behind the firebrand.

Pre-emptive positioning means that as new customers come into the category, they see the firebrand first, as the industry leader—the result of concerted word-of-mouth referral of the firebrand's advocates. For those who know the inside scoop on the market category, the firebrand represents the go-to solution—the one most referred or preferred. For authoritative recommenders, mavens, and experts in the field—especially those who have set up a soapbox or kiosk in the firebrand firm's deep gravity well supersite—the firebrand consolidates its unassailable positioning. It pre-empts all competitive challengers.

eSupply thus characterizes the convergence of the quintessential elements of the Networked Economy: interactive business design;

opted-in, information-sharing stakeholders; real-time processes that produce self-service satisfactions; and closed-loop feedback. When harnessed to the crisply positioned self-service satisfaction of a key customer group, these eSupply elements supercharge your business. It only remains for top executives to convince investors and analysts that they not only understand the Networked Economy but have optimized the business for performance in it—like Austin Powers, they have that old mojo back. Analysts and institutional investors will respond positively, pushing valuations to appropriate heights.

Loyalty Lock-ins

Firebrands use a variety of lock-ins and rewards to maintain dot.com mojo by creating customer loyalty and keeping customers from switching to competitors, as we illustrate in Figure 4-18.

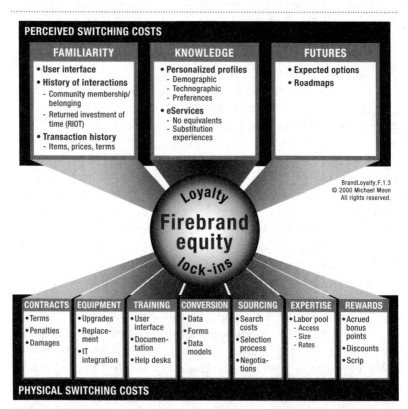

Figure 4-18 A *firebrand's loyalty lock-in* uses perceived and actual physical switching costs, as illustrated, emphasizing a new Golden Rule of the Networked Economy: you get what you give; the more you give, the more you get

However, brand managers must use lock-ins with extraordinary sensitivity and tact because they rely on negative incentives—physical switching costs: contracts, equipment, training, and others.

Lock-ins also work psychologically, through *perceived* switching costs such as familiarity with user interfaces, community membership, having to change preferences at a personalized Web site, or abandoning a roadmap of expected future developments.

Let's look at some loyalty lock-in examples to better understand how they work.

AUTOMOBILE

I'm currently driving my third BMW (and if you recommend this book to enough of your associates, I will soon acquire my fourth). I especially like the experience of driving a performance car with the elegant refinement of a luxury automobile. Living in Marin County just north of San Francisco brings many benefits, including a robust network of German auto maintenance specialists to tend the large numbers of BMWs, and a German car dealer, Sonnen, particularly notorious for its insensitivity.

As a result of these two factors, I can schedule a regular maintenance call with no more than a couple of days advance notice (a plus, given that I travel and lecture extensively) and pay highly competitive rates that make maintaining my BMW no more expensive than maintaining a lesser automobile. Granted, German-made parts remain more expensive than aftermarket parts for American makes, but they account for a small part of the overall bill. I am locked in to buying German-made BMW parts but I don't mind because the price premium remains insignificant compared to the labor costs. In fact, given the amount of pleasure and high level of reliability I enjoy, BMW has earned its price premiums; I do not begrudge them one bit.

COMPUTER SOFTWARE

I use Microsoft Office along with everybody else in the personal computer-using world. Microsoft has spent hundreds of millions of dollars improving performance and stability of its Office products, to the point where they now work pretty well. The fact that I can create a Powerpoint, Word, or Excel document and other people can read it provides tremendous value.

Microsoft's loyalty lock-in comes with a price tag I find only barely acceptable. Unlike makers of widely used graphic design and publishing software—Adobe and Quark, for example—Microsoft does not open its applications to third- and fourth-party developers to a meaningful degree. Microsoft's hypercompetitive vigilance has blinded the company to the value of such platform partners.

For example, our small company has standardized on Outlook Express e-mail. The way that it stores contact data and conducts other housekeeping activities make it needlessly cumbersome to use—a common occurrence, because software designers often find it difficult to elegantly serve divergent needs. I'd like to be able to throw away the contact management piece and plug in a real database, but Microsoft's Soviet technology approach prevents this. I'd also like to index my e-mails with keywords to facilitate easy search and retrieval—access denied, fourth-party developers thwarted. While Microsoft attempts to extend its products through Visual Basic, this ignores the other half of the house using Macs.

This failure of Outlook Express symbolizes Microsoft's inability—or unwillingness—to support uncommon levels of personalization. We might more easily tolerate this in the case of a software product with true alternatives, Quark versus InDesign, for example. Lacking true alternatives to Office, however, people feel unnaturally beholden to Microsoft. In fact, brand research shows that most people characterize their relationship with Microsoft as that of a slave to a master. Microsoft has thus sown seeds that have now grown into a global pool of toxic discontent and unbridled resentment—the result, in part, of abusing their loyalty lock-ins.

PERSONALIZED WEB SITES

In 1996, Apple Computer asked us to conduct a comprehensive audit of media producer activities with the goal of ascertaining what kinds of information and experiences graphic designers, videographers, desktop publishers, Webmasters, digital photographers, and other creative professionals need to increase their productivity, revenue, and profits. They also asked us to architect a Web portal for the design and publishing community—a deep gravity well supersite—that systematically addressed the needs of this community of practice. Apple wanted to use the portal to disseminate information that would let these professionals better understand the return on investment they get from the Macintosh platform and to collect benchmark data about Macintosh productivity.

While personal anecdotes and occasional benchmarking studies pointed to a Mac advantage, Apple wanted to collect the quantitative data necessary to make a formal business case. We designed and instrumented a deep gravity well supersite as a data collection system. Mere use of the Web site produced volumes of data which, using our strategic data model, could translate into meaningful benchmark studies.

We designed a comprehensive survey form to profile user demographics, interests, and information needs. The site would use the profile to actively serve personalized tables of contents for up to 12 domains of concern (media formats, for example) for each individual subscriber. The tables of contents would update themselves automatically as a subscriber viewed specific elements. If subscribers took the time to rate articles, they could earn eCreds good for downloads.

Personalizing a Web site illustrates a key loyalty lock-in principle: you get what you give. By taking the time to profile themselves, join discussion groups, or rate what they found on the site, subscribers earned a set of Web resources and experiences customized to their professional needs and worldview. Research shows that when a Web user personalizes a site, she will make it a default, go-to destination. This goes way beyond mere bookmarks. If the Web site plays an integral role in the person's work life, she may visit the site a dozen or more times a day—that's a loyalty lock-in.

Value Capture

The ability to price a product or service in terms of customer willingness to pay provides unparalleled opportunity to rapidly grow a market and earn extraordinary levels of profit without creating the perception of gouging customers. The fact that most of a firebrand's eServices and the satisfactions they produce derive from eSupply—pre-existing digital assets and self-service processes—makes possible value-based pricing, including its most potent form, dynamic pricing.

A firebrand manager and a self-service customer can collaboratively configure a highly personalized satisfaction—the result of successful use of an eService. In the course of tailoring such an eService, the customer will add additional resources or capabilities to a generic eService. Some of these add-ons should come free of charge, but others should come at a cost, ranging from small to large, as appropriate. In effect, the firebrand manager can "version" digital brand resources for a variety of asking prices.

Figure 4-19 depicts a number of seller tactics by which to version digital brand resources. As bakeries discovered long ago, a customer might pay a premium for freshness or earn a discount on day- or week-old material. Some customers will pay a premium to stand in the short line as frequent flyers. On the Web, use of power search and display functions or fast-track indexes (similar to the personalized tables of contents we designed for the Apple site described above) might serve as equivalents. Each uses the seller tactic categories to guide consideration of versioning strategies for your digital brand resources. Remember that the best guide for versioning and calibrating price sensitivity for a particular version will come from real customers paying real money in a self-service environment.

eSUPPLIED	LOCKED-IN	FIREBRANDS
• User-created value • Closed-loop feedback processes • Virtuous/vicious circles; winner takes all • Frictionless 24 x 7 replenishment	• Contracts • Equipment • Training • Conversion • Sourcing • Expertise • Rewards	• Relevant • Simple • Trusted • Low risk • Self identity

BUYER FACTORS

SELLER TACTICS — versioning techniques

Firebrand value capture

value-based pricing

TIME	INTERFACE	ACCESS	RICHNESS	FORMAT	VERSIONS	SUPPORT
• Delayed release • Pre-publication specials • First-use premiums	• Search tools • Power functions • Fast-track indices • Sonification	• Time zones • Open or restricted locations • Site licenses • Speed bumps, performance limitations	• Image resolutions • Complete-ness • Cross references • Indexing granularity	• Print • Multimedia • Live/streaming media • Localized	• Lite/deluxe • Industry specific • Professional/consumer • Protected/keylocked versions	• Live help • Training • Support groups • Guilds • 4th-party publications and courses

Figure 4-19 Firebrand managers use a variety of *versioning techniques* to maximize total sales revenues without compromising customer satisfaction or profitability. They can use eSupply, locked-in customers, and brands to capture maximum value

Figure 4-20 shows that some customers will pay extraordinarily high prices for the same product or service that you may have to pay other customers to take. Airlines have mastered the art of yield management, pricing each seat of each flight based on historical data of travel patterns, newly understood seasonal factors (impending storms, Super Bowl), customer loyalty profiles (status in a frequent flyer club), and featured promotions. Firebrand managers face a similar problem. If nobody buys the seat before the plane takes off, the airline loses money. In the Networked Economy, for the eService firebrand, the airplane takes off every ten seconds.

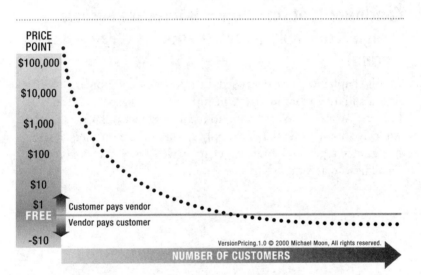

Figure 4-20 The versioning of eSupply means that a firebrand manager could charge one customer thousands of dollars and give the same product or service away to another customer for free, or even pay a customer to accept it

Firebrand managers must use yield management techniques to maximize their profits. Ultimately, they will price products and services based on how opted-in a stakeholder has become (how much personal data the stakeholder shares), the volume and quality of their contributions to the community of practice that surrounds the firebrand (discussion groups, etc.), their level of firebrand advocacy (the number of additional new customers they create by order), and the quality and depth of the buying and using experience-related data that they provide. The more they prime the eSupply pump with their contributed resources, the better the deals they get.

Conceivably, luxury good manufacturers such as Mercedes, Gucci, and Baccarat could give away very expensive products in the full confidence that they will get a return on investment—through the magic of eSupply—of 10 to 100 times the gift's cost. Some forward-thinking economists have used this idea to explain what they see as the economic principle of the Networked Economy—what they call the "gift economy" where prestige accrues to the individual or organization that gives gifts to people who in turn bring back transactions and meaningful eSupply interactions.

Conclusion: Dot.com Mojo = Interactive Business Design × (eSupply + Loyalty Lock-ins + Value-Based Pricing)

In this chapter, we have discussed the important components of a firebrand and the firebrand's relationship with eMediaspace and stakeholders. We also called attention to the importance of harnessing the explosive brand potential of eSupply. An interactive business design brings it all together. In the next chapter, we show you in concrete detail how to accomplish this.

Chapter 5

The Seven Best Practices of Firebranding

We have examined the elements of a firebrand and the functions they serve as the enterprise seeks to serve customers and other stakeholders in eMediaspace. Now we set forth a road map for building a white-hot firebrand. While we start in small steps, the pace quickens through these seven best practices, leading you to the exciting—or dreadful—conclusion that the successful firm in the Networked Economy must wholly re-invent its core business processes, build or re-engineer basic IT infrastructures, and employ a burgeoning array of practices and capabilities all oriented toward one goal: a totally satisfied, interactive, self-service customer.

Figure 5-1 depicts the seven best firebranding practices we discuss in this chapter: 1) building a corporate firebranding system, 2) implementing net-integrated communications, 3) implementing integrated projects management, 4) mastering Web-integrated database marketing and sales, 5) globalizing your firebrand, 6) building an entrepreneurial eServices platform, and 7) implementing real-time value creation.

SEVEN BEST PRACTICES OF FIREBRANDING

Real-time value creation
Real-time data feedback on brand productivity

Entrepreneurial eServices platform
Self-directed 24 x 7 satisfactions

Globalized firebrand
Atomized, self-directed education and information delivery

Web-integrated DB marketing and sales
Analysis-driven stakeholder programs

Integrated projects management
Wide-area workflows, status reporting, and time-activity tracking

Net-integrated communications
Unified, congruent messaging and feedback across all media

CORPORATE FIREBRANDING SYSTEM

Milestones.Firebrand.B.1.3
© 2000 Michael Moon,
All rights reserved.

Product	Environmental	Print	Electronic	Interactive
•Ingredients •Packaging •Tangible good	•Outdoor •Signage •Uniforms	•Advertising •Annual report/ 10K/10Q •Business forums •Collateral	•Ads •Demos •Presentations	•Copy/ editorial •Design/layout •Interfaces •Streaming/ dynamic media

BRAND RESOURCE REPOSITORY

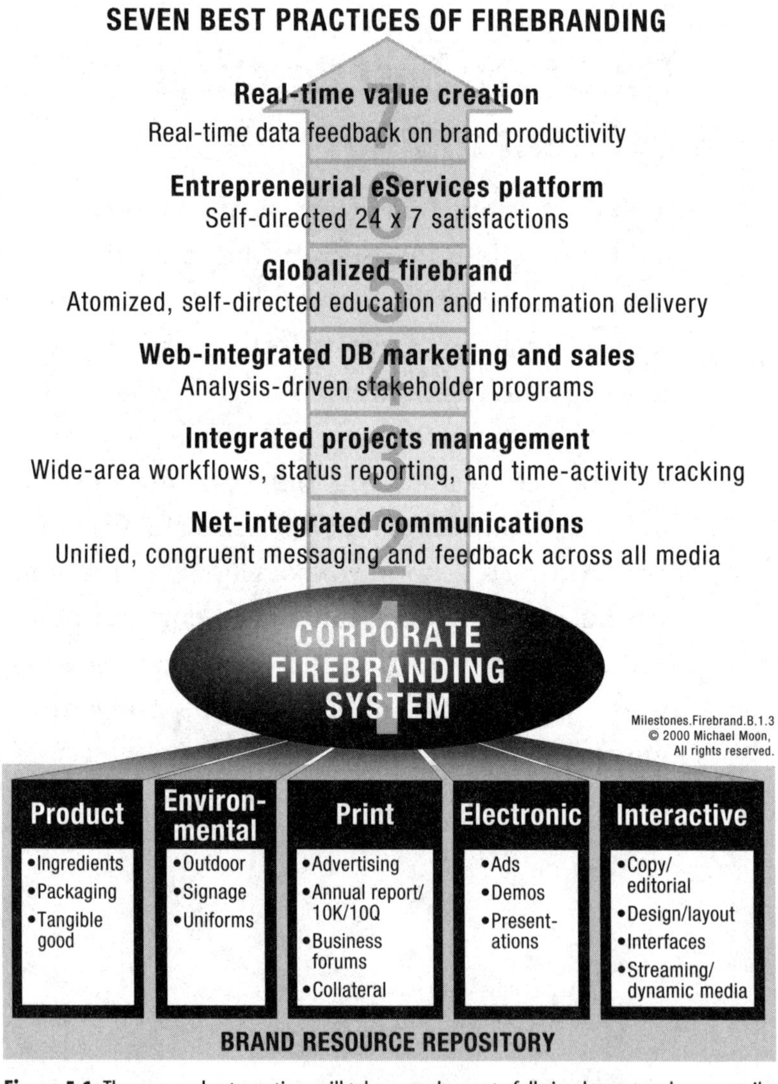

Figure 5-1 These seven best practices will take several years to fully implement and may entail re-engineering significant portions of marketing, sales, service, training, and development

Best Practice #1: Build a Corporate Firebranding System

A successful firebranding strategy starts with things your company already possesses: customers and a corporate branding system. Whether you've built your brand around a product or a service, you have already created marketing materials, brand identity elements, advertisements, Web sites, sales training programs, and other mechanisms. Each of these elements should take your brand identity and market positioning to customers, business partners, investors, and other stakeholders. This means that key customers can quickly associate one word and one idea with the principal satisfaction they derive from the buying and using experience of your product or service. In other words, these mechanisms all attempt to communicate another fundamental element that your company probably has: a crisp, focused positioning, as illustrated in Figure 5-2.

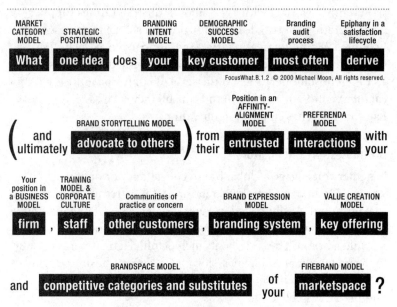

Figure 5-2 Classic positioning strategy focuses one idea with one word with one customer. As applied to firebrands, a company must link these three elements to one defining eService interaction. For definitions and references for the terms used here, see the glossary and index

Unfortunately, we find this is rarely the case. Instead, our brand audits reveal a hodgepodge of muddy and unfocused ideas, quasi-positions, and trial balloons to determine what might strike a customer's fancy. Why can't businesses see this systematic undermining of their branding process? Typically, we find that the CEO or chief branding officer simply has no way to see where and how the company uses—or abuses—brand resources.

Marketing executives spend hundreds of hours a year developing a positioning strategy and materials only to find, for example, that Sales uses only some of the things they produce, often creating new material of its own that fails to maintain brand identity integrity. Field and customer-service representatives further dilute and undermine Marketing with their own efforts. In the worst case, every line function and department may employ its own positioning strategy and brand identity elements, creating a worldwide muddle of logos, slogans, packaging, sales presentations, Web sites—you get the not-very-pretty picture.

Recently, I worked with a $3 billion industrial fittings supplier with operations in two dozen countries and a dozen business units. I counted 38 unique treatments of the company logo, including six different color schemes, italicized and non-italicized fonts, and 15 different stationery sets. At this level of confusion, only the radical intervention of a global brand consultancy such as Siegelgale or Landor Associates could straighten things out.

Brand Resource Repository

Whether you engage a global brand consultancy or do it yourself, you need to have a centralized repository for all resources related to your brand. As illustrated in Figure 5-3, this *brand resource repository* gathers together everything your company's various groups use to build a brand. These elements include official treatments of your logo and wordmarks, taglines, slogans, stationery, business forms, Web pages, and templates for all printed, electronic, and online sales and marketing collateral.

A brand resource repository represents a significant undertaking. Not only does it constitute a large, complex database, it requires a highly trained team of specialists who will populate and manage the repository. We'll discuss this in more detail later in the book. You may want to consider outsourcing this function.

Figure 5-3 Emerging best practice dictates that companies centralize all their brand resources in a central database

A brand resource repository lets individuals find and retrieve the materials they need. It also serves other important firebranding functions. It propagates throughout the enterprise and among trade partners a consistent brand identity. It specifies precisely how and where to use which brand resource across all media and branding channels. These specifications may include industrial design and product-related packaging, environmental or outdoor expressions of the brand (billboards, uniforms, signage, point of sale displays or kiosks), electronic and broadcast elements (TV, radio, video and audio cassettes, music CDs), printed materials, and interactive resources such as Web sites, multimedia CD- and DVD-ROMs, software interfaces, and a host of new digital formats.

A brand resource repository returns its investment in three significant ways. First, the repository reduces costs by eliminating duplicated efforts. Secondly, it builds value as it enables the enterprise to extend a consistent brand identity to partners, investors, and customers everywhere, in a timely manner. Finally, the repository creates new, incremental profits as managers use it to structure and systematize a firebranding process, providing practices and procedures that let them quickly update existing products or services and launch wholly new ones. A firebranding team can now accomplish in hours what used to take weeks or months, and can successfully react to the discontinuities and short-lived opportunities that characterize the Networked Economy.

Business Case for Brand Resource Repository

My firm tracks several thousand enterprises, large and small, and their deployment of some two dozen technologies related to branding. About a year ago, we studied Autodesk's deployment of a brand resource depository. Autodesk makes AutoCAD, the number one software tool for drafting and design. The company sells AutoCAD through a network of distributors and trade partners around the world, its international sales adding $200 million alone to annual revenues. Consequently, each distributor and trade partner relies on Autodesk for promotional and marketing materials.

But Autodesk and its partners face an unusual problem. The company updates AutoCAD every 12 to 14 months. This creates a seven-month selling window. Before deploying its brand resource repository, Autodesk spent two to three weeks propagating collateral for its next upgrade to sales and marketing partners around the world. When we analyzed the opportunity cost, we discovered that this delay, due to propagation, shortened the effective sales window by two to three weeks, costing Autodesk $1.3 million in potential profits.

After deployment of a $250,000 brand resource repository, Autodesk eliminated the delay and produced four-times the return on their investment in the first year.

The leading vendors of brand resource repositories include CDXC, MediaBridge, and WebWare. Go to www.Firebrands.com for contact information on these and other solution providers.

In addition to the Firebrand Positioning Model mentioned above, let's review the critical elements of a corporate firebranding system that builds on things most companies already possess, and show how they must change to support creation of a firebrand.

Firebrand Planning Process

Traditional brand planning has evolved as a set of ad hoc processes oriented around campaigns and product launches or in response to compelling events—a new product launch by a competitor, for example. Large, global packaged goods companies have evolved formal processes that run in conjunction with a broader business-planning cycle not focused on brand planning. Because customer behavior can change so radically, and because competitive threats can emerge so quickly, the Networked Economy requires brand managers to formalize planning in a process that builds a firebrand one quarter at a time. In fact, we know of several pure-Internet-play dot.coms that reassess their business model and branding strategy on a weekly basis, asking one essential question: *What new value can we add that will further endear if not lock-in customers to our brand?*

Figure 5-4 illustrates lessons learned by companies that have successfully built vibrant, global brands. Professional business managers will see many parallels to the discipline of a quarterly business operations review. The firebrand planning process focuses on brand productivity and progress relative to branding goals.

This firebrand planning process requires a strong and well-positioned *branding authority* to drive a quarterly review, incorporating a *brand audit process*. The brand audit uses both quantitative and qualitative research methods to investigate customers of both *its* brand and its competitors' brands. It also includes an assessment of existing or expected competitors. Brand managers seek to understand their competitors' business designs, brand theory, brand architecture, and branding process, by applying the same models—which we present in this book—that they use to understand and develop their own brands.

An effective firebrand planning process requires a planning cycle shared by managers throughout the enterprise and across divisions, coordinated through a group calendar that takes into account the various seasonal and business cycles that affect enterprise operations. The firebrand planning process also requires task-driven training. This includes software tools and process templates that enable brand managers to quickly analyze data and communicate results.

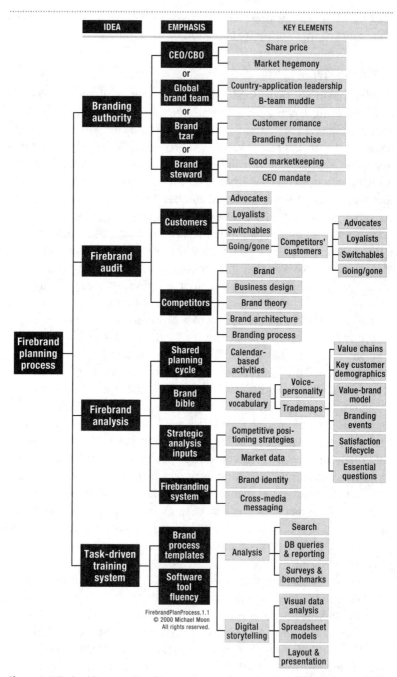

Figure 5-4 Firebranding prescribes that management elevate brand-planning to the same level as a quarterly review of business operations

Brand Identity

Brand identity represents the fruit of a considerable investment in a corporate- and product-identity development program. With rare exceptions, this requires the engagement of a strategic brand consultancy; a company that systematically analyzes business communication needs and develops a comprehensive set of tools, templates, and systems to express the voice of a brand. This consultancy transforms a static brand into a vibrant, emotional reflection of the principal satisfaction enjoyed by a company's key customer segment. Successful firebranding demands that brand managers address brand identity creation in the new dimensions of digital and online media and in the new, interactive customer relationships that emerge in the Networked Economy.

For example, as Federal Express expanded into international markets and began to compete with DHL and other international couriers, the company found a need to re-think its brand to stand out in a cluttered and highly competitive market. Customer surveys and focus groups conducted around the world revealed that the "federal" in Federal Express carried negative associations, especially in Latin American countries. In fact, most customers did not say "Federal Express." They had begun to say "FedEx"—as noun and verb— and identified highly reliable, on-time delivery as the principal satisfaction of the service. This research also showed that the orange and purple color scheme had become memorable across most cultural contexts. Purple and orange each resonate deeply with aristocratic and religious associations in many societies. The research also showed that customers found the business form confusing, with too many options and unclear terms.

The brand identity consultancy took these inputs and others and reformulated a brand identity system that included uniforms, trucks, business forms and stationery, outdoor kiosks, signage, sales presentation and bid proposal templates, and packaging materials.

Rising to the new challenges of the Networked Economy, Federal Express also developed a CD-ROM that contained all of the new brand identity elements, business forms, and templates necessary to re-create all of the company's brand expressions, plus the necessary design, layout, and presentation tools (obtained through a company-wide site licensing agreement with the software vendors). Code-named PRPL (Personal Reference and Presentation Library), the CD-ROM, and now a companion extranet, make the brand identity system available to all

Federal Express employees, advertising agencies, and other trade partners around the world. In other words, the company successfully transformed its static brand identity and moved many steps down the road toward building a firebrand.

Smart Media Factory

Traditional brand building relied on traditional media elements and practices: one-off brand identity elements and associated resources (photographs, illustrations, film clips, sound bites, etc.) created by hand at great expense by craft artisans and stored haphazardly in analogue media (film, paper, magnetic tape). If the element incorporated licensed intellectual property (celebrity endorsements, cartoon characters, etc.), the terms and conditions of such use rarely remained attached to the asset. Instead, this licensing information stayed under lock and key in a file cabinet with the contract.

As illustrated in Figure 5-5, these new capabilities facilitate the systematic application of technology and best practices to the creation and use of digital brand resources. In practice, brand managers implement a smart media factory as an extranet that connects dozens of brand resource creators (in-house or outside contractors and vendors) to the brand resource repository and the brand management team.

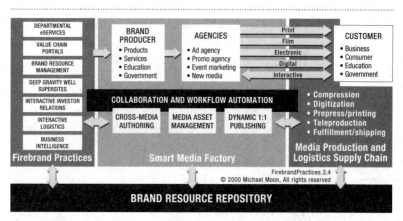

Figure 5-5 The smart media factory employs dozens of automation techniques and practices which relentlessly pursue the systematic elimination of labor from the design, production, and distribution of brand resources

The smart media factory automates almost every aspect of the brand resource design, creation, and production process. This entails standardization on a set of design and authoring tools that produce agile, multipurposed media assets—digital media files that contain the creative works and designs used to build the brand. Because they exist in digital form, the brand creators and managers can store them online, route them anyplace in the world across the network, modify them at will, and update them as necessary, without damaging the original version. Their agility reflects great care in designing these elements to plug-and-play in four-color and black and white print, three-color RGB broadcast and online formats, and other media including textile, silkscreen, and injected plastic molding. The smart media factory feeds the brand resource repository, allowing swift creation of Web pages, brochures, signage, large format posters, packaging, data sheets, TV advertisements, as well as streaming audio and video clips suitable for training, employee communications, and investor relations. (For more information about the technologies, tools, best practices, and recommended vendors for the smart media factory, go to www.firebrands.com.)

This gives a brand manager the power to ensure that everyone uses a consistent set of brand resources in all their communications with customers and other stakeholders. More important, the smart media factory reduces time to market and slashes the costs of creating brand resources. A smart media factory also makes the creative and production process more predictable and scalable. Brand managers can quickly expand or easily shrink their operations to take advantage of the myriad short-lived market opportunities and partnering activities that characterize the Networked Economy.

Cross-Media Messaging Framework

Many firms still communicate with the market using different teams and agencies with expertise in particular marketing practices, media, and distribution channels. For example, a medium-sized firm will use several different agencies for print and broadcast advertising, interactive advertising, public relations, investor relations, publicity and promotions, packaging, and trade shows. Different groups within the firm often create their own business forms, product or service documentation, and training materials.

In the Networked Economy, building a firebrand demands creation of a cross-media messaging framework. This framework uses agile, multipurposed assets (stored in the brand resource repository) to communicate crisp, consistent branding messages across all media and into all areas where customers (and other stakeholders) touch the firm, its products or services, and its agents.

For example, a fashion apparel manufacturer would use a cross-media messaging framework to ensure that its Web sites, in-store kiosks, point-of-purchase displays, packaging, annual reports, trade and consumer advertisements, special promotions and catalogs, and business forms and corporate HQ interior design build and reinforce the brand identity and positioning (one word and one idea linked to one key customer segment).

Effective deployment of a cross-media messaging framework will force many firms to re-engineer key business processes and their subordinate workflows associated with marketing, promotions, sales, public relations, field service, and training, often with the help of special consultants. Warning: A simple e-mail solution does not suffice. The cross-media messaging framework uses a sophisticated, *database-centric workflow and collaboration infrastructure* that integrates with the brand resource repository. The brand resource repository usually provides this additional capability. If not, a professional services and systems integrator can provide a compatible third-party solution. These systems must fully support the Apple Macintosh platform because the branding community has standardized on this best-of-breed solution for media design and production.

Best Practice #2: Implement Net-Integrated Communications

Your firebranding strategy must work closely with the most popular aspect of the Internet: e-mail and related messaging systems. This best practice emphasizes using the Internet to integrate all of a company's efforts to both communicate with customers and collect usable data from those interactions—an area that promises almost immediate payback as customers find the process of communicating with your company a more pleasant and productive experience.

How Does Your Company Handle eBusiness Customer Inquiries?

Let's start with the essential question: How does your company handle eBusiness customer inquiries?

According to *Information Week* in its "Research of eBusiness Agenda," a survey of 375 business and IT managers conducted in December 1999, the studied firms responded to customers with expensive, labor-intensive methods: personal e-mails written by an employee or subcontractor; directing a customer to an even more expensive encounter with a teleservice representative at a call center, as illustrated in Figure 5-6.

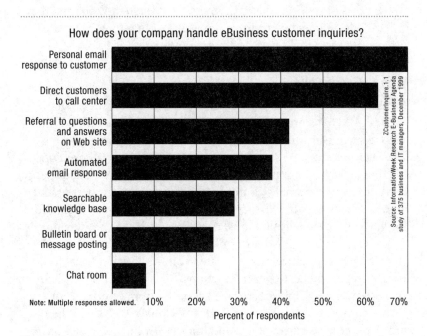

How does your company handle eBusiness customer inquiries?

Note: Multiple responses allowed.

Percent of respondents

Source: InformationWeek Research E-Business Agenda study of 375 business and IT managers, December 1999. ZCustomerInquire.1.1

Figure 5-6 Research of 375 business and IT managers by the industry magazine, *Information Week*, reveals a number of strategies for responding to customer e-mail inquiries

Our research shows that the fully burdened cost of a personal e-mail can range from $3 to more than $500, depending on the knowledge required to understand the nature of the request and the time necessary to formulate a response (which may include extensive research). The fully burdened cost of a call center interaction starts at $2 and quickly scales to $20 or more, depending on the length of the call and the costs associated with physical fulfillment of product litera-ture, annual reports, or other marketing collateral.

The *Information Week* study does not address an even more fun-damental problem: most companies have not established a cohesive strategy for responding to customer e-mails in the first place. They often make it extraordinarily difficult for customers to send e-mail to specific departments or individuals who can answer their ques-tions, offering instead only a generic info@yourfirm.com or web-master@yourfirm.com capability. In fact, over 60% of e-mails sent to Fortune 500 companies never get answered. Our research shows that if customers see a directory of e-mail contacts organized according to the types of requests that customers most frequently submit, they will initiate contact two or three times more often than if the site offers only a generic e-mail address for requests.

Who Ya Gonna Call?

E-mail volumes have surprised and overwhelmed most corporate Web sites. What starts off as a courtesy service by a member of the Web team mushrooms into an expensive, labor-intensive process. The *Information Week* study shows that a relatively small percentage of companies has begun adopting automated generic e-mail response methods. An even smaller number understand that the best practice approach emphasizes self-service solutions that eliminate the need for 90% of the e-mails that most corporate Web sites now create.

Let's illustrate with two examples of toxic branding events and show how best practice net-integrated communications can elimi-nate such painful customer interactions. Recently, one of this book's co-authors, Doug Millison, ordered supplies from Office Depot's Web site and some books from Barnes & Noble's Web site. When problems cropped up, Doug found himself tripping over gaps in their communications systems.

Office Depot: No News is Bad News

Doug usually orders supplies from Office Depot over the phone, because he finds it so frustrating to try to place an order online—something that he had attempted to do a couple of times and in both cases abandoned due to a bad user interface and order form.

This time, he decided to use a coupon he received in the mail offering a 20% discount if he placed a $100 minimum order at the

Web site. He went to OfficeDepot.com but could not find the printer toner cartridge he needed. He picked up the telephone and called to get the product number and used that to place the order online. The system was able to use his telephone-customer account number (which he found on an old invoice and keyed into the Web form) to pre-populate his new Web account application form—a major systems integration accomplishment that few Web sites have mastered. Having a pre-populated form not only reduced his frustration but increased his confidence that they would handle his order efficiently. So far, so good.

After completing the account setup procedure, Doug submitted his order. Office Depot confirmed the order with an automated e-mail reply containing all of the order information and promised delivery date. When Office Depot failed to deliver the supplies as promised, he wrote an e-mail and got no response. The next day, he followed up with a phone call to their call center. The teleservice representative did have a record of the order, indicating at least a basic integration of the Web site and call center—a major accomplishment that many companies have yet to achieve. The teleservice rep promised to get back to Doug with delivery information. When they failed to call him back as promised, he called again. The delivery dispatcher called back to let him know when to expect the ordered supplies. He received the delivery later that day.

As a regular customer of Office Depot, Doug is still willing to do business with them and use their online ordering system, but only if they send him another discount coupon that makes it worth his while to suffer the frustrations of their bad brand-user interface. He understands that he will need a paper catalog to overcome the deficiencies of the online database and expects to use their expensive (for Office Depot) call center service. Office Depot has trained him to interact with them as a now-unprofitable customer, one who insists upon discounts and expensive personal interactions (one e-mail and three phone calls) to satisfy his expectations.

More important, Office Depot has made a significant withdrawal from this customer's emotional bank account, making him more susceptible to the siren song of a competitor who offers a more enjoyable and profitable relationship.

How could Office Depot apply best-practice net-integrated communications to address this situation?

First, they violated a cardinal law of direct mail. They did not test the discount coupon campaign to make sure that it would take a customer through a seamless Web shopping and order fulfillment experience. They failed to preflight-test the customer experience from end to end.

True preflighting would have produced a visual workflow model detailing a variety of customer interactions and how to deal with them. What if a customer can't find a particular product on the Web site? What if the customer has previously established a phone or in-store account? It would have made sense to personalize Doug's discount coupon with his telephone-customer account number. The e-mail confirming his order should have contained a hyperlink to take him to a help desk specifically staffed for problems related to this promotion.

Office Depot could have further optimized his shopping experience by using the discount coupon to drive him to a Web-site order form built specifically for this promotion, pre-populated with the products that he usually buys when he phones in an order. He would then simply check off those items that he'd like to buy. This list would have prompted him to buy more than the minimum of a toner cartridge and a case of paper.

Better yet, Office Depot could have offered him an additional discount in exchange for pre-programming a list of preferred product categories and specific products that he intends to buy in the future—his customer preferenda—and for inviting Office Depot to notify him about special discount promotions. The data from this form becomes a persistent reminder of what he might want to buy every time he revisits Office Depot's Web site—one click puts it in his shopping cart.

Finally, Office Depot could have proactively sent him an e-mail the next day asking if he received his order and, if not, instructing him to click an active hyperlink (embedded in the e-mail) taking him to a Web page that would show the current status of the order and any problem associated with it, such as "back-ordered item," "earthquake," or "Berkeley Spring protest." Much of Doug's frustration came from not hearing from Office Depot about his order status. Their silence forced him to manage their broken system instead of spending his time more profitably on his work (although the experience did provide a great example for this chapter!).

Barnes & Noble: You've Got Problems!

Let's move to our next case study for net-integrated communications: buying books at Barnes & Noble's bn.com Web site.

Doug used to buy books online from Amazon.com. He still uses Amazon.com for research, because of its more robust database of book titles, more descriptive information about books including reviews from other sites and publications, customer ratings and reviews, and the recommendation engine. But he purchases his books online from Barnes & Noble. Why?

Doug publishes a Web site for online journalists at http://www. Online-Journalist.com. Looking for ways to supplement his income, he decided to let people buy books online through his Web site. He joined Barnes & Noble's affiliate program. This means that he can publish book reviews and place an "order now" link that sends readers to bn.com where they can purchase the book, and along the way he collects a small commission on the sale. Doug chose Barnes & Noble's affiliate program for one primary reason: when he orders books from Barnes & Noble through his Web site by hitting the button that takes him to bn.com, he receives an additional discount in the form of the affiliate commission. Strictly speaking, this "double-dipping" discount creates a very clever loyalty program for individuals with Web sites. Amazon.com's affiliate program prohibited him from buying books from his own Web site (thus earning the additional discount), but Barnes & Noble wisely encouraged this practice.

Let's examine how this affiliate relationship demonstrates a few firebrand principles. Doug has "opted-in" to a book-buying service, entrusting billing and shipping information to Barnes & Noble. He has accepted a loyalty lock-in in exchange for discounts. As an affiliate, he has accepted an additional lock-in, making it all but impossible for another online bookseller, including Amazon.com, to unhook him from Barnes & Noble. As an affiliate, he has become a platform partner and will, over the lifetime of this relationship, direct customers to the bn.com Web site, sharing in the value that his relationship with Barnes & Noble creates. They have created a powerful business incentive for Doug to create additional editorial reviews—more reasons for potential book buyers to do business with Barnes & Noble.

Unfortunately, Barnes & Noble has a long way to go before it masters net-integrated communications to the point where it can avoid potentially toxic branding events, even among loyalists such as Doug.

Recently, Doug ordered a biography of Mao Tse-tung from bn.com. As expected, he received e-mail confirmation containing an order number and a hyperlink back to an order status page. A few days passed, but he did not receive the expected e-mail letting him know that his book—guaranteed to ship within 24 hours of his order—had been sent. He clicked the hyperlink in the order confirmation e-mail: the status page told him only that the order was "in process." He responded to the previous e-mail order confirmation by hitting the reply key and asking what had happened to the order. After receiving no response for a day, he telephoned the toll-free service line. The teleservice rep told him that, in fact, the book had not been in the warehouse when the order went through and they had been unable to ship within 24 hours as promised. They told Doug they had the book in stock, would ship it immediately by Next-Day Air (his original order specified standard ground delivery), and that they would waive all shipping charges. The next day he received an e-mail reiterating what the teleservice rep said.

How could Barnes & Noble have avoided this by applying the best practice of net-integrated communications?

Customer expectations derive from a seemingly simple interaction with a Web page showing the book's availability. Perhaps, at that moment in time, bn.com actually had the book in stock but somebody else purchased it seconds before he hit the "buy" button. Barnes & Noble could learn from QVC, the television shopping channel, and display two important pieces of data that would have instantly modified his expectations: number of items remaining in inventory and the number of items sold within the last 24 hours. A simple flag indicating that due to heavy purchase volumes, "You may experience a delay in this order due to its popularity," would have framed his expectations and injected a sense of the live-auction "buy now" imperative so familiar in television shopping.

The order confirmation e-mail should contain three embedded hyperlinks. One would go to the order status page. In this case, the page would have communicated the in-process status.

The second hyperlink would link to a help page of an online form pre-populated with billing and shipping information where Doug could point-and-click to quickly characterize the problem without needing to call and talk to somebody, and automatically route it to the right department. This help page achieves three very important objectives. It reassures the customer of the interactive relationship with the seller, in this case Barnes & Noble. It telegraphs that the seller has anticipated these kinds of problems and has automated their resolution. Third, uniform problem characterization creates statistical data that the seller can use to maintain a closed-loop process quality control of a problematic area. And they should not constrain themselves to just e-mail and Web pages. The order form should also let the customer specify alternate e-mail addresses and reformatting for pager, digital cell phone, and Palm Pilot.

The third hyperlink takes the customer to a help center offering live chat with a teleservice representative—far cheaper to operate than live telephone calls because the rep can handle dozens of simultaneous online chat queries in the same time she can handle one telephone call. More important, in-bound e-mail routing (automated through the order status page described above) combined with live chat enables an organization to outsource customer service during periods of especially high traffic (Christmas, etc.).

Barnes & Noble (or any online retailer) could use the order status page to tell a better story about the customer's order. The simple phrase, "in process," not only might mean many things, but, if left as is, will soon become a more powerful and potentially toxic message: "You've got problems."

Here, Barnes & Noble could learn a lesson from their shipping partners, FedEx and UPS, and provide Web-page notification of the time-stamped status of critical steps in the internal order-fulfillment process: order received at 1:14 PM 9 March 2000; credit card transaction authorized at 1:15 PM 9 March 2000; order posted to Memphis logistics center at 1:16 PM 9 March 2000; list of items packed at 6:15 PM 9 March 2000; scheduled for 7 PM pick-up by shipper, tracking #123456789. At this point, an embedded hyperlink takes the customer to the carrier's shipment tracking Web page, using a cookie or Java applet to show the status of the order as it moves through the shipper's tracking system.

Barnes & Noble should leverage its principal strength against Amazon.com: its network of bricks-and-mortar stores. The order status page should provide the option of picking up the book at a local store that has it in stock, eliminating the shipping charge, or having it delivered the same day by courier. The system would e-mail a "hold for Doug Millison" or, "deliver to Doug Millison at (address)" to the local retail branch. For in-store pick-up, the order status page should offer a bar-coded voucher sent to the customer by fax or Acrobat PDF that the customer prints and redeems at the store when picking up the order. The coupon should also offer a discount on any additional in-store purchases the customer chooses to make. If the customer opts for delivery from the local store, Barnes & Noble could offer same day delivery for an additional fee, or offer free same-day delivery if the customer pays full retail prices. This latter task requires integration of dynamic pricing.

As a next-to-last resort, Barnes & Noble should have offered a variety of live telephone interactions to solve Doug's problem and ease frustrations. The lowest cost and most immediate form comes from voice over IP—essentially a telephone conversation through the Internet. This requires specialized voice IP software and high-speed Internet links, a small but rapidly growing installed base. Failing this, Barnes & Noble should let the customer send an immediate "request for telephone help" message to the next available teleservice representative who will typically call back within minutes. An automated e-mail routing system would alert a teleservice representative and provide customer and order information.

Barnes & Noble would realize two benefits from these otherwise expensive live telephone interactions. Outbound calls cost less to make. Placing the call gives Barnes & Noble the ability to pleasantly surprise the customer—whose frustrations might continue to rise if forced to make the call—and completely change the social dynamics of the interaction. The party who initiates the call generally leads the conversation. In this case, the teleservice representative (armed with the latest available information about Doug's order and past history, including purchases and complaints) can tailor his or her performance to Doug's needs, using pre-scripted questions that branch from a variety of possible customer responses. This lets the teleservice representative speak with authority and reassurance, preventing an unpleasant experience from escalating into full-blown 'net-rage.

How to Get It Right from the Start

We use Office Depot and Barnes & Noble as examples not only because these problems underscore the dangers of not getting it right, but also because they have done a number of basic and advanced things right. They have invested millions of dollars in ambitious eCommerce initiatives. Customers derive new satisfactions from these two firms as a result. For this, we congratulate their efforts. Let's learn from their bleeding-edge experiences, plus our extensive research of companies and their online marketing and logistics fulfillment practices, and draw a roadmap you can follow to net-integrated communications while avoiding pitfalls.

No firm can do everything at once. We outline a three-phase process as illustrated in Figures 5-7, 5-8, and 5-9.

Do It Now

As illustrated in Figure 5-7, in the "do it now" phase, focus first on implementing basic dot.com eServices. These include a deep gravity well supersite with associated workflow and publishing practices, as discussed earlier in this book. This gravity well employs user interfaces optimized for different stakeholder groups, including newbie prospects, first-time customers, repeat customers, heavy-use customers, platform partners, and sales clerks at the firm's bricks-and-mortar locations.

Figure 5-7 Net-integrated communications begins with basic dot.com eServices that include an accessible Web site, an e-mail directory, automated e-mail confirmation, and the ability to offer downloads

On top of these basic dot.com services, integrate automated e-mail confirmations for various types of interactions and transactions with customers and other stakeholders. We emphasize embedding solutions-driven hyperlinks that quickly route a user to a specific area of the Web site or help center. This not only provides convenience, it generates data that closes the loop on a statistical quality control process.

Do It Next

The "do it next" phase should reflect the nature of your business and the type of interactions you have with customers. Deployment of these do-it-next messaging applications may vary greatly depending on a business-to-business or business-to-consumer relationship and the nature of the transaction (product or service deliverable, impulse item versus long deliberation, and the level of expertise required to make an informed purchase decision). In all cases, companies must integrate live-help call-centers with their Web sites, as illustrated in Figure 5-8.

Integrate a "contact us" help page with e-mail addresses, telephone numbers, and physical addresses, as well as logical points of contact organized by type of problem. Essentially a list of frequently asked questions (FAQ) plus a phone directory, the page shows customers (and other stakeholders) how best to use the company's online and offline resources to solve their problems. The page may direct the customer to read a more specialized FAQ, check out an online manual, more clearly characterize the problem, or contact a specific group or individual who can directly resolve an issue or problem.

Because many of your customers and other stakeholders do not yet use e-mail as their sole or primary means of communication, this call center should enable a teleservice representative to send and receive faxes to individuals. These faxes add to the firebranding effort, especially for customers who travel from one hotel to another or who visit locations without ready e-mail or Web access. We strongly recommend that a firm distill each in- and outbound fax as an Acrobat PDF file and place this knowledge asset in a centralized repository where a teleservice representative can access it along with the equally inaccessible inbound and outbound e-mail communications.

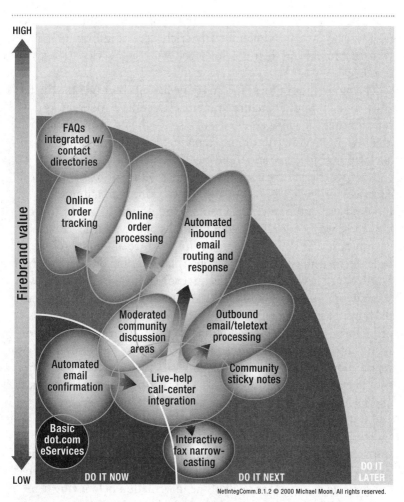

Figure 5-8 Net-integrated communications moves to the next level when it integrates calls to an integrated e-mail management system. The call center provides the platform for increasing levels of automation for order processing, tracking, and fulfillment

Often, the best source of 20-20 hindsight for problem-solving comes from communities of practice and moderated discussions associated with your product or service, or with the market categories in which you operate. We recommend that every company have a moderated community discussion area on its Web site. We also recommend that you consider outsourcing this function as a quick-start technique, letting expert community forum managers quickly spin up effective discussion groups and teach you how they work. At some point you will probably want to bring this task back in-house because it represents such a rich store of information about your customers and their possible need for new eServices (as we discuss later).

The moderator of these forums quite literally becomes the digital voice of the brand. Therefore, you must select these moderators not only for their category expertise but also for their diplomacy, tact, and netiquette. As a community captain, the moderator holds unparalleled power to shape and mold customer perception.

Next, we expand the live help call center with four mission-critical eServices: online order processing and tracking, and automated inbound and outbound e-mail routing and response. We illustrated how these work—or not—in our Office Depot and Barnes & Noble examples above. We underscore the importance of a more robust order form, using purchase preferenda and standing orders to prompt reorders and new purchases. This can evolve into a protected area of a Web site where special terms and conditions extended to the individual buyer or her firm remain hidden from general public view. This order form should provide additional opt-in resources, such as automatic notification of substitutes and discounts, frequent buyer club registration, and the ability to use multiple credit cards. The system should also notify the customer as a credit card expiration draws near and invite the customer to update her profile, which may also prompt additional sales.

The customer profile record should not only contain the basic information (name, address, billing) but also include alternate shipping addresses, as well as a journal of previous interactions and, in appropriate circumstances, all of the information held by the firm about the customer. This should include data collected from various online surveys and links to distilled e-mails and faxes that document the relationship.

Firebranding your Web site shares many parallels with a successful political campaign. Grassroots political action and local politics animate national elections and the candidates who win them. Perhaps just as important, but not anywhere near as well understood, the art and science of rebuttal determines winners and losers in political contests and in cyberspace communities. Both Ronald Reagan and Bill Clinton earned the reputation as "Teflon Presidents" because they both understood the critical importance of answering political charges, reframing an accusation and thereby neutralizing it. In

Western societies, silence or non-response to accusation stands as a tacit acceptance or affirmation of an allegation. For this reason, brand managers must monitor the various sources of conversation and gossip regarding their brands. This includes ongoing participation in Internet Usenet groups and various online forums within AOL, Yahoo!, and MSN as well as the brand managers' own discussion groups.

A new, potent form of digital gossip has emerged, catching many brand managers completely unaware. "Community sticky notes" enable any Web site visitor to append a sticky note comment to any part of your Web site, using a browser plug-in that also lets them read sticky notes appended by other visitors. This allows anyone to affix "graffiti" to your brand messages, including competitors and their customers, as well as your toxic ex-customers. These community sticky notes have become quite popular with screenagers—present and future customers. While a firm has no simple way to eliminate such graffiti, it should use the community sticky note capability to rebut allegations and redirect interested parties to appropriate resources in the searchable know-how database.

Do It Later

The third phase requires substantial reengineering and deployment of significant infrastructure, as illustrated in Figure 5-9.

As an extension of outbound e-mail and teletext processing, brand managers should now consider deployment of voice over the Internet by the year 2002, if not sooner. This application will ride broadband IP networks and the rollout of Internet telephone service by AOL and AT&T Cable. Live Webcam demos can use the same infrastructure.

The call center can also direct customers (and other stakeholders) to appropriate resources at the Web site, organized as a searchable know-how database.

Customers have to know what, how, and why to purchase the right product or service. This database extends the functionality of the "contact us" directory, making it more interactive and more intelligent, answering many queries through a 24/7 self-service center that pre-empts the need for an e-mail exchange or even more expensive telephone interaction. A fully developed, searchable know-how database will reflect deep, penetrating, and intimate knowledge of the customer at each stage of a satisfaction lifecycle.

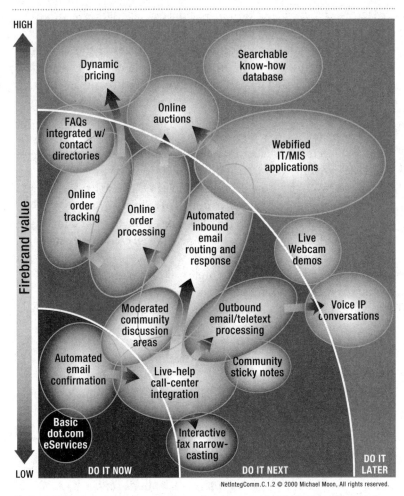

Figure 5-9 Net-integrated communications realizes its potential with dynamic pricing, auctions, and Webified IT/MIS applications—all significant undertakings that require considerable infrastructure to successfully undertake

Designers of such a database start with the *a priori* assumption that someone has a problem and wants it quickly resolved. This someone can come from any number of non-exclusive stakeholder groups—a long-standing customer in a newbie interactive status for a product they already use, for example. The answers they seek may relate to upgrading, replacing, fixing, or simply knowing more about a specific product or an entire category of options. As designers begin to architect the database, the data model quickly manifolds into several hundred, if not several thousand, data entities, and several thousands (or tens of thousands) of data types. We cannot overstate the importance and mind-numbing man-on-the-moon complexity of this effort. Despite the complexity of this challenge, we recommend that you start with a set of basic questions that your most important kinds of customers ask. This will entail retracing the steps that such customers have taken to resolve particular kinds of problems. Textual descriptions will pale in comparison with visual roadmaps, diagrams, and flow charts prescribing a set of informed, expert actions that, when taken, solve an important problem.

Perhaps the most important messaging application of this phase provides dynamic pricing: the ability to price a specific item or service based on availability, demand, customer status and loyalty, seasonal factors, weather conditions, and the competitive landscape. While analysts have talked much about the negative elements of dynamic pricing, highlighting auctions and shopping bots that systematically seek the lowest price items available in a market, we must emphasize the upside potential. When linked with a strategic versioning system, a self-service customer or other stakeholder can use tools to customize a solution and pay a premium for the integrated solution. Brand managers must not only think outside of the box, they must stand outside the box. They must think in terms of satisfactions that customers want to buy and stop talking about products and services that they want to sell. This lets a brand manager and customer collaborate on the just-in-time assembly or performance of a customized satisfaction, many components of which will result from a collection of opted-in eServices and customer-versioned digital assets. (In the firebrands section, we discussed value-based pricing and versioning.)

Online auctions offer another potent way that brand managers can serve customers. They must optimize auctions for profitability, highlighting additional eServices and special buying opportunities for opted-in customers and platform partners. For example, Nike could offer outdated, end-of-run, or odd-lot goods to its channel partners or other stakeholders as a reward for maintaining a good (i.e. profitable) relationship. Or, it could auction odd lots to qualified nonprofit organizations such as churches and community service organizations, creating grassroots goodwill and potentially earning tax write-offs.

As many mortar-and-brick firms have discovered, most of the legacy data systems, including many of the ERP and state-of-the-art client-server applications, do not perform well in a browser-accessed world. These applications have an architecture and a complex user interface that require days if not weeks of user training to master. Webified IT/MIS applications represent a new generation of software developed from the ground up for casual, ignorant, or abuser-friendly Web use. Giving customers and other stakeholders real-time access to the firm's production data systems requires a massive reengineering effort. This can drive real-time manufacturing and automated replenishment for an entire value chain. Webified applications let a Web page make a promise that the factory and logistics system can keep, deepening and strengthening the brand relationship in the process. In turn, real-time demand data (from preview, configuration, purchase, use, satisfaction, and reorder activities) feed capacity planning, procurement, and customer-service load balancing of the iCorp.

Recipes for the Knowledge Refinery

The cross-media messaging system described in Best Practice #1 and the net-integrated communications eServices discussed in this section give brand managers a powerful system to not only send messages to customers and other stakeholders but also to collect valuable data from them. We'll discuss this in much more detail in the sections on integrated projects management and Web-based database marketing. As they implement net-integrated communications, brand managers can lay the groundwork by beginning to develop a strategic data model for use at all appropriate data collection points in their communications with customers and other stakeholders.

A strategic data model describes in precise detail the specific types of data to collect and how to join these data (in database tables) to produce high-level business intelligence. As illustrated in Figure 5-10, the strategic data model structures what pieces of data to collect at each point of data collection so that an enterprise data repository can collate these data into meaningful business metrics.

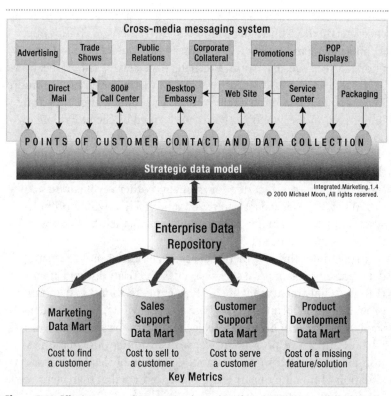

Figure 5-10 Effective cross-media messaging demands uniform data collection at all points of contact with customers and other stakeholders, emphasizing a strategic data model

In the mid-1990s, we benchmarked the customer registration and profiling practices of 87 software, multimedia CD-ROM, and computer manufacturers. We investigated best practices for collecting customer information and applying it to marketing and sales programs. A major software or hardware company will have an average of 37 unique points of data collection, ranging from customer registration postcards, scripted questions at a call center, online forms, trouble tickets at technical support operations, contest entry forms, direct mail and business reply cards, and trade show visitor requests for information. This research showed, among other things, no less than nine unique ways of characterizing an individual's name (e.g., first name, name you like to be called, middle name, middle initial, last name, maiden name, suffixes, credentials, and honorific). We found similar disarray in the ways these companies use data to characterize the name of a customer's firm, addresses (billing, ship to, alternate, temporary, etc.), and means of contact (general telephone, direct line, extension, alternate, pager, faxes, cell phone, home office, and various e-mail addresses). The taxonomy grew even more Byzantine in terms of characterizations of products used, purchase intentions, and nature of activities performed by the individual or company.

Despite collection of all this information, the companies found themselves unable to use the data for marketing, sales support, customer support, product development, and other key business activities. Why? They lacked a strategic data model that would provide systematic data characterization of customers, their business activities, interests, and needs.

To guarantee this systematic data characterization, an enterprise data repository team must start with an entity relationship diagram (ERD). As illustrated in Figure 5-11, an entity relationship diagram provides the blueprint for a database architect who uses it to understand what kinds of business intelligence the database must produce—what essential questions to answer with customer information. A non-existent or incomplete data model inevitably leads to the sorry situation of missing one or more classes of data that managers need for decision support.

For example, Doug remains amazed, after his interactions with Barnes & Noble, that each time he calls, the teleservice representatives seem unaware of his previous calls about order problems and speak to him as if he has never encountered problems with the order fulfillment system. His file should, by now, contain a big red flag and the warning: "Hothead; has experienced problems with his last three online orders." Barnes & Noble doesn't seem to be collecting this class of data.

How do you collect the right pieces of data, especially in eMarkets where a company may only have one opportunity to collect any information at all? By implementing a strategic data model. As you integrate your brand communications through the Internet, you have a golden opportunity to put in place this strategic data model and guarantee collection of truly useful data while avoiding the pain of regret: if only we had known the customer's birthday, if only we knew he used a Palm Pilot and not a Windows CE system, and so on.

Entity Relationship Diagram (ERD)

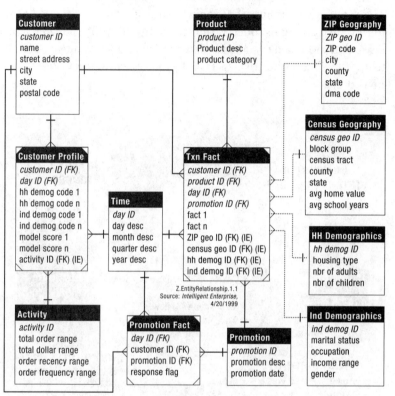

Figure 5-11 This illustration depicts a simple ERD for a customer profile that contains 12 data entities and 67 data items. A fully developed eCommerce ERD may contain 1,000 to 2,000 data entities and 8,000 to 20,000 data items

Net-Integrated Communications: the Big Picture

As customers begin to interact with you through the Internet, you must anticipate the kinds of interactions that customers and stakeholders want to have and put in place the systems that enable successful outcomes. Figure 5-12 shows that development of communications (what to say to whom) derives from data analysis. This requires an enterprise data repository (and a strategy for continually upgrading and extending it) plus data mining tools with which to extract, collate, visualize, and summarize data. You must collect the right data the first time, underscoring the need for a strategic data model—an expensive and complex endeavor, best provided by specialists and led by a credentialed authority in quantitative methods and research. We cannot overstate the importance of designing a strategic data model to reflect the essential questions (queries and reporting) of a professional market researcher grounded in statistics, data modeling, and executive storytelling. It will show line managers and senior executives how to listen to market data.

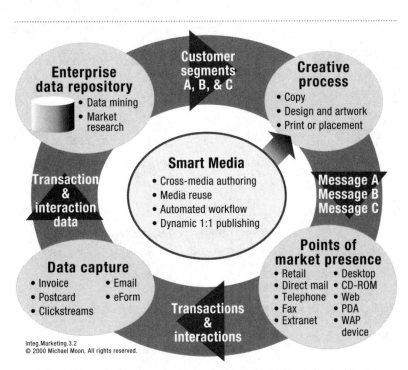

Enterprise data repository
• Data mining
• Market research

Customer segments A, B, & C

Creative process
• Copy
• Design and artwork
• Print or placement

Transaction & interaction data

Smart Media
• Cross-media authoring
• Media reuse
• Automated workflow
• Dynamic 1:1 publishing

Message A
Message B
Message C

Data capture
• Invoice   • Email
• Postcard   • eForm
• Clickstreams

Transactions & interactions

Points of market presence
• Retail   • Desktop
• Direct mail   • CD-ROM
• Telephone   • Web
• Fax   • PDA
• Extranet   • WAP device

Integ.Marketing.3.2

Figure 5-12 This illustration summarizes the central ideas of net-integrated communications: how brand managers use data to target promotions to customer segments and capture feedback data used to continuously improve the brand storytelling process

Analysis-driven communications illuminates the who, what, where, when, why, and "why bother" of your customers. Your creative team translates these insights into copy, concepts, media placements, and a whole range of promotional, marketing materials, as well as other executions that drive a set of interactions and transactions at each point of market presence. Whether online or off, in real time or time-shifted formats, each point of contact with a customer (or other stakeholder) should deliver a consistent brand message and collect uniform sets of data explicitly engineered for collation and analysis in an enterprise data repository (also known as a data warehouse). Thus, data capture via e-mail, postcards, call centers, and Web pages feeds the enterprise data repository. In many cases, interaction data trump transaction data: knowing why your customer bought, what demographic or technographic factors influenced a purchase, how the customer uses the product, and how well this customer matches your highest loyalty, highest profitability customer profile.

Net-integrated communications begin to pay dividends when the brand manager has integrated the messaging applications discussed in this section to the smart media factory discussed in "Best Practice #1, Build a Corporate Firebranding System." This highlights the need for brand managers to make, buy, or rent a brand resource repository that feeds all the members of the branding team, including advertising agencies, direct marketing firms, independent training organizations, affiliates, and other platform partners.

Net-integrated communications calls for an extraordinary level of collaboration and workflow integration among many parties in the smart media value chain. For this reason, the next firebranding best practice in our roadmap emphasizes a set of enabling technologies and practices for taking the firebranding process to the next level of performance and results.

Best Practice #3: Implement Integrated Projects Management

Your firebranding strategy must harness the collective brilliance and creativity of your entire smart media value chain—the people and companies who help you create and deliver your brand storytelling. While this practice focuses on the needs of brand managers and their storytelling partners, the insights and practices also apply to the productivity of knowledge workers throughout the firm.

Integrated projects management emphasizes one key firebranding metric: cycle time. It calls attention to how quickly a company can drive a brand message, promotion, or eService to its intended customer or stakeholder. Cycle time defines the challenge of the Networked Economy: getting the right eService with the right message to the right person just in time and personalized to that individual.

In many cases, cycle time also determines how effectively a company can collaborate with customers and stakeholders.

When properly implemented, integrated projects management reengineers the brand storytelling process to enable creation of a firebrand and illuminates a strategy for reengineering other core business processes (which we will discuss in "Best Practice #4, Master Web-Integrated Database Marketing and Sales").

Which Brand Resource Adds the Most Value to Your Firebrand Equity?

Late in his career, Albert Einstein taught graduate physics students at Princeton University. The story goes that at the end of each year he would pass out final exams—a set of problems for students to solve. One student with a particularly good memory remarked, "Professor Einstein, aren't these the same questions that you gave us last year?" Einstein replied, "Yes, but the answers are different this year."

This anecdote—apocryphal or not—underscores business in the Networked Economy. We ask the same questions and the answers that produce success keep changing.

Brand managers considering what new technologies and eServices to deploy as they build their firebrands face the perennial question: How do we get the right people on the right jobs at the right time with the right tools producing the right materials on time and at budget with a minimum of high-cost, labor-intensive supervision and direct management controls?

In our consulting practice, we often help newly funded business-to-business dot.com start-ups focus their business model, firebrand positioning, and integrated communications strategies for optimum results—a killer IPO or roll-up (profitable acquisition by another company). Using the tools and models outlined in this book, we isolate a critical unserved customer need and help structure a business model to satisfy that need with laser-beam intensity and focus.

Recently, a company came to us for help in launching a business that aims to solve a problem every brand manager faces and which illustrates the importance of integrated projects management in building a firebrand.

We recently helped a dot.com start-up identify a critical weak link found in almost every firebranding program: how to quickly find and engage a professional new media producer or specialist for a particular job. As we worked through the problem, we identified the principal economic actor around which to build their business-to-business eCommerce portal: the production manager (on staff or) contracted to a large brand producer firm (General Motors, Nike, Proctor & Gamble), a large advertising or communications agency (Chiat/Day; Young & Rubicam; Nelson Communications), a production house that serves the agency or brand producer (Capps Studio; R.R. Donnelley), and outsource providers of eCommerce services such as Web design, production, hosting, and transaction management (iXL; IBM Global Services; WorldCom).

Figure 5-13 illustrates a simplified workflow model of a production manager. In this model, we highlight the "units of work" produced by the production manager in collaboration with numerous third and fourth parties.

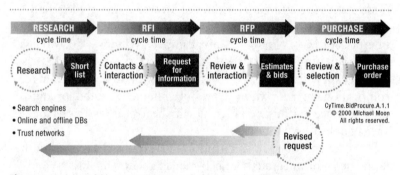

Figure 5-13 Successful business-to-business firebrands will target one knowledge worker with laser-beam precision and automate large portions of this person's workflow. This diagram illustrates the demographic success model of a production manager at a global brand firm or advertising agency, as automated by a new deep gravity well supersite.

For example, a firebranding team has decided to use Flash animation to promote the company's new heart valve mechanism on the Web site. Now the team needs to find a Flash animator with expertise in anatomical illustration, good references, and an ability to start the project within three days. Compounding the challenge, this person must collaborate with and coordinate input provided by the medical device firm, the device's principal inventor, the company CEO, the creative director at the company's advertising agency, the William Morris agent and their client who will provide a celebrity endorsement for this product, plus the regular cast of characters at the outsourced Web site management firm (who must integrate the Flash animation on the company's Web site). Did I mention that the company's creative director also wants to own the intellectual property rights to the animation and license it to the medical device firm for use on the Web only but not for multimedia CD-ROMs, kiosk, or training films (for which the creative director wants to derive incremental licensing revenue, with an ultimate goal of creating the next "Dancing Baby" as seen on *Ally McBeal*)?

The problems falls in the lap of a seasoned production manager who must procure three competitive bids from qualified, available Flash animators. The same production manager, for this project, has to uncover the following: an information engineer who can structure a knowledge base of medical research for one-button quick searches by heart surgeons who visit the Web site; a user interface designer who understands the intimate workings of browsers, Java applets, and database connectivity; a specialist who implements a branded user interface for Mac, Windows, Unix, Palm OS, Windows CE, wireless application protocol (WAP) cell phones, and who-knows-what-else Internet appliance coming down the pike. He also needs to find a sonification engineer who will produce interactive audio for logos, user interface buttons, and high-fidelity heartbeat renditions for a variety of heart conditions.

This dot.com start-up aims to solve part of the challenge, but the larger need for integrated projects management remains.

What Applications Enable Integrated Projects Management?

Integrated projects management characterizes a set of practices and technologies deployed within an integration framework. It gives each economic actor of a firebranding team a comprehensive view of the information necessary to produce the prescribed unit of work. This means that from a database containing all business and project related data, each actor (the production manager in our example) views only the pieces of information needed to produce each specific unit of work (produce a short list of available Flash animators; issue a request for information; issue a request for proposal; issue a purchase order to contract the selected animator's services).

In our "do it now, do it next, do it later" deployment model as illustrated in Figure 5-14, we assume that you possess an intranet server and publishing systems. Increasingly, this means database publishing systems and the systematic elimination of high-maintenance-cost, individually authored HTML pages. It also means standardization on Adobe Acrobat PDFs as the principal container for your knowledge assets—employee manuals, documentation, and all other corporate publications, using an HTML page as a card catalog index to navigate to the appropriate PDF.

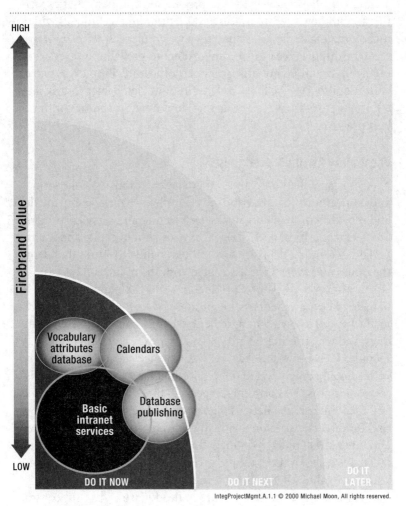

Figure 5-14 Coordinating firebranding projects begins with basic intranet services that include a vocabulary attributes database, calendaring, and database publishing

Do It Now

A basic intranet platform embodies the way a company does business. Along with meetings, the intranet becomes the most important medium by which a company knows itself. As such, the intranet defines, shapes, and colors a company's internal brand (who we are and what we do in the world) and will exert a powerful influence on external offline and online branding efforts. Think of the intranet as your off-off-Broadway theater production company that experiments with new user interfaces and firebranding techniques with the most forgiving and vocal of users—your employees. We cannot overstate the importance of using an intranet to preflight and vet every public firebranding initiative, eService, or feature. Employees become your usability lab. We'll discuss this in more detail later in this chapter. In Figure 5-14, we illustrate the "do it now" necessities of this best practice.

Vocabulary Attributes Database

No team can collaborate unless they share vocabulary—the terms and conventions that describe the customer, what the company does, and how the company organizes itself to find and serve customers. To meet this critical need, every company should create and maintain an expanding database of vocabulary and attributes that define the brand and everything associated with the brand.

For example, every food product has an FDA-mandated label detailing key ingredients. Some number of customers really, really, really want to know each ingredient, where it comes from, what it does, and why this ingredient instead of an alternative. This would require a Web-browsable, keyword-searchable database on every noun, verb, and adjective printed on the product label. Not only will this serve an inquisitive consumer, especially those who may not speak and read English as a native language, it gives each member of the firebranding team—along with all value chain or platform partners and other stakeholders—information necessary for specific tasks and facilitates collaboration among various team members. It takes on particular value when collaborating with other individuals not immersed in the corporate culture of headquarters, like subcontractors and freelancers who must quickly learn the "brandspeak" of the company's particular market and customer. A good vocabulary and attributes database will also contain slang, misspellings, and newly created words used by netizens.

Brand managers will immediately recognize the value of accurate transliteration of key words and phrases associated with the brand into other languages—translations performed by employees and other branding partners. As we will show later, this vocabulary and attributes database will serve a key role in globalizing the firebrand.

Calendars

Calendar applications now available from leading vendors have grown into robust, sophisticated time-management systems. Organizations use them to plan the use of shared resources such as amphitheaters and conference rooms and to track key executive schedules, especially while traveling—all good things.

A calendar should do more, however. It should track significant events in a brand-producing firm's marketspace, cataloging trade shows, conferences, and workshops of interest to brand managers, customers, platform partners, and other stakeholders. This provides valuable insight for planning major market initiatives such as product or service launches, direct mail campaigns, and the like. When properly designed, a calendar application can also organize critical brand planning process milestones that lead up to quarterly reviews.

Database Publishing

Given the high cost of manually creating and maintaining HTML pages, intranet managers must automate the process with database publishing techniques. Prohibit the use of WYSIWYG Web page creation tools such as FrontPage, Dreamweaver, and GoLive by individual users. Instead, train and motivate intranet content creators to place text and graphics into an authoring database such as FileMaker Pro or next-generation XML-based solutions. In this scenario an individual contributor can copy and paste text and graphics into an online, browser-based form connected to a database. Publishing templates, automation scripts, and related tools transform ASCII text and graphics files into HTML pages, then post them to the intranet Web server. Use Acrobat PDF to publish large, complex, or idiosyncratic documents that don't fit one of the widely used template formats.

Do It Next

This section outlines several applications that you should consider deploying once you have a basic Web site and brand resource repository.

Schedules

Many projects of scale and complexity require automation tools to manage them, as illustrated in Figure 5-15. They use a number of project management and scheduling methodologies, including PERT, Gantt, and Critical Path Method (CPM). These tools serve an important function for only a certain class of projects, however, and require trained knowledge workers to use them well. They also force project planners into often-rigid execution frameworks that only work well for highly convergent, linear deployment trajectories—projects from Mars. Most of these tools fail miserably in collaborative, iteratively redefined creative projects—projects from Venus, the kinds of projects that firebranding teams must juggle.

For Venusian projects, we recommend two different types of scheduling tools.

For projects where brand managers have lots of process data (the number of people waiting in line to see a bank teller or use an ATM machine, for example) we suggest that you investigate tools in a category called discrete event modeling and simulation. We have found two software packages useful: EyeThink (High Performance Systems, Inc.) and Extend (Imagine That, Inc.). Using the Imagine That tool, we modeled 1,500 independent variables in a complex seminar marketing program, taking into account the number of direct mail pieces dropped, response rates by territory and type of respondent, room capacities of available seminar venues, and personnel available on prescribed dates. It also serves as a proactive scheduling tool. After we started dropping direct mail, we saw response rates varying. We plugged the response rate data into the tool, which automatically re-scheduled seminar production and staffing logistics.

The second class of tools enables storyboarding of actors, actions, and results over time. Borrowing from the language of theatrical production, brand managers script a specific project or campaign the way a playwright and director write and plan a play. The brand storyteller creates multiple scenarios with variable outcomes for critical junctures as customers (and other stakeholders) interact. Scheduling thus maps a series of trigger events and prescribes a set of actions that the branding team actors can take in order to move the project to the next level and achieve a positive branding event. Storyboarding de-emphasizes the linearity of time and heightens the gestalts of critical brand events and the tactical actions that firebranding teams must take to produce and manager them.

Scheduling thus takes on new dimensions in linear and non-linear terms, two areas of practice that companies must master for success in the Networked Economy.

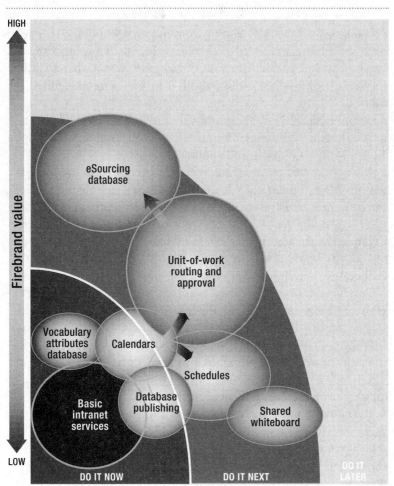

IntegProjectMgmt.B.1.1 © 2000 Michael Moon, All rights reserved.

Figure 5-15 Integrated projects management pivots on the ability to create, route, and use units of work (answers) of other knowledge workers. Scheduling and eSourcing databases can also accelerate knowledge worker productivity

Development of a visual algebra and storyboard vocabulary also represents another key phase in the development of a global brand, as we will discuss later. This enables brand managers to communicate quickly across cultures with a minimum of distortion and misunderstanding. In the broader theoretical context, storyboarding draws on cognitive psychology, behaviorism, and speech act theory. A full discussion of these elements lies beyond the scope of the present volume; visit www.Firebrands.com for pointers to more resources.

Shared Whiteboard and Collaborative Applications

Scheduling puts the firebranding team in synch, but brand managers need to do more: they need to collaborate, share ideas and critiques, and quickly form a consensus about how, where, and when to move forward. They need to do this in both real-time and time-shifted modes.

Brand managers and their teams should first develop collaboration skills and techniques offline, in time-shifted mode, using Adobe Acrobat with its markup and annotation tools.

We predict that as Adobe Acrobat PDF becomes a native file format for most popular graphic design and image editing tools, it will offer sophisticated annotation, markup, and structured feedback mechanisms for the basic unit of work contained within it—in this example, the illustration. Acrobat PDFs have already established themselves as the workhorse in some segments of the graphic design industry because they embed fonts, zoomable high resolution art, graphic design formatting—all viewable across Windows, Macintosh, and Unix machines equipped with the free Acrobat reader. For this reason we strongly recommend that brand managers adopt and master Adobe Acrobat PDF as the principal container for brand resources, the units of work of a firebranding creative team.

One team member can send a PDF for markup and annotation by another team member or group. Using the annotation and markup tools built into the Acrobat application, these team members can suggest revisions or additions, then send back only a file containing their markups (and not the entire PDF). The recipient can collate the various suggestions into a single annotated document that all team members can view on the Web or as a PDF e-mail attachment.

In this manner, a team learns how to collaborate using a rudimentary set of markup and annotation tools. As their collaborative fluency grows and their network bandwidth expands, they can fruit-fully use real-time collaboration tools such as shared whiteboards.

As the software industry shifts to server-centric applications, many of the familiar desktop applications will evolve into collaborative environments. These current desktop applications must undergo a radical transformation in user "affordances" (icons, actions, and assumptions of user know-how tailored for Web delivery and collaboration). No Webified collaborative equivalents of Word or Excel have yet emerged and it remains unlikely that Microsoft will offer an acceptable solution. In this area, Lotus Notes continues to pace the industry. While Notes offers collaboration tools, it lacks the technical underpinnings necessary for fully realized Web delivery.

Unit-of-Work Routing and Approval

These applications serve as the cornerstone for integrated projects management. Software applications that enable or support this practice fall into categories: peer-to-peer messaging with multimedia attachments; third-party applications built on industry-standard relational database management systems (e.g. Oracle); and workflow modeling language.

Peer-to-peer messaging applications ("e-mail on steroids") work well in relatively small groups of up to 100 project participants engaged in a collaborative, iterative process. For example, a graphic designer creates an illustration and sends it to the creative director for review and comment. The creative director bounces it back with annotations on the illustration file itself or in an e-mail form designed specifically for structured comments and feedback.

Beyond simple e-mail, we have tracked user successes with peer-to-peer communications server applications from First Class Inc., Avatar Works Inc. (www.avatarworks.com), and MetaCommunications Virtual Ticket and Job Manager in the smart media value chain. Many of the popular media asset management solutions also incorporate advanced forms of peer-to-peer routing and approval, including those from such vendors as Inso, North Plains, Bulldog, Banta, and eMotion.

Workflow and routing often reflect more complex organizational structures where financial and project data become important elements in the workflow process. For large, distributed work groups, building a customized application on top of a standard RDBMS makes sense.

This requires extensive data modeling (similar to what we discussed in the previous section, "Best Practice #2") to specify which pieces of project data each actor needs to see and modify at which points along a project time line or as a result of triggering events. The actor's role specifies a unique set of data views, rights, and permissions granted in specific context. For example, the creative director mentioned above may have the ability to change specifications of a unit of work but not the billing rate. On another project, that same creative director may not have the ability to change specifications but may have the ability to reset the billing rate. Rights may also change as the project evolves. One actor in a branding team can belong to n number of user classes and have n number of rights in accordance with the role the actor plays in a particular phase of a particular project.

Vendors of media asset and Web site management solutions have built such applications on top of a standard RDBMS such as IBM, Informix, Microsoft, Oracle, and Sybase. Media asset management systems vendors that have taken this approach include AdPlex, Artesia, Art Machine, Banta, Bulldog, Canto, Caere, CDXC, ClickUpdate, Chuckwalla, Deepbridge, DigitalZone.dk, Direct-Data, eMotion, Extensis, Flexstornet, Informix, MediaBridge, Mediasite, North Plains, NXN, Opix.de, Quark, Running-Start, WAM!NET, Webware, and Xinet. Vendors of Web site management solutions with this capability include Interwoven, Microsoft, and Vignette.

Large, global operations with tens of thousands of actors and thousands of external business entities (e.g., traffic managers at newspapers and magazines, merchandising managers at retail outlets) may require the third option, *workflow modeling language*. Equivalent to a programming language, workflow modeling language allows a business-process architect and a team of workflow engineers to quickly create a system that maps to existing organizational structures—specially important if the organization contains trade unions with work rules, or other pockets of potential resistance to workflow changes. Once an architect has modeled a workflow, the architect can reconfigure portions of it to pace change at departmental levels without engaging a comprehensive or traumatic business process reengineering effort. Workflow modeling language vendors include MediaBridge (formerly known as Cascade Systems).

Unit of work routing and approval must have a strong rights management module that handles the legal aspects of licensing and clearances, as illustrated in Figure 5-16. For example, every aspect of an Air Jordan campaign for Nike requires the explicit authorization of Michael Jordan, his manager, his agent, and his lawyer. If the ad contains yet another sports celebrity, such as Derek Jeter wearing Air Jordan, his entourage must also sign off. Needless to say, these people won't likely sit in their offices waiting for the brand manager's phone calls and FedEx packages. But they could use a laptop or other portable computing device to dial up a remote viewing and approval system at a secure Web site—a key function of the brand resource repository.

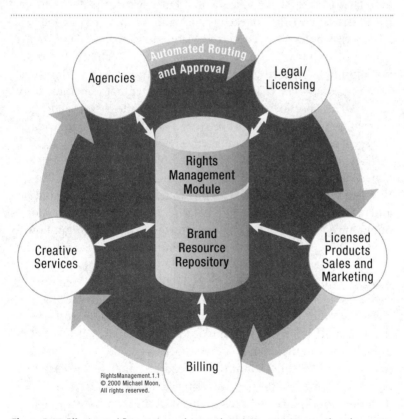

Figure 5-16 Effective workflow routing and approval requires secure access to a brand resource repository with a specialized application for rights management which will incorporate encryption, user authentication, and digital signatures, and may also include digital watermarking, captioning, and fingerprinting

eSourcing Database

As discussed in the Mediafloor example above, production managers must continually scout for available industry resources (new media specialists, information engineers, et al). Brand managers face a similar challenge even larger in scope. An eSourcing database meets this challenge with a three-pronged strategy.

A corporate skills inventory database contains profiles of skills, aptitudes, and ambitions of specific individuals within the brand-producing firm. This database lets a firebranding team quickly locate individuals with highly specialized skills (who can speak and read Mandarin Chinese?). It also lets a brand manager access the friend-of-friend "trust networks" for each participating employee (who knows somebody who can speak and read Mandarin Chinese?). The systematic use of such trust networks can enable even a small firm to touch millions of potential customers without resorting to spam. One of us (Doug) used to publish a daily e-mail newsletter that went directly to about 2,000 subscribers who in turn re-mailed it to their friends, achieving a total readership of between 10,000 and 20,000 individuals in a specific industry niche (interactive media developers).

These trust networks also play a key role in the second component of an eSourcing database: the community bookmarks. The Web can serve as a huge card catalog index to a vast array of online and offline resources—but, to date, it remains a huge card catalog as might have been created by a librarian who, strangely, forgot how to use the Dewey Decimal System. Community bookmarks collect the Web resources preferred and annotated by members of a trust network, organized in password-protected file folders in a Web portal such as www.OneView.com. Before a network starts to use any given resource, it must contain a critical mass of usable stuff—in this case, URLs that link to useful resources. A small team—or even a single, highly efficient net-savvy librarian—could set up the file folder structure (the taxonomy of categories), then quickly assemble a critical mass of bookmarks using standard search engines and dedicated tools like Copernic to jumpstart the community bookmark collection. If she builds it, they will come—and add links, annotate them, and discuss their relative merits and disadvantages.

Trusted relationships thus serve as the parser and arbiter of value in an otherwise toxic clutter of information resources—a key practice for success in the Networked Economy.

A shared vendor industry resource database provides secure browser-based access to proven, go-to solution providers and sub-contractors. This database shares many of the attributes of a customer relationship management (CRM) application, but differs in several important ways. It enables a brand manager to quickly search for highly specific skill sets and issue an RFI (request for information) to determine availability and ballpark costs. A brand manager can use one of two methods to build such a database.

Using the same capability we described in the Barnes & Noble example, an e-mail can contain an embedded hyperlink, linking respondents back to a secure online form where they can profile, using automated pull-down menus and radio buttons, their capabilities for meeting various sourcing needs. Using an Acrobat PDF form at this Web page instead of a dumb CGI form adds additional benefits.

Instead of e-mailing hyperlinks to a Web page, brand managers can e-mail an interactive Acrobat PDF form. The solution provider or sub-contractor can fill out the Acrobat PDF form offline (on a laptop while traveling on an airplane, for example). When she reconnects to the 'net, hitting the submit key tells Acrobat to find and start the e-mail application (if not already open) and use its mail protocols to send an e-mail containing tab-delimited data to a secure e-mail server set up to receive PDF data and sort it into the shared vendor industry resource database. The vendor can also send the PDF on to other individuals or companies in the trust network who wish to enter the database.

Do It Later

As indicated in Figure 5-16, unit-of-work routing and approval serves as the cornerstone for the further evolution of integrated projects management. The fullest realization of this best practice comes in real-time resource allocation, illustrated in Figure 5-17: the ability to put the right person on the right job with the right tools in the right network of collaborators and track progress (the production of units of work), productivity, and costs through a dynamic network of knowledge workers. Before we can achieve this, however, a firebranding team must put in place another layer of IT-enabled capabilities.

Depending on the nature of their business and its age in the corporate lifecycle, as brand managers deploy and begin using unit-of-work routing and approval, they discover several new needs. Let's start with time activity accounting.

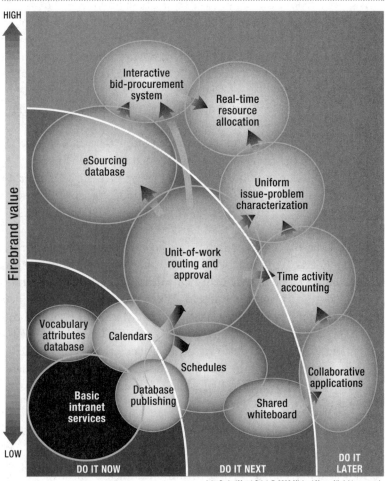

Figure 5-17 Brand managers realize the full potential of integrated projects management when they can quickly source a needed knowledge worker, track time against projects, and uniformly characterize with data an issue or problem

Time Activity Accounting

In the old economy, time activity accounting developed within authoritarian structures (often unacknowledged) designed to manage salaried and hourly employees. In the Networked Economy, brand managers often find themselves unable to hire and keep on staff the kind of talent they need—these individuals increasingly choose to work as independent contractors (eLancers). This means that time activity accounting must evolve to track all knowledge workers, whether employees or contractors, including senior executives.

Most companies have no idea how much things cost or how long projects take. Lacking this information, brand managers find themselves unable to answer the questions, Should we do this activity in the first place?, and if so, Should we outsource it or handle it internally? Time activity accounting provides the data to answer these questions. More importantly, time activity data provides a way to assay the investment of knowledge work in a particular unit of work.

In our consulting practice, we have investigated a variety of brand resource management activities, estimating how much of whose time a particular unit of work contains. A purchase order for $100 worth of office supplies averages $125 in overhead activity-related cost. Somebody had to research what to buy, where to buy it, create a purchase order, issue it, file it, track its receipt, authorize release of funds for payment, and maintain purchase history data. When applying this type of analysis to multimedia assets in an eBusiness Web site, even relatively simple sites, individual assets can quickly skyrocket to tens of thousands of dollars or more in fully burdened costs, the largest portion of which comes from routing, approval, and change orders that result (iterations of creative executions—the heart valve device Flash animation we discussed earlier, for example).

While management may encounter difficulty persuading knowledge workers to systematically categorize how they spend their time, this practice offers extraordinary benefits. First, the simple fact of keeping a detailed record of how they spend time automatically prompts knowledge workers to focus on higher priority tasks, in the same way that keeping a food journal automatically leads to healthier eating habits for a person who seeks to lose weight.

Beyond that, time activity accounting provides statistical data by which to measure cycle time for key projects and identify choke points and broken processes that impede progress and impair productivity.

Uniform Issue-Problem Characterization

Murphy's Law remains intact in the Networked Economy. Things that can go wrong, will, but now they go wrong in Internet time, around the world in seconds. Knowing that even the most well-structured workflows will encounter bumps and problems, integrated projects management must proactively address multitudinous contingencies.

We first understood the power of uniform characterization of problems and issues in our benchmarking of software development practices in the early 1990s. Software developers face particularly difficult problems when they encounter a program bug or glitch. They can spend countless hours trying to identify what went wrong and, in the process, cannot discern the scope of the problem, asking such questions as: Have we exceeded the parameters of our development architecture? Have we simply made a mistake in linking two or more processes? Have we encountered an "undocumented feature" of the hardware system, the operating system, the programming language, or the debugging system?

After identifying a problem of a particular scope, the developer must then communicate it in succinct, concrete terms to the appropriate resource: the technical support team, for example, who in turn can re-create the condition on their own equipment. Then, they can analyze the problem and suggest solutions.

One particular computer company that we studied built a distributed database application with a front-end user interface that displayed an online form with radio buttons, ballot boxes, pull-down menus, branching sections (if they answered this, that section of questions lights up) that systematically characterized the user, user's level of skill, tools used, platform configuration, and other important technical aspects of the problematic environment, plus a structured way to characterize the problem, its associated behaviors, and other salient facts. This problem-characterization mechanism provided highly consistent data on the nature of problems that various types of software developers experienced. It enabled analysts to correlate problems and issues to underlying deficiencies in training, development strategy, tool selection, and programming practices, including the consumption and use of manuals, technical notes, journals, and online libraries.

This experience suggests a possible solution for brand managers who need to optimize integrated projects management in a network of interactive relationships with members of the branding team, platform partners, and ultimately, customers. We highly recommend that brand managers ask, "How do we characterize, in data, a dissatisfaction that holds up the workflow?" To the unit-of-work routing and approval system, the branding team must add a capability similar to the programmer's bug report application described above, that will let members of the team characterize with data, in uniform terms, the difficulties they encounter. Using these reports, brand managers can analyze their firebranding team productivity and apply resources as necessary to improve the workflow.

More important, what brand managers learn about how to listen with data to their own firebrand team activities (through uniform issue-problem characterization) teaches them how to use the same approach (and large portions of the same data model and application infrastructure) to learn how to better serve customers and other stakeholders as they encounter problems and issues associated with the buying and using experience of the brand producer firm's product or service. Loyal customers and platform partners will gladly invest large portions of time to characterize a problem if they believe that the brand producing firm will use this information to solve this problem, not only for themselves but for other customers (especially those in their friend-of-friend trust networks). Brand managers should motivate and reward use of this application with cash bonuses, discounts, frequent flyer miles, and other goodies.

By the way, if the use of the programmer's bug report example strikes you as strange, we remind you that brand management in the Networked Economy depends on effective management of complex software development projects—your Web site, for starters, and all of the business IT applications accessed through the Web site.

Interactive Bid Procurement and Real-Time Resource Allocation

Web-based market exchanges and trading hubs represent only the tip of the iceberg of the emerging Networked Economy. Every conceivable capital transaction—including purchase, lease, or rental of capital equipment or service equivalent—will have two or more Web-based dedicated, global market exchanges or hubs. But brand producer firms will still want to create direct relationships with suppliers, especially those that add the highest value to their firebranding efforts. Integration of unit-of-work routing and approval and the eSourcing database produces an interactive bid-procurement system that permits brand managers to do this.

An interactive bid procurement system uses the resources built in net-integrated communications, and earlier phases of integrated projects management, to fully automate supply chain research, requests for information and proposals, purchase order management, project tracking, progress billing, and financial analysis. The scope and complexity of this type of integration requires the services of enterprise applications vendors such as IBM, Oracle, Arriba, CommerceOne, and i2.

Cycletime data from workflow analysis and time-activity accounting data permit a more thorough examination of sources of profit and barriers to profitability—profit zone analysis (discussed earlier in the book). This leads to the Holy Grail: real-time resource allocation.

Brand managers seeking to create a global firebrand must take advantage of opportunities and challenges that emerge out of nowhere and demand immediate action.

The Networked Economy takes the adage, "To err is human, to really foul up takes a computer" to the next level: "To screw up in front of a billion people is a daily occupational hazard." Brand managers must have the ability to instantly create and focus their A-team on an opportunity or challenge within minutes or hours of its emergence as a branding priority.

Such discontinuities can include overwhelming demand for a hot product, as in the case of Stephen King's eBook online release earlier this year that caught online distributors unprepared. As requests to download the book snowballed and surpassed server capacity, brand managers could have quickly conscripted hundreds or thousands of employees or on-call temporary workers to fulfill these orders through their individual e-mail accounts. In this case, brand managers could have enjoyed the buzz of this "strategic shortage due to overwhelming popular demand" then spin the story of their ability to marshal resources to fulfill that demand—the best of both worlds, if they had had net-integrated communications and integrated projects management fully in place.

As it happened, the online distributors of the book benefited from driving massive traffic—of first-time online Stephen King book buyers—to their sites and creating the kind of shocking outrage that characterizes the quintessence of a firebrand (the ability to attract worldwide attention to a single idea) we discussed earlier. And they learned the hard way why real-time resource allocation plays a fundamental role in successful firebranding.

Knowledge Worker Productivity and the Satisfaction Lifecycle

Earlier, we discussed how customers (and other stakeholders) evolve and grow through the five major development stages of a satisfaction lifecycle: need, purchase, payback, full use, and advocacy. As a customer moves through the satisfaction lifecycle, she asks a set of essential questions that represent requests for information, experiences, and self-service interactions.

We noted that this customer satisfaction lifecycle parallels five seller activities: market creation, sales cycle, post-sales support, account management, and strategic partnering. As brand managers address integrated projects management, they build and deploy infrastructure and practices that drive their value creation process (offer-market development, demand creation, sales conversion, solution fulfillment, strategic development). At the heart of value creation we find knowledge worker productivity. Increasing knowledge worker productivity defines the mission of integrated projects management.

Peter Drucker, in his book *Management Challenges for the 21st Century* (Harperbusiness, 1999), set forth a general theory for knowledge worker productivity, which we distill in Figure 5-18. At every step along the path of a project, brand managers, their creative team, and associated knowledge workers must answer two essential questions: Who owes me what types of interaction, information, experience, fulfilled how? and, I owe to whom what types of interaction, information, experience, fulfilled how?

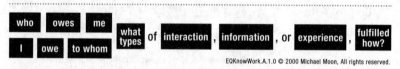
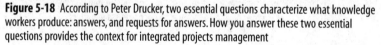

Figure 5-18 According to Peter Drucker, two essential questions characterize what knowledge workers produce: answers, and requests for answers. How you answer these two essential questions provides the context for integrated projects management

As illustrated in Figure 5-19, integrated projects management systematically catalogues the essential questions asked by the firm's knowledge workers (what they need to know to do their jobs) and the essential questions asked by customers and other stakeholders (what they need to know to get served and satisfied). These questions link to information assembled from the brand resource repository and other business IT applications. In the next section, we'll discuss how to build on this infrastructure to achieve web-integrated databased marketing and sales.

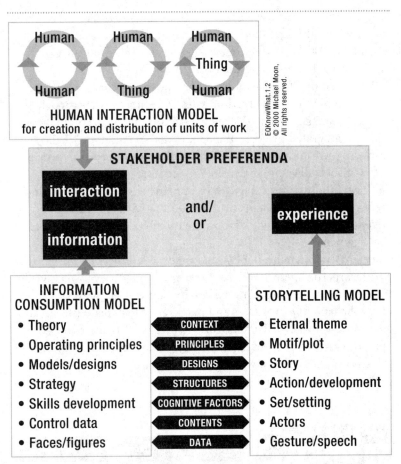

Figure 5-19 Customers and knowledge workers seeking answers to their essential questions demonstrate similar preferences for interaction, information, and/or storytelling experiences. Use this model to design answers to the specific preferenda of key brand stakeholders

Best Practice #4: Master Web-Integrated, Database Marketing and Sales

A firebranding strategy moves into high gear when self-service satisfactions result from customers interacting with a firm's core business processes—production data systems and an enterprise data repository. Earlier, we defined brand storytelling as the systematic application of product or service design, stories, media, and business IT applications to the buying and using experience of customers (and other stakeholders) throughout a satisfaction lifecycle. Web-integrated database marketing and sales enables this in a stakeholder-driven process. The ability to implement Web-integrated database marketing and sales, or not, separates companies able to continue on to fully develop their firebranding strategies and successfully compete in the Networked Economy from those companies that will fall by the wayside.

Do It Now

You must start with a clean enterprise data repository, which may take months of hard work to accomplish. Do not proceed further until you have this basic capability.

Enterprise Data Repository

As illustrated in Figure 5-20, we assume that the brand producer firm has some form of an enterprise data repository and an aggressive, high-priority strategy for upgrading it to full firebranding capabilities. As previously discussed, an enterprise data repository consolidates and conditions data from all available and appropriate sources, enabling brand managers to accomplish two things: analysis of customer needs, wants, and desires; and validation of brand storytelling effectiveness with cycletime metrics.

At the heart of the repository lies a database record containing data as specified by the strategic data model discussed in net-integrated communications. This database record, when populated with good data, gives the brand manager extraordinary power to fine-tune the firebranding process. Our audits of this capability reveal a problematic area that seems to overwhelm marketing departments and all but the most senior IT staff. To make an enterprise data repository firebrand-ready, you need to do the following.

You must have clean, up-to-date data. You must buy or lease economic and demographic overlay data to better analyze customer relationships and their desirability. By desirability, we mean customers with demonstrated high profitability, a profile that suggests high levels of future profitability, or customers who, once locked in, guarantee steady growth in market share (what we discussed previously as share-determining market sector). You will also need trained and motivated users of business intelligence—reports and queries, derived from data collected from customers as they move through a satisfaction lifecycle.

Figure 5-20 Database marketing has one immutable law: use one database and maintain it religiously. Often this requires outsourcing database management to firms fully equipped to do the job right

Since most firms lack the software and the knowledge to accomplish this, we highly recommend that brand managers outsource the management of their master file (a collection of all of the data from your various systems of record and list sources). Brand managers should engage a list-maintenance firm to source, purchase, and integrate economic and demographic data overlays.

For example, BMW USA and other automobile companies purchase motor vehicle registration data from R. Polka and use the data to identify current and past owners of BMW automobiles, plus owners of competitive models. BMW also buys demographic overlay data from Experian (formerly known as TRW Credit Information). Equifax and Claritas also sell these kinds of data.

Training smart users of business intelligence usually entails an immersive week-long boot camp and regular, ongoing workshops at Direct Marketing Association conferences. Professional training firms, such as Burke Institute, can also be brought in-house to train users. These training programs teach how to use database query and reporting tools to profile customers in a variety of metrics including cost to serve and lifetime revenue, as illustrated in Figure 5-21.

Lacking these basic resources, brand managers will find it difficult to move to the next phase of Web-integrated database marketing and sales.

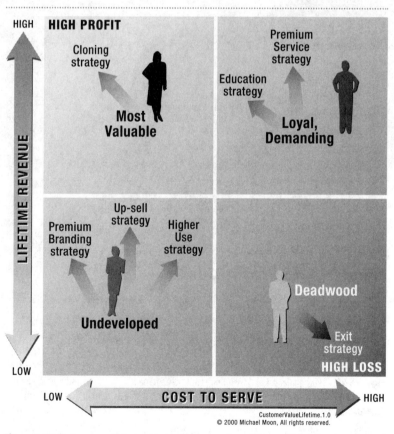

Figure 5-21 Customer analysis should reveal an economic or demographic profile of various groups and should drive a segment strategy as suggested above

Do It Next

In this phase, illustrated in Figure 5-22, two important developments converge: the training of marketing managers on how to use data and the implementation of a uniform data collection mechanism that we call a universal brand stakeholder subscription service.

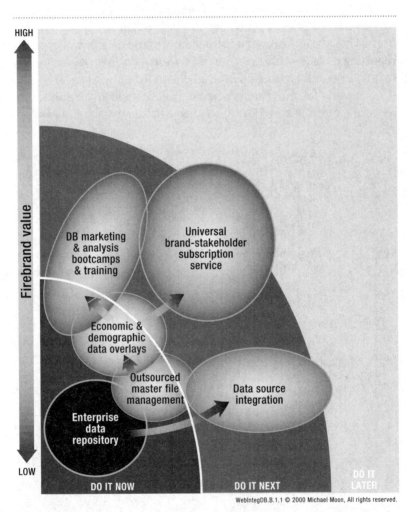

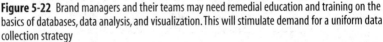

Figure 5-22 Brand managers and their teams may need remedial education and training on the basics of databases, data analysis, and visualization. This will stimulate demand for a uniform data collection strategy

Universal Brand Stakeholder Subscription Service

This firebranding best practice calls for managers to engage prospects, customers, and other stakeholders as subscribers to one or more eServices. This means borrowing a set of best practices from magazine circulation management, especially those controlled-circulation professional and trade magazines given to qualified subscribers at no cost, to implement a universal brand stakeholder subscription service.

This service has the look-and-feel of the online subscription forms for popular professional and trade magazines, but with a major difference: here, each answer triggers a pre-programmed set of branching questions. Firebranding requires that you collect 2,000 or more pieces of data from a customer (or other stakeholder) over a 5- to 10-year lifecycle, as specified by the strategic data model. The goal remains simple: slice the salami one thin slice at a time. Technically, this means that you must have online interactive forms driven by dynamic middleware—you cannot use CGI for this function.

In the net-integrated communications best practice, we discussed the infrastructure that would allow you to deliver messages and collect data from customers and other stakeholders at many points of market presence. All these data reside in the enterprise data repository which uses the data to pre-populate portions of the universal brand stakeholder subscription service form and periodically prompts users to validate (or update) old data and add new data as necessary. Obviously, strict and clearly delineated privacy practices must accompany this subscription, as necessary to earn and keep the trust of your interactive customers and stakeholders.

When properly implemented, this subscription service produces a fully opted-in customer—somebody who has shared intimate personal and professional information, in a trusted relationship, expecting that the brand producing firm will use the data to satisfy her wants, needs, and expectations. From a branding perspective, this requires that brand managers position this opt-in subscription service as a way of pre-programming a deep gravity well supersite to serve the individual customer or stakeholder. Research shows that this process of subscribing (to personalize information presentation and organization) yields a customer (or other stakeholder) who returns to the deep gravity well supersite 25 times more often than the visitor who does not subscribe and personalize the experience.

If Barnes & Noble successfully implemented this best practice at its bn.com operation, they would offer kiosks in their bricks-and-mortar locations that would encourage and reward frequent book-buyers (such as ourselves) to pre-program book genres, categories, authors, and ideas of standing interest, representing a standing request for information and offers.

For some bibliophiles, Barnes & Noble might also offer two more valuable eServices made possible by the universal brand stakeholder subscription application.

Barnes & Noble could use the bibliography of a prominent book to offer that book's purchaser additional resources to more fully explore the subject, including not only books but also article reprints, technical papers, and the like. In the spirit of firebranding, Barnes & Noble could take a giant step further by commissioning the book's author to more fully annotate these bibliographies, in essence deputizing the author as an affiliate who earns commissions on additional sales created by the annotated bibliography.

Barnes & Noble could invite loyal customers to use bn.com's book database (of both in-print and out-of-print titles) to organize their personal library collections. Such a system would let a customer rapidly catalog a personal library by typing in the name of an author, then checking off the titles already owned, or by typing in a book title for which the database automatically adds information.

Barnes & Noble would reap several benefits from this. First, it would prompt its loyal book buyer to purchase titles she doesn't own yet. Second, with a simple mouse click Barnes & Noble could enable the customer to make her books available to second-hand and collectible book buyers. A personal library catalog might also prove invaluable to the customer in the event that a catastrophe—fire, flood, earthquake—destroyed the precious collection. In fact, if Barnes & Noble had such a service, it could easily sell an insurance policy on the collection and reap recurring incremental revenue (even if the customer never bought another book), while providing peace of mind to the loyal customer. Book publishers or authors could let Barnes & Noble query loyal customers about their satisfaction with books they've recently purchased and about their desire and price sensitivity for future books or newly versioned digital compilations of heretofore disparate elements—interviews, magazine articles, journal essays, etc., dynamically compiled and delivered in keylocked Acrobat PDF or other downloadable book formats.

Data-Sources Integration

Data-sources integration represents the most difficult technical challenge a firebranding team will face. Larger, older firms with lots of legacy data systems—and burgeoning new points of market presence—will find it even more daunting. Figure 5-23 shows the degree of integration of front-line sales and other key business processes, an aggressive trend toward enterprisewide convergence of data collection and use. Over the past 10 years, data warehousing and data mart specialists have addressed these issues and continue to refine their solutions. Brand managers must nonetheless understand that strategic brand resource management systems must include a strong middleware platform—the technical capability to quickly integrate legacy data sources to Webified n-tier client-server applications such as a brand resource repository and dynamic publishing system.

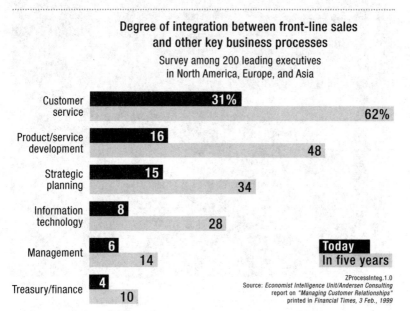

Degree of integration between front-line sales and other key business processes
Survey among 200 leading executives
in North America, Europe, and Asia

Customer service: 31% / 62%
Product/service development: 16 / 48
Strategic planning: 15 / 34
Information technology: 8 / 28
Management: 6 / 14
Treasury/finance: 4 / 10

Today
In five years

ZProcessInteg.1.0
Source: *Economist Intelligence Unit/Andersen Consulting*
report on *"Managing Customer Relationships"*
printed in *Financial Times, 3 Feb., 1999*

Figure 5-23 Research published by Economist Intelligence and Andersen Consulting clearly points the way to a wholesale convergence of data throughout the enterprise, led by customer service and product/service development

Do It Later

Trained, motivated brand managers with good data will reap handsome rewards when they close the loop between outbound messaging and inbound customer feedback and transaction analysis. Figure 5-24 illustrates the capabilities needed to close this loop.

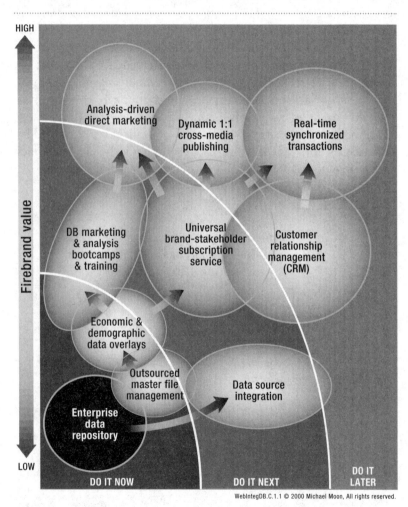

Figure 5-24 Web-integrated databased marketing and sales has one overarching goal: synchronization of customer interactions and the firm's timely response, with the ultimate goal of becoming a real-time value-creation process

Analysis-Driven Direct Marketing

We owe our understanding of this practice in large part to Despina Gurlides, former VP of Research at Miller-Huber, a prominent agency for customer loyalty programs, and current VP of Interactive Research at productopia.com. This capability emphasizes the systematic development, pre-testing, and post-mortem analysis of every major direct-response marketing effort. When driven by a skilled, direct-response professional, a company will develop and promote many combinations of offer, incentive, discount, personal letter, follow-up telephone call, free 30-day trial, etc., testing them with various segments (also called "test panels").

Going back to our Office Depot example and its $20-off promotion, analysis-driven direct marketing would have let the company target Doug's historical purchases (paper, toner cartridge) and instead of offering him a money-losing $20-off package, they could have offered a subscription that would automatically send him paper and toner cartridges every 110 days, based on his purchasing pattern. They could also have offered a "spring campaign preparation kit," adding pads, pens, folios, and other supplies that he might not have considered purchasing (although he has a history of purchasing some of them; Office Depot could have proactively added some items based on purchase patterns of other customers like him) but which he would consider purchasing if offered a discount.

Analysis-driven direct marketing uses rigorous data analysis to identify, refine, and optimize the job of marketing: telling the right story to the right person at the right time, maximizing return on sales.

Dynamic 1:1 Cross-Media Publishing

Web-integrated database marketing and sales aims to achieve one overarching goal: tell the right story to the right customer, in the right format and at the right time, propelling them forward through the satisfaction lifecycle and deeper into a lifelong, trusted relationship with the brand producing firm. Dynamic 1:1 cross-media publishing represents the next major step towards accomplishing this goal.

A stakeholder—prospect, customer, investor, trade partner, employee or family member—comes to the deep gravity well supersite seeking a solution to some kind of problem or seeking entertainment. With rare exceptions, they dive into the gravity well with an expected outcome in mind. The stakeholder submits a request for information, experiences (result of storytelling), or a self-service satisfaction (downloads a user manual, purchases a new product, or other financial and non-financial interactions and transactions).

Whether or not the stakeholder has previously interacted with the firm or used the universal brand stakeholder subscription service form, a dynamic 1:1 cross-media publishing system, illustrated in Figure 5-25, can automatically produce customized Web pages (HTML and XML enabled), print documents, and rich media (streaming or downloadable audio, video, and animation).

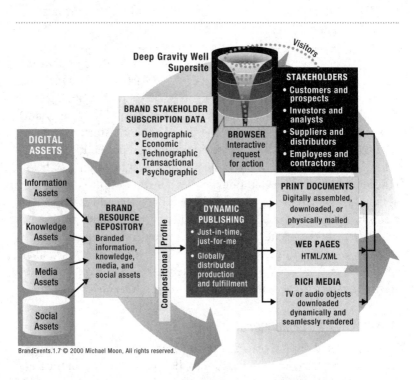

Figure 5-25 A simple set of interactions by customers or other stakeholders at a Web site reflecting achievement of Web-integrated database marketing and sales will produce print, online, and rich media publications just-in-time, just-for-the-individual

Dynamic publishing starts with full access to the digital assets of the brand resource repository. These include static and multimedia objects specifically engineered for systematic re-use and re-expression in multiple venues and formats, and conditioned to meet all branding specifications—color fidelity, graphic design, typographic treatment, current model, year and available product, etc. The customer request prompts the dynamic publishing system to grab the parts it needs and put them through a highly automated workflow that produces a customized output (brochure, Web-based interactive annual report, remixable audio).

These customized outputs represent just-in-time, just-for-me media productions. To accomplish this, the publishing system needs to know what to assemble and how to assemble it. The compositional profile provides the recipe, using five types of data from the brand stakeholder subscription form.

- ► Demographic data describe the individual's age, sex, education, income levels, professional activities.

- ► Economic data describe a business or household entity in terms of number of employees or occupants, nature of business, annual revenues or budgets, and industrial or other forms classification.

- ► Technographic data describe the technical capability of an individual stakeholder, specifying computing platform or device, type and version of browser, installation and version of browser plug-ins, type and speed of Internet connection, and encoding protocols.

- ► Transactional data describe the details of the customer's past orders and what direct marketers call RFM, recency (how recently they have ordered), frequency (how frequently they have ordered), and monetary (how much money they have spent each time).

- ► Psychographic data characterize an individual's beliefs and opinions about particular subjects or themselves, collected through surveys, contest entry forms, and clickstream data analysis.

Dynamic 1:1 Publishing in Action

Over the past two years, we have studied several dynamic publishing projects in our consulting practice. From these studies we distill a portrait of best practice that firms will widely deploy by the year 2001.

For purposes of this example, let's consider a typical event in a retail stockbroker's office. The stockbroker receives a call from an old client, Eduardo Jimenez, a successful Latin American businessman who runs a prosperous import-export company headquartered in Fort Lauderdale, Florida. As a Hispanic man in his late 50s, he has begun to plan his estate with his children and grandchildren in mind. The broker steers him into a portfolio of mutual funds, bonds, and a few buy-and-hold long-term growth stocks—a typical balanced portfolio optimized for long-term asset appreciation. Satisfied that they have established the parameters of the plan, the broker promises to send Don Jimenez a package of literature including prospectuses for the various investment instruments and marketing materials for the brokerage house. Upon confirming the mailing address, the broker hits the "fulfill now" button on his computer screen and says good-bye to Don Jimenez.

Instantly, the broker's application sends a packet of data to the firm's digital logistics and lettershop fulfillment house to publish, assemble, and mail the appropriate publications. In the past, this would have entailed a fulfillment specialist walking into a warehouse to choose literature items, packaging them with a cover letter, and shipping them to the customer. Due to the high opportunity cost of not having a key prospectus or brochure in stock, the brokerage house would routinely print and warehouse an abundant supply of literature for just this purpose.

In one such case that we researched, we found that 63 percent of all printed, four-color collateral for a major brokerage house remained unused and went to recycling for pulp. At an average of $2.17 per piece, the unused collateral exceeded several million dollars a year—"just a cost of doing business."

The digital logistics system now in use receives the packet of data from the brokerage house and begins executing a dynamic 1:1 publishing process.

The compositional profile characterizes Eduardo Jimenez as a middle-aged, Hispanic man with a principal residence in Fort Lauderdale and the proud owner of an 80-foot yacht. Using this data, the publishing system uses a publishing framework and dynamically inserts headlines and copy targeted to his profile. These copy and marketing themes resonate with the traditions of honor, intergenerational patrimony, and pride in the family legacy. The publishing system dynamically inserts images, illustrations, and photos following a nautical theme, with one extra twist: a middle-aged Hispanic male plays the role of the captain, dressed in blue blazer, ascot, and boat shoes. One scene depicts him clearly in charge, directing crew members—all blonde-haired and blue-eyed. This conveys an important dimension of the worldview of prosperous Hispanic men in predominantly Anglo societies: they have arrived. They command the respect and esteem of others. Their authority and rightful place stand unquestioned. Don Jimenez will see these images and subconsciously respond "Híjole, these guys get it!" This demographically targeted messaging will instill an extra level of trust and confidence, bolstering his commitment to, and relationship with, the brokerage house.

Later, hyperlinking from an e-mail message, Don Jimenez arrives at a set of Web pages dynamically assembled just for him. This Web site displays a complete history of his account activity and various calculators, pre-populated with appropriate information, permitting him to visualize and understand his investment strategies and options. He can also specify that the system send teletext information to his pager or wireless application protocol (WAP)-encoded text to his mobile phone, to notify him of breaking news related to his portfolio and interests.

While this example mimics the Premier Pages at Dell.com, it takes the dynamic publishing model a few steps further. With a mouse click, the system can publish the pages in Spanish—a feature enabled by Unicode double-byte characters and a database containing vetted Spanish translations. For key user interface features and graphics, mouseover movements produce voiceovers (describing functions and interpreting captions) in perfectly inflected Spanish—using the Beatnik interactive audio technology. Using the same compositional profile, the publishing system will produce portfolio reports, white papers, and other collateral on the fly, assembling and distilling PDF documents on high-speed servers. The whole process happens fast enough to build updated-at-the-very-last-minute portions of the materials as soon as Don Jimenez clicks the "download" button, binding them to pre-existing documents for immediate download. The system also gives Don Jimenez the option to have a PDF e-mailed to his lawyer and children, or printed and mailed to these same parties.

Because the brokerage house understands the importance of audio-visual brand resources and their ability to cross cultural divides, this same dynamic publishing system can quickly assemble English- and Spanish-language streaming video and audio programs, including items licensed from CNBC, CNNFN, and Bloomberg, as well as syndicated radio stock analysis and the brokerage house's own internal subject matter experts. Audio assets may also derive from telephone interviews with satisfied customers and corporate executives at the featured company. The Web site may deliver MP3 audio objects encoded from streaming audio sources. Instead of pre-encoding, the customer previews the streaming audio; then the system distills the requested MP3 objects.

Customer Relationship Management (CRM)

Often referred to as front-office applications, dozens of leading software vendors now offer a variety of solutions called customer relationship management (CRM). Many of these CRM applications grew from help desk solutions used principally by customer service and technical support specialists. Other CRM applications evolved from contact management and sales force automation solutions, helping front-line field sales or service executives manage their relationships with customers by offering calendars, schedules, etc. Most of these CRM applications represent three-tier client-server systems and have not yet evolved into fully Webified n-tier applications. As a result, they remain clumsy and non-intuitive when delivered on the Web. CRM will grow rapidly, especially when linked to the universal brand-stakeholder subscription service and dynamic 1:1 cross-media publishing.

Real-Time Synchronized Transactions

Building upon the universal brand-stakeholder subscription service, CRM, analysis-driven direct marketing, and dynamic 1:1 cross-media publishing, firebrand firms must synchronize internal and external transactions in real-time. Managers may soon discover that they can't get there from here: core business processes and production data systems will not work 24/7 in an n-tier client-server infrastructure accessed via the Internet. Major stumbling blocks include: the basics of how to characterize a customer with data, how to compute interest, taxes, and tariffs across two or more production data systems (each in a time zone other than Greenwich mean time), passing data from one system to another without violating security protocols and database integrity—the list goes on.

In practical terms, when a customer pays for an item with a credit card, all other systems linked to that transaction should immediately track this transaction. Going back to another example we discussed earlier, Barnes & Noble's systems apparently could not handle this requirement. They didn't know Doug's status as an Affiliate. They only had a portion of Doug's transaction history and didn't know he was spending $200 per month on books, nor did they have a record of his past customer-service problems and frustrations. And they lacked a way to communicate quickly with a local bricks-and-mortar store to request a same-day courier delivery of the items he wanted. This whole situation erupted when Barnes & Noble sold Doug a product not in inventory—a product data management breakdown.

While data integration remains a huge and vexing challenge, two additional factors exacerbate the difficulty: the need for a robust, fault-tolerant server network, and the need for a middleware platform into which hundreds, and potentially hundreds of thousands of affiliates, platform partners, and individual customers can plug in. In addition, supply chains and demand chains need to integrate and interoperate with this middleware platform and server network.

Web-integrated database marketing and sales represents a compelling investment for the small- to mid-sized firm whose legacy data and bureaucracy have not reached suffocating proportions, although they will need some sweetener for this bitter pill: the true cost of deploying the wrong system often exceeds the price of simply throwing it away and starting over again. If you come from one of these firms, make sure that your CEO understands both the business and technical implications of real-time, synchronized transactions and the critical necessity of getting there sooner rather than later. We believe that a small- to medium-sized firm able to successfully reposition itself as a fully Webified enterprise (actually performing real-time synchronized transactions) can command dot.com-style valuations of 100x (or more) earnings.

This daunting reality of enterprisewide data integration helps explain why dot.coms with a native, built-right-from-the-ground-up n-tier, client-server business process will rightly command stratospheric business valuations for the foreseeable future. Traditional firms—those with substantial legacy data systems and which have not developed the capability to re-engineer or engineer from scratch systems that meet these requirements—should consider merging with a dot.com start-up that has already mastered web-integrated database marketing and sales.

Best Practice #5: Globalize Your Firebrand

Your firebranding strategy must address worldwide markets. Even the smallest firms can find customers outside the U.S. More important, even within U.S. boundaries, the increasing number of immigrant groups who speak English as a second language suggest the need for a "global" approach. Many firms have simply ignored this, focusing instead on the need to establish a deep gravity well supersite eCommerce presence with the intention of developing a global strategy in a later phase. Such a strategy may have merit, but in this section we hope to persuade you to develop a global firebrand framework before creating legacy systems that will make it more difficult and costly later on.

Large firms that already market products and services in international markets have already encountered many of the challenges and issues of creating a crisp, consistent, focused brand identity in international markets. As we suggested in "Best Practice #1, Build a Corporate Firebranding Systems," effective global brands require the expertise of brand consultancies experienced in developing international, cross-cultural brand identities. For more on this, we suggest that you read David Aaker's book, *Building Strong Brands*. Here, we focus on the firebranding needs of the small to medium-sized firm, asking the question, What can you do to globalize your brand identity?

In all cases, effective delivery of a globalized firebrand requires effective deployment of an n-tier, client-server computing infrastructure that we call the iCorp.

Strong Branding Authority with Worldwide Focus

In Chapter 3 we discussed how branding authority evolves (or devolves) through a corporate lifecycle. This discussion highlighted the best practice of a CEO leading the branding process as a fiduciary responsibility. This means that the CEO uses effective brand management to bolster shareholder confidence and maintain share price.

We also discussed the need for a crisp and focused positioning strategy that distills the one idea (a desired or expected satisfaction) and imprints it in the minds and hearts of one customer segment. As that relates to a self-service satisfaction of your branded Web site, your firebrand positioning will frame one interaction (that produces the desired or expected satisfaction). Many companies discover that the offline brand positioning conflicts with the positioning of the self-service interaction. This can lead to the creation of a second and usually weaker digital brand or, even worse, a muddled and confusing extension of the offline brand.

For example, BMW has created a focused, offline brand positioning around the experience of the "ultimate driving machine." As the company continues to build its online firebrand, they must ask, what one self-service satisfaction does our firebrand reflect and amplify? Classic positioning theory would dictate that BMW reinforce its "ultimate driving machine" positioning online. But people visit the BMW Web site not to find the "ultimate driving machine" but instead to satisfy a different need: "Which model should I buy?" "I have a problem for which I need a solution." "I want a join an enthusiasts club or community of practice." Offline and online brand positioning must match.

In Chapter 4, we discussed the firebrand planning process, highlighting the need for an ongoing brand audit and analysis as well as a task-driven training system (companywide use of software applications and templates for training).

Building on these elements, a CEO-led branding team or a brand tsar (a founder, chairman, or executive VP with a personal stake in the branding process) leads an effort to expand the firebrand to a worldwide audience. The CEO or brand tsar must have extensive international experience and should probably speak and write fluently in some language other than English. Given that most senior executives do not fit this criteria, we make three recommendations.

First, they should follow the example of CEOs in Asian and European countries who learn the languages of their important international markets. Augment this by reading books that explain the subtleties of doing business in particular national markets and regions.

Next, they submit themselves to the coaching of a strategic brand consultancy that partners with the firm on a long-term basis. This engagement might include the structuring and management of their quarterly brand planning conferences.

Finally, I have found that the fastest, most effective way to learn the nuances of another culture results from studying the religious traditions that frame the moral and ethical context of a society and its legal system. If you seek success in China, for example, know the basic tenets of Taoism, Confucianism, Buddhism, and Maoism (Mao Tse-tung's personal interpretation of Marxist-Leninism).

Global Storytelling

Brand managers must learn the nuanced art of thinking globally and telling stories locally.

Eliminate "American Imperialism"

We strongly recommend that you engage a global brand consultancy, ideally one with mastery of both online and offline brand positioning. Only a handful of integrated communications agencies have the breadth and depth necessary to tell a cohesive, compelling, relevant, and effective story across all of the world's major markets and cultures. In the Networked Economy, these agencies play a pivotal role in helping companies build global firebrands. Their highest value comes in two critical areas: vetting a brand to eliminate traces of "American imperialism" and branding globally while speaking locally.

Popular commercial brands emerged as a unique business expression of American culture that companies outside the U.S. have largely mimicked over the past 50 years in the same way that cultures around the world have embraced and integrated other uniquely American idioms such as Hollywood films, rock and roll music, and computer software. When a company takes one of these brands into a foreign market, it bears the deep imprint of American culture, morality, ambition, and social class structures. If not modified, these values often polarize a market into pro- and anti-American camps.

Nike, a brash, aggressive brand, encapsulates the ferocious competitiveness of American spectator sports. When Nike began to build its brand in the international soccer market, it brought this same American story and dressed it in soccer garb. They produced a television commercial that showed Satan kicking a soccer ball that shot like a comet right through the goalie's chest to score a goal. It so shocked parents and children in Europe that Nike had to pull the ad. The underlying story that Nike was trying to sell—that Nike provides an inhuman competitive advantage—proved too American for the market.

Apple's "Think Different" campaign ran into similar problems, especially in cultures that have experienced centuries of abuse by strong kings and autocrats as well as shameful persecution of their artists and intellectuals. Instead of reflecting the noble ideals of ingenuity and creative self-expression, some Europeans saw the campaign as a reminder of the entrepreneurial spirits their local cultures have suppressed and the cynical mistrust of the great personages of history. When Americans see a picture of Albert Einstein, he represents genius and the ability of ideas to change the world. Rosa Parks, and Jackie Robinson crossing home plate, symbolize the indomitable American spirit of freedom. But Europeans tended to view these celebrities with a cynical, "Yeah, but—," pointing to Einstein's misogyny, Robinson's struggle against racial hatred, etc.

Every brand either consciously or unwittingly conveys a worldview and a set of human values that reflect the culture of their origin. Thus, American executives must work doubly hard to pierce the "tranquilized veil of obviousness"—the basic unexamined assumptions of what constitutes a human being and a life well-lived within their culture of origin. They can learn a lot from European brands such as Gucci, Ferrari, Michelin, Heineken, and Japanese brands such as Mighty Morphin' Power Rangers, which arrive on American shores with the advantage of having developed storytelling that transcends the culturally imposed filters of their country of origin.

Brand Globally, Speak Locally

An international brand consultancy will have fluency in how slogans, keywords, and phrases can translate into elegant local idiom. To achieve this, brand managers must often rethink or redefine the voice of the brand in terms of more abstract values and principles that local brand storytelling can translate into the appropriate forms. In practical terms, this means surrendering attachment to one particular word and embracing other expressions that resonate with its spirit but may not necessarily translate in literal terms. We see this most clearly in the translation of brand names from English into Chinese or other Asian languages that don't use the roman alphabet.

For example, Pepsi in China becomes "Bai xi," meaning "one hundred happinesses." Far from a clumsy translation, the Chinese phrase conveys the abundance of the sort of all-encompassing "happiness" we express in the phrase "Happy New Year!"

When Federal Express expanded into international operations, it needed to rapidly globalize its brand. They engaged Landor Associates to help in this pivotal transformation. Extensive field research revealed a number of plusses and minuses associated with the Federal Express brand identity. The bright purple and orange color scheme stood out as one of the most distinctive features of the brand. These colors carried rich cultural significance around the world, associated with royalty (purple) and celebration and religious devotion (orange). At the same time, they discovered that many customers had begun using a shortened version of the company name, FedEx, and used it as a verb, "I'll FedEx it to you today. (While lawyers try to persuade brand managers to suppress verb use of a brand name, for reasons of intellectual property protection, they miss entirely a more important point: the most potent, vital expression of a brand always comes in the form of a verb. Encourage its use as such and tell your lawyers to go bark up another tree. They don't know diddly about branding.)

Landor's field research also revealed some negatives. The Federal Express drop-off kiosks got lost among competitive kiosks. The company's business forms were confusing—difficult to read, with too many options. And, most important, the term "federal" carries a particularly distasteful association in Latin American countries with histories of citizen abuse by "federales"—military organizations used for domestic political control.

The upshot? They kept the colors, simplified the forms, and increased the height of the kiosks to let them tower over the competition. And, they settled on FedEx as the brand name for the global brand. To articulate the new brand identity, they produced a highly successful CD-ROM called PRPL (Personal Reference and Presentation Library) containing digital files of all brand identity elements in both black and white and color versions, all business forms, plus pre-built templates for signage, posters, uniforms, stationery. The CD-ROM also contained more than 100 PowerPoint and Persuasion slide shows complete with graphics, several hundred megabytes of clip art, a library of letters, thank-you notes, and formal businesses proposals, plus QuickTime movies and multimedia animations suitable for use in presentations and electronic kiosks. Now, FedEx makes this material available to international partners through an intranet.

International Voice of the Brand

For many international customers, your Web site will serve as the first, and often the primary, point of contact. Don't assume that overseas customers know your firm's background, history, leadership, or major customers. Fill them in on the back story, but with an important caveat: customers in some countries outside the US may consider it more critically important to form a personal relationship with a key executive, as a peer. This means that key executives should have their own personal home pages nested with the firm's Web site to help tell the firm's story in human terms, beyond the mere functional details of what the firm does, sells, etc. Putting a human face on your firebrand represents a key step in globalizing it.

Before taking the obvious step of translating your Web site into various languages, we highly recommend a necessary but painful first step. Systematically impose a writing style guide for all text published on the Web site that produces short sentences (less than 20 words) and active, transitive verb constructions. This makes it easy for an individual who reads English as a second language to quickly comprehend the sentence. This practice also produces text optimized for on-the-fly machine translation, such as Babelfish and other Web translation services. We anticipate the emergence of next-generation translation software packages that will dynamically translate "digerata" English text into a variety of languages for publication in a Web site and in e-mail.

Here, a vocabulary and attributes database begins to pay big dividends. By adding an interactive capability, a company can invite its international stakeholders—and employees fluent in those languages—to help fine tune translations of key words and phrases intimately linked to the brand.

Whenever possible, reduce wordy narratives to crisp, well-designed infographics that use a minimum of text but which convey the scope, ratio, and relationship of key ideas, processes, and interactions. These convey the most important aspect of any good translation: context that produces meaning for the content.

If you have used infographics in this manner, giving visitors to the Web site the ability to receive local language text for the diagrams represents far less work than a full translation. Even better, use a technology like the Beatnik Player to provide interactive "voiceover" translations—triggered by mouseover moves—for key concepts depicted in an infographic.

Training

McDonald's demonstrates that a global service brand results from systemization of training for front-line staff and all management levels. Every store manager graduates from Hamburger University and attends refresher courses at regular intervals. Andersen Consulting has grown its global business through the systematic training of new hires. Federal Express uses a recruitment and selection model to choose their drivers, then trains them systematically.

Systematic recruiting, selection, and training drive an effective global firebranding effort. The brand-producing firm must train its marketing, sales, and service teams, as well as the vendors that work with them, to support a concerted global firebranding program. This lets a company's front-line sales and service actors hit their marks and deliver their lines in accordance with the brand theater script and deliver the same buying and using experience around the world. This means giving them tools like FedEx's PRPL and the training necessary to use such tools well.

At the same time, brand producing firms need to "train" customers and potential customers in successfully buying and using the product or service in question, enabling them to answer their essential questions as they move through the satisfaction lifecycle.

Happily, one infrastructure serves both purposes: the brand producing firm's deep gravity well supersite. The Web site and associated intranets and extranets deliver training and education to emerging communities of practice, including employees of the brand producer firm and self-service customers. This requires development or licensing of specialized eServices: atomized, self-directed learning mechanisms in native languages for maximum reach within particular national markets.

Atomized, Self-directed Learning Technologies

Effective self-directed learning starts with a realistic assessment of the student's present capability. This calls for standardized, diagnostic aptitude tests. The results of this test guide development of three important elements: the course plan, presentation formats optimized for the student's connative learning style, and offerings of traditional offline support services (classroom instruction, books, etc.).

Atomized, self-directed learning represents a multimedia application stack built on top of your brand resource repository and cross-media messaging ("Best Practice #1, Build a Corporate Firebranding System"), unified messaging ("Best Practice #2, Net-Integrated Communications"), unit-of-work routing and approval ("Best Practice #3, Implement Integrated Projects Management"), and dynamic 1:1 publishing ("Best Practice #4, Master Web-Integrated Database Marketing and Sales").

This application stack delivers many resources: an extensive library of streaming audio and video programs; structured forums (live chat, bulletin boards, and e-mail); a well-managed database of essential questions and links to answers and related resources; shared two- and three-dimensional objects (models of products and processes—to describe and document a complex piece of machinery or surgical procedure, for example); and workbooks that may include portions (tests, for example) produced on-the-fly by the dynamic publishing system. Time-activity accounting ("Best Practice #3, Implement Integrated Projects Management") lets managers audit the learning process and isolate problem areas.

Employees will use these self-directed learning modules to learn how to deliver the desired buying and using experience. Customers will use the same system—with views tailored to their particular needs as customers—to answer essential questions as they move through the satisfaction lifecycle for a product or service. Brand managers will use the same training system to identify problems related to the training process and, by extension, to monitor how effectively they manage the buying and selling experience of customers.

For example, employees who interact with customers but who do not know how to use the advanced features of a company's voice-mail system run the risk of needlessly frustrating customers. The same holds for e-mail and other messaging systems. Such an atomized, self-directed learning system would enable a brand manager to test employees to determine their levels of competency with these tools and automatically configure curricula designed to remedy their specific shortcomings—using the uniform issue-problem characterization capability of "Best Practice #3, Implement Integrated Projects Management."

The ESL Opportunity

This same platform, used to train employees and guide customers through a satisfaction lifecycle, can also be used to draw employees and other stakeholders into a deeper relationship with the brand.

What better opportunity to use the story of a brand as the subject matter for an overall English fluency educational program? This delivers a number of benefits.

Such a program immerses an employee in the brand, its satisfactions, and the stories that bind customers and other stakeholders to the brand, while raising the employee's level of English reading, writing, and speaking. As they become fully immersed in the brand, they become more productive and better able to handle a range of tasks and responsibilities. This also represents a learning resource that an employee's family members—important stakeholders in weaving a worldwide trust network and friend-of-friend referrals—can use to improve their English skills. Not only do they become more fluent in English, they also become effective brand advocates and evangelists. These family members will also feel much more comfortable about investing in 401(K) and other ESOP benefit programs, creating an important, low-cost source of capital for the firm.

In non-English-speaking countries, customers and their families often perceive fluency in English as a critical economic skill of direct and immediate benefits. Not only do customers learn how to successfully buy and use a product or service, they can command higher wages or take advantage of new business opportunities. One can only imagine the brand loyalty that could result. ESL as a branding strategy can also mitigate the perception of a U.S. brand as a reflection of American cultural imperialism.

IT Infrastructure to Support Global, 24/7 Operations

Globalizing a firebranding also means engineering core business processes and IT infrastructures to support worldwide operations within and across national boundaries. This requires two key elements: an n-tier client-server computing architecture and global logistics fulfillment.

Throughout this book we have discussed the need for Webified applications and an n-tier client-server infrastructure. We have linked a variety of applications and capabilities to this infrastructure, emphasizing the need for robust, 24/7 mission-critical performance. Let's examine this in greater detail.

As illustrated in Figure 5-26, any number of individuals from various stakeholder groups access the iCorp infrastructure through eMediaspace using a variety of IP devices, including computers, handhelds, telephones, mobile wireless systems, and a burgeoning array of consumer devices in the pipeline.

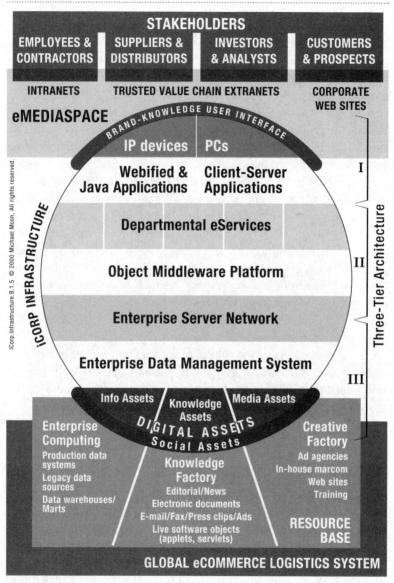

Figure 5-26 This model depicts the basic infrastructure of every successful enterprise in the Networked Economy. It highlights several technical deployments that represent make-or-break decisions for your firm

Our model highlights the principal branding device for a fire-brand: the *brand knowledge user interface*. As discussed previously, each stakeholder may have a user interface optimized for his or her productivity as well as specific rights and permissions for accessing iCorp infrastructure and applications. This interface not only serves as a human interface, it also serves as a de facto "user manual" for self-service customers and other stakeholders. This means that fire-brand managers must take extra care in providing user documentation, tutorials, vocabulary, intuitive search capabilities, and extensive information engineering.

While this model emphasizes a single user, it can also support iCorp-to-iCorp interactions necessary for value chain relationships.

The run-up to Y2K and the publicity surrounding it compelled many companies to upgrade their core IT systems to three-tier client-server deployments, most notably strategic applications such as enterprise resource planning (ERP). A three-tier client-server architecture distributes computing power across a network. Mainframe computers do what they do best (fast number crunching and processing), network servers manage network functions (e-mail, etc.), with personal computers used as terminals on the network, accessing mainframes and servers as necessary when local processing power does not suffice.

Many CIOs have discovered that requirements for eCommerce do not naturally fit with those of a three-tier client-server system. In many cases, three-tier applications require extensive user training in arcane and complex practices, with remote access and security addressed only as afterthoughts. Many of these applications do not function correctly via Web browser access, due to Internet latency and the peculiarities of browser applications.

Nonetheless, many companies have begun to Webify these applications, using a new class of software called application servers or more robust middleware platforms which we will discuss in more detail later in this chapter. Beginning in earnest in 1999, the software industry responded to customer needs for Webified applications that represent native n-tier applications developed with Java and using an industry-standard CORBA (Common Object Request Broker Architecture). They now offer core applications designed from the ground up specifically for use through a Web browser, as opposed to creating a special piece of software (the "client" in client-server) that a specialist must install and maintain on an individual's personal computer.

In contrast, *n-tier architecture* exploits the strengths and overcomes the weaknesses of computing through the Internet. It enables application developers and systems managers to quickly link up any number of (the "n" in n-tier) separate computer systems or applications into a cohesive and integrated system. A system may include an entire data center with mainframes or something as simple as a Palm Pilot. Instead of a local area network, n-tier enables movement of data over a wide-area network such as the Internet taking into account latencies, security needs, and the differing requirements of end-use platforms and browsers.

Departmental eServices represent the front-line of the iCorp. Every departmental function of a corporation in the Networked Economy will become a 24/7, interactive, self-service facility. Personnel, purchasing, legal, technical support, publishing services, product development, testing—each becomes an interactive service provider, available to both internal employees and external stakeholders (especially those of the firm's supply chain), over the Internet. Business managers should think of each department as something to outsource and then ask the make, buy, or rent question: should we outsource this departmental activity, or should we make it a fully interactive department and become an outsource provider to our trade partners?

For example, General Electric purchases over $40 billion of business and industrial products and services annually. GE has created an online procurement system, called TPN, that has eliminated internal, paper-based purchase requisitions and purchase orders. GE built the system to eliminate transaction costs associated with paper handling, estimated at above $120 per purchase order. Because of the volume of GE purchases, their suppliers give them huge discounts and most favorable terms. In turn, GE offers its 17,000 external trade partners the use of TPN for their own procurement, sharing the GE discount and terms. GE thus transformed a cost center into a profit-producing, external-customer-serving business unit.

We anticipate that every departmental function will undergo a similar transformation.

As the iCorp transforms itself into an interactive eService provider for employees and other stakeholders, it needs a platform with which to encode and program business logic and rules for each interactive eService. Our research shows that the only effective way to execute this strategy exploits a robust object middleware platform. This special class of software resides on servers at the heart of an n-tier architecture. Based on CORBA, it allows internal or external applications developers to quickly integrate new business functions or applications that work together seamlessly with each other and with existing applications. This middleware platform enjoys a huge and growing library of specialized adapters that enable an application developer to quickly hook up and interoperate with an existing mainframe, minicomputer, or server application or database. This means that a company can continue to use legacy mainframe and minicomputer systems, using the middleware to Webify them as well as to integrate new, n-tier applications—all seamlessly integrated to the Web browser-based brand knowledge user interface. Additional middleware adapters and plug-ins let application developers drive all of the applications discussed so far in this chapter. For this reason alone, your choice of object-based middleware becomes the most important business decision that your company will make in the next five years. The wrong choice will mean that you will fail to adapt to exigencies of the Networked Economy.

In the right hands, object middleware facilitates one of the most stunning developments in the Networked Economy: blindingly fast plug-and-play mergers and acquisitions—the ability to quickly buy and assimilate new businesses. For example, Nations Bank went from a small, regional banking operation to a global competitor in large part due to their middleware capability. They could quickly integrate the banking systems of dozens of newly acquired banks and quickly offer new services to their customers.

N-tier client-server computing requires an extraordinary network of enterprise-class servers. These servers must provide high reliability, high availability, and rapid scalability. Reliability means that they don't crash and, if they do crash, they notify other servers on the network to pick up the slack. Availability means that if hundreds or thousands of users access computing resources, the server can reprioritize resource allocation to serve the increased demand. Scalability means that a firm can easily add additional servers, storage subsystems, and other peripherals as required, providing the ability to quickly expand capacity, including the option of distributing some of a firm's computing load to outsource providers. For these reasons, most companies with mission-critical, high-performance computing needs have standardized on one of four versions of Unix, from IBM, Hewlett-Packard, Compaq, or Sun Microsystems.

The iCorp amasses huge quantities of data, much of it not usable in its current form. Even in the forty-fifth year of the Information Age, over 90 percent of business information still resides in paper: faxes, invoices, purchase orders, documentation, and other business records.

In our iCorp infrastructure model, we identify several categories of data that require management. This underscores the need for an enterprise data management system.

Media assets derive from the creative factory, comprising photos, illustrations, and other art elements used in corporate communications and branding.

Knowledge workers create *knowledge assets*, characterized by unstructured data usually stored in word processing, spreadsheet, presentation, e-mail, and other application software outputs. Knowledge workers consume these assets, transforming them into answers or more questions.

Information assets represent rows and columns of structured data derived from production data systems. IT and MIS departments design systems that condition this production data and make it available to employees and other stakeholders through a Web browser. Production data becomes an economic asset when it helps build the brand, facilitates trusted interactive relationships, and enables transactions—all activities that have economic value by which to benchmark these information assets. As discussed previously, the customer database record becomes the most important information asset of the iCorp. Without it, the iCorp flies blind.

Social assets represent a digital file that contains an active request for action, a promise or the fulfillment of a promise (an answer). If mishandled, a relationship suffers. Social assets include voice-mail, e-mail, faxes, and other forms of business communications, but only while the relationship remains active. After the particular cycle ends, these items become knowledge or media assets—a completed unit of work.

Projected enhancements to Oracle and IBM RDBMS will make it easier to manage all of these digital assets by automatically transferring them, as knowledge workers create and store them, from personal computers to the enterprise data management systems. This means that all units of work produced by knowledge workers will reside in an enterprise repository, enabling higher levels of automation, unit of work routing, and timed-activity accounting for individual knowledge workers.

This iCorp IT infrastructure model describes the computing architecture of many successful dot.com start-ups, further explaining the valuations that they enjoy, especially when traditional companies target them as acquisitions to quickly enter the Networked Economy.

In terms of globalizing your firebrand, this iCorp architecture plugs into a global logistics infrastructure—an array of companies that operate in the background to assemble, package, ship, install, support, and train, if necessary, end use customers in all markets. An iCorp fueled by its middleware platform and n-tier client-server architecture can quickly take advantage of these outsource logistics suppliers.

In addition to logistics fulfillment, these logistics suppliers may provide a spectrum of other services necessary to a global firebrand. For example, Federal Express offers its call center, staffed with employees fluent in all of the languages for parts of the world where they do business, on an outsourced basis to its customers, including small- to mid-sized firms. We expect these global logistics fulfillment firms to expand such offerings to include net-integrated communications capabilities, integrated projects management facilities, globalized Web-integrated database marketing and sales systems, and even distance learning and skills development curricula including ESL and basic end-user computing skills.

Best Practice #6: Build an Entrepreneurial eServices Platform

Your firebranding strategy will soar when you have mastered this best practice. It represents the integration of the previous five best practices, giving you the ability to rapidly drive new eServices to the shocking delight and wow of customers and other stakeholders. This best practice requires that the brand producing firm master the art and science of commercializing a potentially disruptive innovation. Firms do this by creating highly effective teams, engendering a culture of support for ingenuity, and a federal structure within which to test the viability of a new eService offering and launch it. This best practice incorporates many of the lessons learned from dot.com incubators and accelerators such as Softbank, IdeaLabs, CMGI, Divine Interventures, Garage.com, and others.

Do It Now

The entrepreneurial eServices platform begins to take shape with the addition of three important capabilities: "Get IT solution" showcases, cycletime audit methodology, and T.I.G.E.R. units, as illustrated in Figure 5-27.

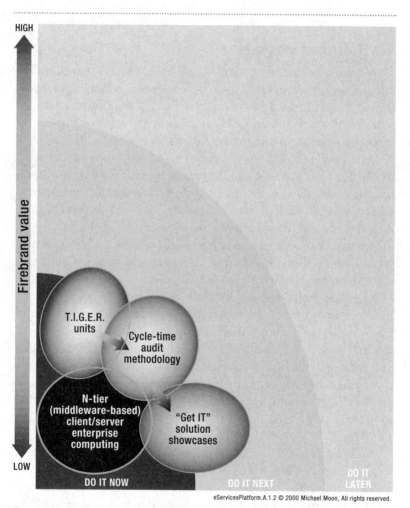

Figure 5-27 Brand managers can quickly harness the power of teams, technology innovations, and activity-based audit methodologies in this do-it-now stage

N-Tier Client/Server Enterprise Computing Platform

Before beginning to implement this best practice, the brand producing firm must first have in place the iCorp infrastructure described in "Best Practice #5" (Figure 5-26), plus net-integrated communications, integrated projects management, and substantial portions of Web-integrated database management and sales from best practices described earlier.

"Get IT" Solution Showcases

The explosion of enabling technologies has made it extraordinarily difficult for companies to track new developments that might form the basis for successful new eServices. "Get IT" solution showcases represent a way to systematically expose current and potential firebrand managers and eService entrepreneurs to new technologies.

In practical terms, this means a systematic, ongoing research activity of what's hot and new, and the presentation of these things. Traditionally, companies have relied on professional and trade magazines, conferences and exhibitions, and seminars and workshops to introduce members of the organization to these new technologies. Given the rapid pace of new technology innovation, these traditional methods no longer suffice. In response, Web portals like c|net, ZDnet, and others have emerged to help spread the news.

Firebrand managers need to take a more proactive course. They must actively seek out new technologies, applications, and solutions that can fuel the next round of firebranding. This requires three things: a road map that highlights various categories of technologies and solutions (the ones we discuss in this chapter), a business intelligence gathering process managed by a specialist in technology trends and solutions research, and a filing system managed by a librarian to consolidate and track information about new technologies and solutions.

We strongly recommend that the firebranding team meets regularly to examine what new technologies and solutions might have fruitful applications for their brand. We track several dot.com startups that do this on a weekly basis and have designated one individual to serve as the lead scout. The scout scours the 'net for promising new developments, participates in dozens of online forums where she can pose "What's new and cool?" questions to a community of peers, and scans 50 to 75 magazines per month, clipping and filing articles.

We also recommend that firms convene a "Get IT" showcase at least quarterly, where marketing, sales, and service executives can learn from demos of promising new technologies, tools, and solutions. These showcase events can take place in corporate lunchrooms or amphitheaters, or in a rented hall. In many cases, it makes sense for half a dozen companies to sponsor an all-day "solutions fair" to showcase as many as 20 presentations from the most promising vendors and solutions providers uncovered by research. For example, take the applications described in net-integrated communications (e-mail, call center integration, discussion forums, etc.) and invite the 15 or 20 vendors to demo their solutions.

The "Get IT" solution showcase has one aim: introduce promising new solutions to a member of your firebrand team who will say, "Eureka! I'm going to drill that into this market!"

T.I.G.E.R. Units

How do brand managers test to see if a particular idea has eService potential? They come from individuals and small groups inspired with the possibility and who subsequently take concrete action to realize their dream.

Management consultants and theorists have long documented how most organizations do not encourage this behavior but instead ignore, if not outright suppress, these kinds of expressions. In fact, many of the extraordinary dot.com business successes derive from entrepreneurial thinking that could not flourish within the originator's corporate environment, finding expression only after leaving the firm. The venture capital community has grown extraordinarily wealthy by funding such entrepreneurial efforts. We see no reason why medium- to large-sized firms cannot replicate the incubator function now prevalent in the dot.com community and harness this talent and business opportunity for their firebrands.

Figure 5-28 illustrates a way that a firm can evaluate and harness innovation to meet business objectives. Most firms ask themselves if they have the resources to commercialize a new innovation. By resources they usually mean people and capital equipment. Clayton Christensen, Harvard professor and author of the book, *The Innovator's Dilemma* (Harvard Business School Press, 1997), argues that management must instead closely examine two other dimensions of their ability to commercialize innovation.

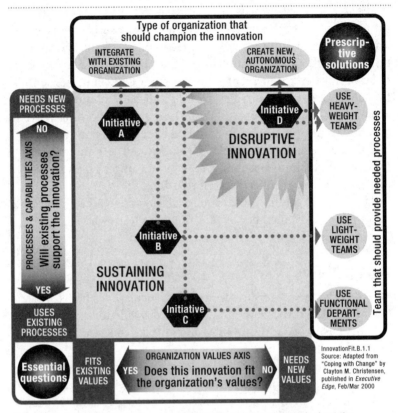

Note: the left and bottom axes pose questions the manager must ask about the innovation. The right side shows the appropriate response to the situation on the left axis. The top shows the appropriate response to the question posed on the bottom axis.

Figure 5-28 Firebrand managers must ask whether a new eService represents a disruptive innovation or a sustaining one, and investigate how well it fits with organizational values

Managers must ask two questions. Does the innovation fit organizational values? Will existing processes support this innovation? If the innovation shows a strong fit but needs new organizational processes to support it, managers must create "heavyweight teams" to build the new supporting processes. If the innovation shows strong fit and existing organization processes can support it, managers can simply deploy it within the existing organization.

But if an innovation does not show good fit and if existing processes won't support it, management must create a detached, autonomous organization to successfully commercialize the innovation. Corporate culture and the established distribution of power and authority (as discussed in the section on corporate lifecycles earlier in the book) thus play an important and largely overlooked role. For this reason the innovation advantage falls to mid-sized firms that retain an entrepreneurial spirit and in which the CEO can tolerate and support heavyweight teams that champion a new, disruptive innovation.

As they execute a firebranding strategy and seek to develop new eServices for stakeholders, brand managers can use Christensen's questions to determine what kind of innovation these eServices represent and thus decide whether to establish teams inside or outside their existing organizations. We call these teams (both heavyweight and lightweight) T.I.G.E.R. (Teams Integrated Getting Excellent Results) units.

A T.I.G.E.R. unit tests the viability of new eServices based on innovative ideas that originate elsewhere in the brand producing firm—from the company's visionary CEO or technical personnel, perhaps. The team includes three to seven people who put the idea for a new eService through a role-playing exercise that can determine whether or not the company should take on such a project, and how to deploy it if they decide to do so.

For example, the Discovery Channel set out to deploy a media asset management system that would make it easier to find and retrieve film, video, sound, and still image media assets for internal use or for licensing to other companies that need such capability. The general manager commissioned a T.I.G.E.R. unit comprised of six people who played the following roles:

▶ The business manager who had the vision for a new online licensing business unit, a new satisfaction she wanted to bring to market

▶ An IT professional who would have to support the new service with technical infrastructure, insisting on certain standards and deployment practices

▶ The librarian/archivist who would run the application

▶ The on-air promotions person who needed speedy access to specific kinds of scenes

▶ The international marketing manager who needed to replace certain segments of the show to meet local needs

▶ A program producer looking for footage and other media assets for use in a broadcast or print project

First, the team discussed their needs for the new service and created, on paper, a description of the system they thought would fit their needs. At the urging of the Discovery Channel manager who mandated the team, they conducted a competitive assessment and benchmarked how a dozen independent stock media houses organize their assets for speedy retrieval, the kinds of requests they receive from various types of customers, and their billing practices.

In the process, they discovered many requirements that they had not anticipated in their earlier brainstorming. In particular, they discovered the need for a robust, master keyword indexing system by which to facilitate intuitive retrievals by non-technical creative staff and producers. They also discovered the need to link still image and video assets into logical groups, and several other system requirements. They used this new information to put together a new system specification.

Next, they performed business modeling. How many people would use the system? How much time would it save various types of users? How much incremental revenue would such a system produce if offered to external paying customers? How many new products or programs could they produce by reusing existing material (as opposed to going out and producing new material)? They also investigated the costs of digitizing, indexing, and storing these media assets online. Here they discovered that full commercial realization would require several thousands of hours of digitization and indexing—an expense that, in the absence of the ROI benchmark they had developed, might have scuttled the project. They knew they could recover the expense but achieve a multifold return on investment in both hard and soft dollars.

The team then used role playing to explore how deployment of the new system might proceed, examining issues related to the user interface, specialized client software for Macintosh and Windows platforms, integration with video post-production systems, server and network bandwidth capabilities, and a number of other technical issues. They also modeled personnel and workflow issues, identifying possible choke points, policies and procedures that might have to change, and identified the need to move to a two-shift schedule for digitization and cataloguing.

They presented an operational business plan that specified cash flow requirements, resources, deployment milestones, a list of possible problems and contingency plans, and a return-on-investment calculation. The general manager approved the project and the Discovery Channel built the system.

The Discovery Channel learned the hard way how to harness the power of a T.I.G.E.R. unit. We offer a three-phase roadmap you can follow to guarantee a never-ending stream of viable new eService offerings.

Brand managers must create and support a T.I.G.E.R. unit for each major firebranding initiative. We recommend that brand managers use a formalized recruitment and selection methodology to identify the essential connative and cognitive skill sets necessary for a successful team.

In this context, *connative* means native or instinctual modes of expression and interaction with others in a group. For more on this, we highly recommend either of Kathy Kolbe's books, *Connative Connection* (Addison Wesley Pub. Co. reprint) or *Pure Instinct* (Times Books, 1993). According to Kolbe, four elements of connative expression mix to give each individual a unique connative style, and when they operate within the parameters of that style, they achieve their most productive and satisfying results. The four connative elements include quick start; fact find; implement; and follow-through. Kolbe has mapped over 4,000 professional job roles in over 1,000 task-oriented teams, each with an optimum mix of these connative styles among team members. PricewaterhouseCoopers, SAP, and Norwest have licensed and adopted Kolbe's methodology.

In this context, cognitive characterizes mental aptitudes and skills such as the ability to synthesize information to create new solutions, to think abstractly, to logically organize an argument—the kinds of abilities that standard IQ or aptitude tests measure. T.I.G.E.R. units must also balance the reader/thinker and talker/listener cognitive skill sets identified by Peter Drucker in his latest book, *Management Challenges for the 21ˢᵗ Century*. Reader/thinkers assimilate information principally through reading, and express themselves in writing. Talker/listeners assimilate information through personal interactions (meetings, phone calls), and express themselves by talking.

Having assembled a T.I.G.E.R. unit, the brand manager gives it the task of preflighting a potential eService for deployment.

As in the Discovery Channel example, the T.I.G.E.R. unit includes the business manager who assumes overall responsibility for taking the new eService to market. For example, somebody in your customer service group might want an online forum devoted to a particular set of customer needs. They have the knowledge, passion, and commitment to drive this forum (a new eService) to the customer base.

The business manager needs a reality checker, generally the IT specialist who can think in terms of the technical infrastructure and resources necessary to field the service and who can identify technical roadblocks that will need to be overcome.

This T.I.G.E.R. unit needs at least one person who represents the principal stakeholder to which the business manager wants to target the new eService. This stakeholder representative should have an intimate knowledge of the kind of problem that this new eService seeks to solve. In the Discovery Channel case, the team needed three people to voice the stakeholder needs.

The team also needs a support and communications facilitator who handles administrative tasks and manages the group to-do list, calendar, research, and other functions.

Cycletime Audit Methodology

Every T.I.G.E.R. unit needs a set of tools and training in how to conduct an activity-based cycletime audit. This audit collects and collates data related to the workflows of the stakeholder to which the manager wants to target a new eService. For example, at the Discovery Channel this meant studying the time and motion of the on-air promotions manager, the international marketing manager, and program producers. This audit methodology should identify potential productivity gains, cost savings, and overall improvements in production cycle times, including the value of an increased ability to accommodate change and respond to new opportunities.

We have used interactive PDF survey forms, machine-readable faxes, and structured MS-Word documents as data collection devices. We have also used online browser-accessed forms and applications built with FileMaker Pro and used by an in-field consultant. No matter what kind of form the team uses to gather this audit data, the team must develop an effective data model specifically designed to specify how to produce cycletime benchmark reports from raw data.

Do It Next

As illustrated in Figure 5-29, brand managers must take proactive measures for the collection of market feedback from customers, platform partners, and other stakeholders. This requires a variety of automated survey research capabilities and a group of individuals and companies willing to engage in the survey process.

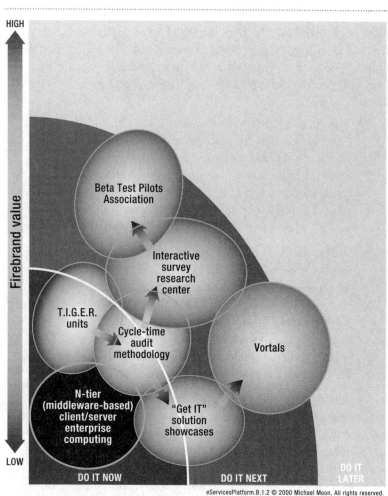

HIGH

Firebrand value

Beta Test Pilots
Association

Interactive
survey
research
center

T.I.G.E.R.
units

Cycle-time
audit
methodology

Vortals

N-tier
(middleware-based)
client/server
enterprise
computing

"Get IT"
solution
showcases

LOW

DO IT NOW

DO IT NEXT

DO IT
LATER

Figure 5-29 Interactive surveys and analysis of clickstream data help brand managers build their firebrands in record time

Interactive Survey Research Center

We cannot overstate the importance for a firebranding team to master the art and science of "listening with data." This starts with learning how to use market data well and, more important, how to frame questions that data can answer. This requires a working knowledge of quantitative and qualitative data research methodology—how to collect and collate data to produce meaningful, insightful business intelligence.

With this basic understanding and methodology in place, you can now begin building a highly specialized set of applications that we call the interactive survey research center. This represents a database application with several specialized query and data visualization tools that massage and analyze data. The interactive survey research center contains:

▶ A unified, research-oriented data model that specifies what data various types of research initiatives must collect and which enables an analyst to combine uniform sets of data from multiple survey instruments and initiatives. In practical terms this means that all survey instruments use uniform ways of characterizing individuals, businesses, industries, professional or lifestyle activities, reading and Web use patterns, etc.

▶ A database record of the exact wording of each question ever used in your surveys. This historical record tracks all instances of a question's use in various research initiatives, plus response rates and confidence indices for each. This enables a relatively inexperienced brand manager to quickly assemble new surveys from questions of proven data-collection value. This record also contains annotations that explain best use, problematic areas, and alternate ways to collect the same data.

▶ A collection of paper, digital, and online survey instruments, including questionnaires, warranty registration and contest entry forms, and all other forms used to collect customer and other stakeholder information at all of the brand's points of contact in eMediaspace. The research manager will digitize each paper-based form as a searchable, annotated Acrobat PDF—making it a highly valuable nugget of knowledge. We have used formatted MS-Word documents and e-mails as highly effective survey instruments, encouraging users who receive them as e-mail attachments to input their response to our questions in designated cells of the document.

A survey engine represents an authoring and composition suite that quickly generates online interactive data collection forms for use on your Web site and on the sites of your partners and affiliates. For more complex and heavily formatted surveys, we recommend using a scriptable FileMaker Pro database, Quark or Adobe page layout applications, Acrobat Distiller, and an automated e-mail data transmission applet.

Integration to an e-mail management system lets an analyst quickly invite a group of people to participate in a survey, using a hyperlink embedded in the e-mail message that takes them directly to an online form (HTML or interactive PDF) in a protected area of the brand producer's Web site.

A stated research methodology specifies how your company conducts quantitative and qualitative research. It includes ironclad declarations of confidentiality, proper data use, criteria for representative data samples, and other elements as necessary. This will evolve to include an interactive tutorial that teaches the basics of conducting quantitative and qualitative research, and certifies eService entrepreneurs, employees, or other trusted stakeholders to conduct research in the brand customer base.

Software application templates for data analysis and presentation let even inexperienced members of the firebranding team prepare meaningful, high-impact reports. As knowledge assets, they contain tremendous amounts of "process knowledge" about how to conduct effective research, and therefore firebrand managers should take every measure to protect these assets by placing them in the protected database of survey instruments.

A directory of research services contains profiles of individuals and firms with specialized knowledge and research practices. This directory should include ratings offered by usability labs, independent interactive survey services, competent leaders of focus groups, sources of list rentals for sample populations, interactive form designers, and other resources. A research librarian should also use a search facility such as Copernic or Sherlock to quickly search the Web, find likely links, screen them for suitability, and organize the results by topic. Or use a community bookmark database such as the one found at www.OneView.com.

An online PDF library of all previous research reports organizes an institutional knowledge bank. A research librarian should use Acrobat's annotation and markup tools to add additional commentary and analysis. These PDFs should contain active hyperlinks to online discussions and forums as well as to periodic distillations of such discussions that the librarian appends to the PDF. These PDFs might also include article reprints, conference transcripts, and digital copies of the survey instruments used to produce past research reports. A research librarian should also secure, as a matter of course, reports from trusted third-party research firms with a license for internal distribution of such reports.

With a fully developed interactive survey research center, firebrand managers can quickly survey hundreds of thousands, or millions, of people on hundreds of topics. It offers an unparalleled ability to spot emerging trends, propose "what if" solutions, determine price sensitivity to numerous offers, track customer progress through a satisfaction lifecycle, and measure competitive inroads.

Beta Test Pilots Association

Every firebrand manager knows the tremendous value of an opted-in customer—an individual who has agreed to correspond and interact with the brand producer firm. As someone who has conducted survey research for 13 years, I have discovered that a certain number of customers love to participate in extensive and time-consuming research activities, especially if they believe that their investment of time will influence, if not directly drive, next-generation product or service development.

The Beta Test Pilots Association represents the formal organization of these opted-in customers and other stakeholders. It works on a simple premise. The firebranding team offers to give the customer free cool stuff months in advance of other people in exchange for completing extensive online survey forms. In order to participate, the firebrand manager has to know what kinds of really cool stuff to offer the customer and what kind of questions the customer is qualified to answer. The enrollment form for the Beta Test Pilots Association details demographic, economic, technographic, and psychographic data of an individual and his or her household or business.

A firebrand manager, often with the aid of a research analyst, will formulate a research strategy and a set of questions to answer. They then query the Beta Test Pilots Association database for a suitable sample, striving to replicate a sample that matches the demographic success model of the key customer segment targeted by a new eService.

Using the net-integrated communications capabilities discussed earlier in this chapter, and database records housed in the enterprise data repository, the firebrand team quickly invites thousands or tens of thousands of individuals to participate in a research project. This will produce highly usable data within hours; in less than a week, it can produce comprehensive sets of data that validate or discount a business assumption or the value of a new eService.

Vortals

A vortal represents a vertical market or focused subject-matter portal—what some analysts call a "vertical portal." Each stakeholder group gets its own vortal, a home page with a user interface that drives deep into a gravity well that offers a very narrow, very deep selection of materials and interactive experiences tailored for this stakeholder group. Think of a vortal as a telezine; a special interest digital magazine designed to satisfy each stakeholder group. The vortal provides a rich destination for these stakeholders.

Firebrand managers must understand that vortals represent the fruit of a complex publishing workflow and should consider partnering with an established trade or special interest magazine publishing group to help design and ultimately operate the vortal. The vortal becomes a platform and public address system for individual eService entrepreneurs, T.I.G.E.R. units, and firebrand managers to speak to their constituencies in a professional and effective manner. A vortal can also showcase firebrand research and invite stakeholders to join a Beta Test Pilots Association.

Keep in mind that *vortal* does not represent merely a new name for the same old corporate Web site. A vortal will have a user interface, search tools, navigational affordances, and presentation formats uniquely engineered for a specific stakeholder group. Each vortal draws its sustenance from a common set of infrastructure resources. Think of planets orbiting the sun, each planet a vortal, the sun an iCorp infrastructure.

Just as the Get IT solution showcases provide a way to expose the firebranding team and company at large to innovations that may spark new eServices, so the vortal may also serve to propagate new ideas and distilled insights from the larger stakeholder universe.

Do It Later

As illustrated in Figure 5-30, your entrepreneurial eServices platform invites and rewards customers, employees, and other stakeholders to become active platform partners with a variety of techniques deployed in this phase.

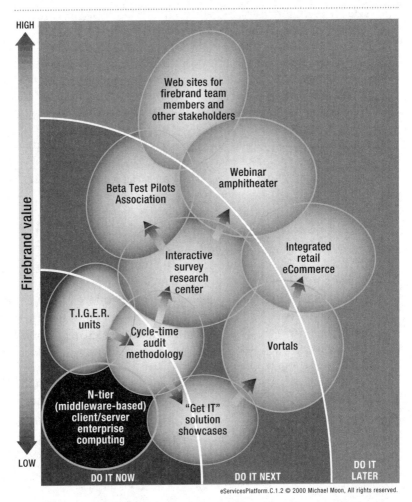

Figure 5-30 Firebrands light up cyberspace when employees, brand advocates, and other stakeholders become platform partners, quickly driving new eService satisfactions to market

Web Sites for Firebrand Team Members and Other Stakeholders

Earlier, we discussed how individual members of a firebranding team will create meaningful interactive relationships with individuals of customer organizations and within the brand's various stakeholder groups. This places a new emphasis on the "personal brands" of individuals of your firebrand team, expressed in a personal Web site: a place where they tell their part of the firebrand story and introduce themselves personally regarding their hobbies, pets, or favorite books—all currencies of relationship that compensate for the lack of in-person contact.

Following this example of individual firebrand team members, individuals at the brand producing firm's platform partners can establish their own personal Web sites, sharing the same underlying deep gravity well infrastructure and resources. This allows thousands of independent consultants and other platform partners to find productive engagements with opted-in customers (and other stakeholders) of the firebrand, thus extending the value of your firebrand and locking in more tightly both buyers and platform partners. In some cases, the firebrand firm may operate an online store, earning transaction fees as it sells the products and services of its platform partners.

Webinar Amphitheater

A Webinar amphitheater marries dynamic 1:1 publishing and streaming media to the firebrand. It enables individual firebrand team members and other stakeholders to present, in streaming audio and video formats, subjects of interest or concern to any stakeholder group. Think of it as a venue for live multimedia presentations, and, after such presentations have been recorded, a library with a powerful search capability by which to quickly identify and sequence multimedia knowledge assets to answer specific stakeholder questions. Individual stakeholders fill out a subscription form, profiling themselves as economic actors with specific areas of interest, and complete a satisfaction scorecard that closes the loop on information consumption by the stakeholder. We emphasize the bi-directional flow of information between knowledge producer and knowledge consumer.

The Webinar amphitheater allows community captains and platform partners to reach their constituencies. These live multimedia seminars combine teleconferencing systems, dynamic publishing, streaming audio and video, and shared two-dimensional and three-dimensional objects—using the same platform that delivers atomized, self-directed learning that we discussed in the previous section of this chapter.

The live presentation capability will find particular value in corporate shareholder meetings and analyst briefings.

Integrated Retail eCommerce

Vortals and a Beta Test Pilots Association will attract large numbers of platform partners—third- and fourth-party providers of after-market products, services, and training—in addition to the community captains and other brand advocates who will participate. Smart firebrand managers will want to give them the opportunity to sell their products and services through the firebrand deep gravity well Web site. This means that even if you have brands that don't require online retail sales, you will need an integrated retail eCommerce capability—the ability to showcase merchandise and services and sell them off the page. In particular, professional service firms may find a healthy market for reports and publications related to the firebrand product or service.

In the earlier section on net-integrated communications, we discussed building an online collateral store that, in addition to providing sales and marketing collateral to trade partners and the press, could also sell merchandise carrying the firm's brand identity. This same infrastructure can sell similar merchandise from the brand producer firm's platform partners as well as the offerings of other third- and fourth-party providers.

For the small- to mid-sized firm, we recommend that brand managers first investigate outsourced eCommerce services as a way of quickly deploying this capability without significant infrastructure investment and implementation.

An integrated retail eCommerce effort ultimately means that a firebrand can quickly plug and play into every meaningful point of market presence and do business. This may include a branded presence on interactive kiosks in retail stores and other public locations as well as on the emerging generation of mobile Internet devices.

The entrepreneurial eServices platform mimics in several important ways the economic function of an Internet incubator company. It exists principally to launch new eService businesses that bring new satisfactions to market. As a firebranding practice, it gives the firm a systematic method to quickly bring new eServices to market and to launch new businesses that prove too disruptive or stand too far afield from the brand's crisp and focused positioning. In many cases, these entrepreneurial eServices will require their own unique firebrand positioning because they do not fit within the laser-beam-focused position of the firebrand.

Best Practice #7: Implement Real-Time Value Creation

Your firebranding strategy coalesces at this point. The earlier hard work on infrastructure and applications integration has engaged ever-growing circles of personnel throughout the enterprise in the branding process. Empowered with tools, systems, and practices, front-line managers leverage the iCorp infrastructure, creating highly charged moments of truth for individual customers and other stakeholders.

In order to compete in the Networked Economy—when it fully emerges by 2005—the companies that survive will integrate their business processes to the business processes of other firms throughout the world. Just as blood circulates through the human body, information will flow through the digital economy, carrying with it all the key nutrients necessary for healthy, active life. This will require a fully re-engineered, completely Webified IT infrastructure and a burgeoning host of applications and eServices that deliver self-service satisfactions 24/7.

At this seventh and final stage of firebranding, business operations become closely wed to market developments and customer interactions. In practical terms this means that core business processes throughout the enterprise operate with same-day data, adjusting every aspect of the enterprise operations to the business events of the day. While this may sound futuristic, it nonetheless describes how Cisco, Dell, Amazon, AOL, and others operate today. In this section, we apply the hard-won lessons of these bleeding-edge pioneers in terms more broadly applicable to a wider range of businesses.

Unlike previous sections of this chapter, we choose not to offer practices in "do it now, do it next, do it later" phases. If your company has had the luxury of beginning with a clean slate and implementing a fully Webified, n-tier IT and financial reporting infrastructure as described in the previous six practices, you will find the capabilities of "Best Practice #7" relatively simple extensions of what you have put in place already.

If, on the other hand, you have legacy data systems and a partially Webified IT infrastructure, you may find these practices daunting or unattainable. Since most readers will fall into this category, what practical advice can we give? As we see it, four courses of action emerge. One: do nothing, with the goal of retiring or cashing out before the Networked Economy completely envelops your firm (shifting all of your stock options into more long-term instruments). Two: package your firm as an acquisition or roll-up candidate. Three: locate a smaller, fully

Webified firebranding firm in your market and acquire it. Four: Get to work re-engineering your IT infrastructure from the ground up to implement these seven best practices.

Real-Time Brand Intelligence

We owe underlying insights for this practice to Dorian Cougias, now chief technical officer at True North, one of the world's largest advertising and communications agencies. In "Best Practice #4, Master Web-Integrated Database Marketing and Sales," we described how Cougias, at a previous agency, helped BMW USA instrument its Web site for brand intelligence, to answer such questions as, Which specific pages and multimedia experiences did consumers at households with more than $80,000 annual income visit most frequently?

Using specialized software originally developed for the Defense Department, real-time brand intelligence instruments each Web page and multimedia brand resource to report activity in real-time. This software originally tracked real-time infrared imaging events across Eurasia, identifying cannon, mortar fire, and rocket launches. In some cases, sophisticated pattern recognition algorithms could identify infrared signatures by type—most notably, ours versus theirs, short-range versus long-range ICBM. When you think about it, no real difference exists between tracking 20,000 real-time infrared events and 20,000 users throughout a deep gravity well supersite. Revising Wendy's famous "Parts Is Parts" campaign, we can say, "Data is data."

A fully instrumented Web site can correlate the activity of opted-in customers and other stakeholders to key developments and milestones of the satisfaction lifecycle and a switchable/loyalty index. Switchable customers demonstrate a distinct activity pattern. They ask different kinds of questions. They dwell on certain topics and issues. They use certain key words and phrases. They do not ask certain questions, nor do they dwell on certain topics, nor do they use other key words and phrases. Where do you start developing profiles of loyal, switchable, and prospective customer behavior? As described in our discussion of the deep gravity well Web site and its user interfaces, the site search facility can guide users to frame queries in terms of their role as an *economic actor* (current customer, prospect, employee, press, etc.), their *level of engagement* (browsing, researching, decision-making, problem-solving, optimizing), and their *area of principle focus* (specific product, a community of practice, a product ingredient, etc.).

How individuals frame these queries begins to identify them as information consumers. Each subsequent query further refines this profile. Analysis of these queries by stakeholder groups provides one type of real-time brand intelligence. When coupled with instrumented Web page data collection and the data gathered at points of presence in the net-integrated communications infrastructure and web-integrated database sales and marketing activities, baseline data emerges by which brand managers can track real-time branding events.

This will parallel the grocery-checkout scanner-data tracking conducted by A.C. Nielsen and other large consumer-research firms. These firms have instrumented checkout bar code readers at some 2,000 supermarkets and other retail outlets to collect data about actual purchases, in 10-minute increments throughout the business day. These research firms consolidate this data and sell it to big brand firms like Proctor & Gamble, Coke, and Kraft. Brand managers at those firms use the data to validate sales improvements that result from their marketing and merchandising programs. Using these scanner data, a brand manager can quickly identify the best mix of print, broadcast, and online media for individual geographic markets. This same practice will become standard for Web commerce when the equivalents of bar code scanners and traffic aisle monitors propagate through key points of market presence.

Front-Line Fiscal Dashboards

We first ran across this application at Dell Computer in 1997. In 1999, Cisco Systems has adopted a similar application. In a nutshell, it works like this.

Front-line marketing and business managers have an operating budget, reflected in a spreadsheet. When a manager wants to initiate a program—a direct mail program, for example—they estimate mailing size, response rates, and the increased sales that typically result from first-class delivery versus bulk, four-color versus black and white or two-color, die-cut piece versus standard form. The manager draws upon previous campaigns, each meticulously documenting these factors plus the nature of the message, the market segment, position in product life cycle (hot, brand-new stuff or end-of-cycle stuff), and ultimate sales rates. After determining the best strategy and mix of variables for the new program, the manager reviews it and signs off on it. The manager then integrates the data that characterize the new initiative and rolls it up into a consolidated daily expense report for the company CFO. Much like a credit card clearing process, the manager receives a sub-second authorization within certain budget limitations or available balance limit imposed.

Using this data, a CFO can quickly rein in expenses should sales begin to soften or if the firm loses a major contract. The CFO can signal to front-line managers an expense reduction goal which then allows the front-line manager to scale back the project, use lower-cost materials and fulfillment methods, or put the project on hold.

In this manner, Dell's CFO has pushed fiscal accountability to the front-lines. These spreadsheets include calculations for internal rates of return on treasury funds. An extensive training program ensures that all front-line managers use this dashboard.

Integrated Daily Financials

Daily reports from the front-line fiscal dashboards give the CFO and CEO important insight into how to scale business operations in real-time. This goes way beyond mere short-term expense reduction to allow senior management to see two important processes operating in real-time: How quickly do we as a company exploit new market opportunities (cycletime metric of branding productivity)? and, What areas of our operations should we outsource for the day, week, month, or indefinitely? Just as servers now provide "fail-over" redundancy, software that identifies a server in the process of failing and shifts its data processing tasks to another server on the network, so integrated daily financials allow executive and middle managers to shift operations to available resources throughout their supply or fulfillment value chains.

We have begun to see this in Web site replication and media caching for sites that expect to see huge spikes in Web visitors (immediately following a Super Bowl commercial spot, for example). We see similar practices in credit-card processing and inventory management.

Integrated daily financials enable senior executives to run simulations on events that may occur in a few days or weeks, or in the event of a strategic development in their market—merger, plant closing, or other significant event. Tracking specific market segments and bell-wether accounts that tend to pace industry activity enables early warnings for everyone throughout the organization and designated external stakeholders. Certain financial or business-process events can trigger a net-integrated communications capability, messaging e-mail, pager teletext, voice, and fax to all designated individuals.

This might include a streaming Webcast of the CEO response to a fast-breaking corporate development or news event. This might also trigger a call to action among a network of contingent workers, contractors, and freelancers in the event of natural disaster or, on the positive side, a sudden surge of demand for a product or service. More importantly, such a system could notify these contingent forces to clear their calendars for action within a specified time range. We might call this real-time "eSourcing" of contingent and subcontracted labor. We described the infrastructure to implement this in integrated projects management—now we see it in action in real-time.

Integration of Employees as Business of One

Thus integrated to a real-time income statement via the dashboard—if management takes an enlightened approach (and chooses not to use these systems to enslave or coerce desired behaviors)—front-line staff can begin to act more as autonomous business units than as mere employees completing sets of assigned tasks. Full attainment of real-time value-creation requires that front-line staff act autonomously, but they will need the guidance of corporate policy and training.

Management will embed business rules and operating procedures in the underlying software algorithms that enable the dashboard systems and come into play throughout interfaces to the enterprise integrated projects management infrastructure and to external branding systems. Middleware application servers contain many of these business rules and operating procedures.

In our discussion of integrated projects management, we showed how the two essential questions of a knowledge worker (Who owes me what kind of information? To whom do I owe what kinds of information?) apply to the example of an eSourcing database application for a production manager of an advertising agency or creative services department. This eSourcing application modeled the production manager's information consumption and the production of answers for other knowledge workers. Using this as a template, the firebranding iCorp begins to model other key knowledge workers of its firebranding team, organizing the resources of the iCorp and the Networked Economy for the optimum productivity of one economic actor, i.e., a marketing manager or other key knowledge worker. This approach will transform this economic actor's role into an autonomous, self-correcting, proactive business unit with one employee—this particular knowledge worker. Cycletime metrics then reveal how many requests for answers this knowledge worker receives, how quickly she provides answers, and the relative satisfaction of other stakeholders with those answers.

This inevitably leads to the knowledge worker renegotiating compensation, emphasizing payment for results and initiatives that produce new results—all tracked and quantified in real-time firebranding processes. Compensation structures must also evolve to track performance with fact-based data and reward business-of-one employees based on performance. This framework will stimulate employees to invest in a skills portfolio (acquired and developed via the atomized lifelong digital learning systems described in "Best Practice #5, Globalize Your Firebrand"), and negotiate skills-based and performance-based compensation contracts.

While it may strike the reader as implausible that most companies will choose to operate this way, in fact many of the successful raging-bull dot.com start-ups operate in this manner today. They accomplish large portions of their administrative, marketing, and technical business functions through a network of contractors and contingent workers (each of whom operate as a business of one). Stock options of a pre-IPO dot.com can wonderfully concentrate the minds of these entrepreneurial eLancers of the Networked Economy.

Interactive Investor Relations Web Site

In our discussion of the deep gravity well supersite, we prescribed the deployment of an interactive annual report and a variety of investor relations applications. This represents posting static SEC-mandated financial data and interactive calculators for measuring financial performance.

Now, these interactive annual reports and related disclosure documents evolve into live-data formats. This means publishing the data in XML following a regulatory standard schema template for tagging data and metadata. This would enable anyone visiting the Web site to drag-and-drop an entire table of data from a Web page to a spreadsheet, resulting in a populated spreadsheet with all of the algorithms, macros, and formulae from which the various numbers and ratios derive—in short, a complete transfer of data and metadata from the published financial report to a database or spreadsheet of an investor, analyst, or other stakeholder.

When the interactive investor-relations capability integrates the Webinar multimedia theater and dynamic 1:1 publishing capabilities previously described, the CEO or CFO can address a select group of analysts, trade partners, or employees on very specific issues. This will also allow the firm to create highly customized publications assembled just in time for each designated participant in such a discussion. This could include dynamic binding of analytic tables, simplified large-print formats for elderly IRA and 401(K) holders, as well as translations into other languages spoken or read by employees, their spouses, customers, and other interested parties.

The fully developed, multimedia, interactive annual report fills two very important firebranding functions that now become doable thanks to the infrastructure development and re-engineering accomplished through these seven best practices.

First, the interactive annual report should define in the most concrete and tangible forms possible the quintessence of the brand: what single, all-inclusive, differentiated satisfaction do customers buy and ultimately bond with, forming lifelong loyalties? The substance of the report oozes the firm's crisply focused brand positioning, the many voices of customers that give depth and meaning to the branded satisfaction, and independent market data that validates the firm's growing position and brand strength in the marketplace.

Second, the interactive annual report serves as the cornerstone for internal business education curricula and the atomized lifelong learning programs that facilitate higher and higher levels of literacy, numeracy, and firebranding expertise (storytelling). We highly recommend that the enterprise uses the annual report and related financial statements as a pedagogical device. Teach literacy using the content of your annual report and related materials. Teach numeracy and financial analysis skills using the numbers of the annual report. Teach storytelling and brand management using the investor-relations materials as examples of communication strategies and tactics.

Suppose a 14-year-old in Guangdong or Benares or Jakarta or Mexico City learns the basic skills of English literacy, technical English, and business from a particular firm. Can you imagine that teenager's lifelong affiliation, and even devotion, to the company that gave her this opportunity? Do you suppose that they would use the product or services of this corporation? Would they freely recommend if not outright defend the brand even in the face of hostile rebuke? Would they not make a motivated employee or subcontractor? Would their emotional bank account give them the capacity to forgive an occasional faux pas?

Obviously, the impact of such an interactive investor-relations Web site extends far beyond the investor and analyst stakeholder communities. This vision may also leave readers wondering, "It sounds great, but what do I do today?"

Engage a consultancy to develop an interactive tutorial, gauged to the reading and comprehension levels of a high school sophomore, that teaches how to read and understand a financial statement. This tutorial should include a workbook and comprehension tests. It should represent a curriculum suitable for a community college class delivered to students who speak English as a second language. This single application can focus several deployments that will repay immediate dividends and bring returns for years to follow.

Conclusion

This chapter has outlined a roadmap that constitutes nothing less than a wholesale revision of business and commercial activity as we know it. As pundits have remarked, the Internet will have an effect as profound as the printing press and the Industrial Revolution. For many, it means not just that we stand at the cusp of a new era, but at the edge of a chasm that dwarfs the Grand Canyon.

We have tried to emphasize short-term tactical deployments of technologies and practices within a framework that reflects a vision of the Networked Economy and what it takes to succeed in the coming era, based on the best available information, and painting as complete a picture as we can at the present moment. We anticipate having to revise and update this framework at least every 18 months or in book form, and, using our Firebrands.com Web site, to collect data and front-line reports from firebranding pioneers to disseminate more frequent dispatches.

Keeping in mind the way early maps of the New World look fanciful and erroneous today, so, too, will the firebranding roadmap seem awkward and out-of-date ages from now—for it charts a realm that is constantly evolving and being refined as more and more pioneers send back their reports from its frontiers. We invite you to join this community of trailblazers.

Chapter 6

Firebranding in Action: Five Prospective Business Models

Depending on the kind of business and a host of other factors—including nature of the offering, corporate lifecycle phase, number and type of customers, maturity of the industry, and more—firms will employ different mixes of firebranding strategies and techniques. In this chapter, we provide a conceptual starter kit or template for firebranding five different kinds of generally applicable business designs. We anticipate that your firm will fit within the parameters of one of these composite models. We'll continue to elaborate on these models at Firebrands.com, based on our ongoing industry research.

Knowledge Refinery

This business sells expert advice, branded information, or other professional or personal service—all provided by highly trained and highly paid knowledge workers. Each knowledge worker *collects* facts, data, and information, *performs* a set of logical operations consistent with commonly accepted industry practice, and *produces* a result of value to the client as well as a result that peers would generally recognize as "good work."

The term "knowledge refinery" describes the nature and structure of a business organized to enhance the productivity of professional service providers—knowledge workers who transform data into answers or skillful actions that meet or exceed client standards of quality, value, and satisfaction.

Professional service firms in this category include real estate agencies, law firms, accounting firms, market researchers, and schools. Personal service firms in this category span a broad spectrum of providers, including hair dressers, wardrobe consultants, house cleaners, gardeners, carpet cleaners, plumbers, pest control—the list goes on and on.

During the 1980s and 1990s, this sector underwent a radical transformation through aggressive and largely successful franchising efforts by thousands of entrepreneurs. In each case, the franchise systematized the informal or tacit knowledge of a highly effective service provider, organized a comprehensive training and management program, and branded the service as a powerhouse franchise and the definitive go-to solution provider in that category. Popular business press described this as the "McDonaldization" of the personal and professional service sector.

The knowledge refinery picks up where these franchising operations left off, applying principles of ecommerce, firebranding, and knowledge worker productivity. It asks and begins to answer these questions: How do we, as high labor-cost businesses, make money while we sleep? How do we use technology to extract the labor content, and therefore our dependency on increasingly scarce, high-cost labor, from the service that we provide to our clients? This entails escaping the work-an-hour-get-paid-an-hour business design. The Networked Economy will support many innovative ways for service organizations to provide new satisfactions, largely of a self-service nature, to clients within existing markets as well as those heretofore beyond current markets.

The knowledge refinery aggregates several eService applications that facilitate two kinds of interactions between client and service firm: *self-service interaction by the client,* and *system-assisted services provided by a representative of the firm.* An n-tier client-server computing infrastructure and a set of business IT applications support these two outcomes. In the Charles Schwab example in the "Platform Partners" section of Chapter 4, we showed how the firm provides tools that let customers serve themselves (research, asset allocation, transactions, etc.) as well as more sophisticated tools for use by independent financial planners, estate executors, and other Schwab affiliates.

The brand storytelling process emphasizes the underlying *methodology* (processes, practices, etc.) that enables the knowledge refinery firm to provide its services. A market research firm might offer a white paper that analyzes various market research methodologies, strengths and weaknesses of each, the firm's unique blend of these techniques, and the firm's use of special technologies, databases, and practices that constitute the "secret sauce" or source of differentiation from competitors in the category. Their brand storytelling also emphasizes how satisfied customers and communities of practice successfully use their services and talk to each other about how to maximize the value of the knowledge refinery: in effect, these customers tell the brand story. Anticipating that brand advocates and community captains will want to help tell the brand story, the knowledge refinery's branding team should provide tools and support their efforts to tell the brand story and to help them make more money and gain wider prestige from their brand evangelism. The knowledge refinery might give them privileged market or user research data, for example, or special access to an interactive research capability within its deep gravity well supersite.

The business model for the knowledge refinery will emphasize the production of a vertical portal designed support the firm's front-line staff and its primary client base. This deep gravity well supersite organizes information and services in order to answer the essential questions that the knowledge refinery's service providers and clients need to answer. It provides a variety of documents, FAQs, databases, bid procurement systems, industry directories, links to other Web resources and experts. (See Chapter 5 for more details.)

To this basic structure, the knowledge refinery adds an interactive survey center to create new knowledge through ongoing client and market research. A subscription management database lets an individual client personalize a set of online resources to meet her particular needs, plus resources necessary to help a client understand how to maximize the benefits of personalization.

As the knowledge refinery's community of practice grows and creates new knowledge (housed at its deep gravity well supersite), the branding team adds atomized, self-directed training modules and eServices to help keep its own front-line staff current, and to keep clients up to speed. Community captains will likely become the primary customers for these learning applications; they use them as new currencies of exchange among community members.

Dream Factory

Dream factories sell a broad range of capital equipment, appliances, home furnishings, industrial products, office supplies, consumables, etc. They transform their knowledge of customers, technology, manufacturing processes, and the market into products that customers will want to buy and use, and they use information and storytelling to add new value to these traditional products.

In the old economy, these companies used a variety of research techniques to understand what consumers wanted, then manufactured and tried to sell products that met those expectations. The biggest successes—products like the iMac or Sony Walkman—represent the fruit of companies tapped into the aspirations of customers and an understanding of how to mold technology to create products that fulfill these dreams. The term dream factory describes a business organized to pull customers more intimately into the product development loop.

During the 1980s and 1990s, manufacturing productivity soared due to several factors. Factory automation, enterprise resource planning (ERP) systems, and total quality management (TQM) gave manufacturers the ability to identify hidden costs and inefficiencies. Supply chain integration, just-in-time manufacturing, and large-scale outsourcing of core manufacturing and business processes made manufacturers extraordinarily nimble and capable of adjusting to short-term peaks and valleys in demand, sometimes retooling manufacturing lines for shorter and shorter product runs.

The dream factory leverages these developments, applying principles of ecommerce, firebranding, and knowledge worker productivity to the design, production, delivery, and use of insanely great products. By integrating customer input to the design and manufacturing process, the dream factory moves the firm closer to real-time value creation.

The dream factory asks and tries to answer these questions: How do we design and build products that customers do not know they want (right now) but upon seeing them fall madly in love and can't get enough? How do we use technology to weave our company into the fabric of our customer's business or lifestyle? How can we induce a collaborative visioning-to-reality partnership based on trusted interactions, reciprocity, and an ongoing fair exchange of value spanning decades?

Dream factories take advantage of industry atomization, the process that has deconstructed products into assemblages of interchangeable parts that each manufacturer will optimize in different ways to particular performance criteria (cost, quality, performance, durability, etc.). A single Dell PC, for example, represents the fruits of mixing and matching hundreds of different types of industry-standard components (microprocessors, hard drives, monitors, etc.), usually delivered to the factory within hours of a customer's order. The Dell PC thus emerges as a branded framework or platform that customers use to design solutions that meet their particular needs. This framework also gives customers the ability to perform future upgrades and enhancements.

Dream factories need, therefore, tools that let customers design and build solutions based on these frameworks. Dell offers a design-your-PC configurator at its Web site. Just about any manufacturer can apply this type of tool, however. Apparel manufacturers, for example, can let customers design solutions within a wardrobe system (a framework for lifestyle expression), reflecting their skin and hair colorations, body type, lifestyle profile (urban hip, suburban town and country, etc.), and offer online wardrobe consultations for specific events (prom, resort vacation, polo match, etc.).

The dream factory abolishes geographic barriers that have traditionally separated producers and consumers, buyers and sellers. A worldwide tailored logistics system completes the final leg between factory and customer. More than just a package delivery system, worldwide tailored logistics systems perform a variety of localization and personalization services that local governments or distribution partners may require. These services may include configuration, installation, training, and just-in-time integration of other third- and fourth-party products.

The business model for the dream factory will emphasize a broadly defined customer loyalty program—the delivery of satisfaction over an extended lifecycle and the capture of value in the form of trusted survey feedback, upgrade or add-on sales, subscription fees paid for access to personalization tools, and transaction fees or commissions on third- or fourth-party products or services sold through the brand firm's deep gravity well supersite. This business model relies heavily on strategic sourcing of atomized components, industry standards and protocols for integrating these components, an active and profitable group of platform partners (third- and fourth-party firms that make money selling their goods and services into the brand's loyal customer base), and strong, well-organized communities of practice led by brand advocate C-captains.

The dream factory's deep gravity well supersite will emphasize opt-in customer registration, universal subscription management, uniform issue-problem characterization, esourcing databases, zoomable images for digital detailing of products, and an interactive survey center.

Where the knowledge refinery's brand storytelling focuses on community, and how customers can help themselves and each other find the answers they need, the dream factory strives to pull the customer into a long-term, intimate relationship with the brand firm and its value-creation process—a one-to-one partnership between customers and designers. The storytelling will also emphasize the virtues of the manufacturer's integration framework for branded business solutions or lifestyle expressions. The dream factory succeeds when the customer sees this integration framework as a fundamental aspect of his or her social identity.

Satisfaction Theater

This business entertains shoppers and customers, using all the tricks of traditional retailing, guerrilla theater, and firebranding. These integrated retail operations stock, showcase, sell, and in some cases provide training and service for the products they resell.

During the 1980s and 1990s, the retail sector underwent dramatic changes. Successful retailers became either superstores and warehouse clubs (Wal-Mart, Costco, Home Depot, Staples, Good Guys, etc.) or highly specialized niche operations (Crate & Barrel, Victoria's Secret, Starbucks, The Gap, etc.).

The large warehouse clubs radically altered their business designs. Costco, for example, charges an annual membership fee that equals the total net profit that a grocery store might derive over a year's time from a single customer. Wal-Mart used automation technology and supply chain integration (with automated inventory replenishment and data mining) to wring tremendous costs and inefficiencies from their supply chain and pass these savings along to customers. Home Depot and other superstores bulked up their inventories to ten to fifty times greater variety than the local Mom and Pop stores, giving customers fantastic levels of choice at incredibly low prices.

Niche retailers narrowed their focus to a handful of high-quality, highly differentiated products and added uncommon levels of knowledgeable front-line sales staff to earn price premiums on otherwise commodity products. Going into Starbucks for the daily java jolt represents far more than just a cup of coffee; it has become a highly ritualized, communal experience by which to start the day in high gear.

The satisfaction theater pulls together several technologies and firebranding practices for the principle benefit of the sales clerk—the actor who wows customers with a virtuoso performance of product knowledge, helpful hints, and who, for consumer products, serves as an exemplar of the lifestyle reflected in the brand. Perhaps the most revolutionary aspect of the satisfaction theater entails the dramatic rise in social status of the sales clerk—now called a consultant or associate and who enjoys a collegial, peer-to-peer relationship with the customer.

The satisfaction theater asks and tries to answer these questions: How do we motivate, inspire, and manage the brilliant theatrical performance of our front-line sales staff? How do we recruit, hire, and train these star performers? How do we use technology to empower and embolden their performance, as opposed to the way retailers in the past used technology to control, manipulate, and coerce the right behaviors for the benefit of managers?

The satisfaction theater combines many of the firebranding practices from net-integrated communications, Web-integrated database marketing and sales, and the entrepreneurial eServices platform. It starts with the assumption that a customer will come through the doors of a retail establishment seeking some ineffable *je ne sais quoi*, or else is on a hit-and-run mission to get what he needs and get back to work. These two buyers will encounter a wired, network-savvy sales clerk who can quickly navigate the store's vertical portal Web site that contains mountains of information, analysis, customer reviews, and streaming how-to demos on every product in the store, or that's available through a worldwide inventory supply chain.

If the customer doesn't find an available sales clerk, the floor plan, fixtures, and merchandising displays will gently but firmly direct the customer to an interactive kiosk, as suggested in Figure 6-1, that offers a branded knowledge user interface to the public portion of the store's vertical portal Web site. The search engine, vocabulary and attributes database, uniform issue-problem characterization function, eSourcing database, and a universal subscription form (pre-populated with information previously provided in the case of an opted-in customer) all work together to quickly profile and identify a buyer's particular purchase intent and its profit potential. Page views and other user interactions related to high-profit items immediately trip a change in music or issue a beeper signal to sales clerks, notifying them of a high-profit, high-commission sales prospect, "now active in the category."

In satisfaction theaters with high traffic (a fast-food restaurant, for example), electronic point of purchase (ePOP) systems will dynamically present featured products or combinations triggered by statistical data derived from historical transactions—by time of day, day of week, season, and other recurring events. Pilot studies for McDonald's showed that these kinds of displays can increase sales for the highest margin products by as much as 15 percent for breakfast, lunch, dinner, and late-night diners.

A few price comparison dot.com etailers will soon dominate Web-only retailing, offering customers the products they want at the lowest possible price for immediate delivery. The satisfaction theater represents the revenge of the clicks-and-mortar retailer who can now offer unprecedented levels of personal service, customization, and hand-holding by bringing the deep gravity well supersite into the store. Earlier in this book, we showed how Office Depot, Barnes & Noble, and Big O Tires have begun to use satisfaction theater principles.

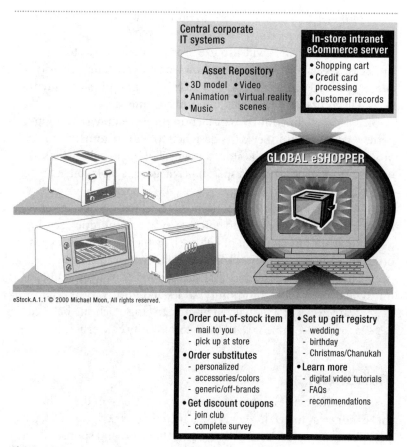

Central corporate
IT systems

Asset Repository
- 3D model
- Video
- Animation
- Virtual reality
- Music scenes

In-store intranet
eCommerce server
- Shopping cart
- Credit card processing
- Customer records

GLOBAL eSHOPPER

- **Order out-of-stock item**
  - mail to you
  - pick up at store
- **Order substitutes**
  - personalized
  - accessories/colors
  - generic/off-brands
- **Get discount coupons**
  - join club
  - complete survey

- **Set up gift registry**
  - wedding
  - birthday
  - Christmas/Chanukah
- **Learn more**
  - digital video tutorials
  - FAQs
  - recommendations

Figure 6-1 Retailers must bring eCommerce into the store, using eKiosks in the manner suggested here

The satisfaction theater uses three more firebranding practices to gain tremendous competitive advantage.

Dynamic one-to-one publishing of personal catalogs lets a customer profile herself (in terms of coloration, clothing sizes, lifestyle etc.) and get in return a personalized view of the store's inventory, merchandised and presented in ways that this customer will find particularly attractive. This personal catalog remains available online through an at-home Web browser or at the in-store kiosk (with a large HDTV display). The store can also print and bind a copy using one of the many outsourced print-on-demand eServices. The personal catalog will also contain zoomable images that, using technologies like ImagePump from Xippix Inc., provide unprecedented levels of detailed inspection prior to purchase when the customer views the catalog online.

Satisfaction theaters will also use broadband networks to bring simulcast special events (fashion shows, product debuts, celebrity demos, musical or theater performances, etc.) into the store. Invitations will go first to registered, opted-in customers.

Brand storytelling for the satisfaction theater emphasizes shoppertainment—grand spectacles designed to pull customers and prospective buyers into the store and enroll them as subscribers to future events, eServices, and special privileges available only to opted-in customers.

The satisfaction theater uses brand storytelling, spectacle, and highly personalized services to enhance local communities, serving as an important mechanism of culture by which communities pass on from one generation to the next social norms, values, and practices. The satisfaction theaters that succeed in the Networked Economy will express local community values and norms within the larger framework of a globalized brand, striking a delicate balance between global commerce and local community concerns.

Storydwelling

Storydwellings serve as entertainment destinations on the Web. They make money in many different ways, including subscription fees, pay-per-view products, sales of licensed merchandise, and sponsorships. In some cases, promotion of other lines of business (movies, products, services, etc.) constitute the return, not profits per se.

Storydwellings target "screenagers" of all ages. We use the term *screenager* (a word coined by Dave Pola in 1994 at the pioneering interactive media industry magazine, *Morph's Outpost on the Digital Frontier*) to characterize an individual who has played more than 1,000 hours of video games, computer games, or online games during his formative years. Screenagers quite literally connect the red, green, and blue dots of digital media in ways that reflect a new worldview. Our research shows that they have "crossed the chasm" of interactive technology adoption, and represent the first cohort of the digital divide—people who "get it" that interactive digital media constitute a seamless extension of one's basic concept of self and social identity.

Storydwellings find their roots in the interactive multimedia CD-ROMs of the early 1990s. Both authors of this book played key roles in the shaping of a new community that emerged as programmers, designers, and authoring tool makers that came out of the PC software, video game, computer-based training, and consumer electronics industries to develop and publish interactive multimedia CD-ROMs—the precursor to today's Web design and development trade.

Using rich audio and visual media assets, novel navigation concepts, not to mention logical structures that mirror imagination and dream, the most popular CD-ROMs pulled their users into an immersive, other-worldly experience—a remarkable feat of "controlled hallucination" on the part of a user only 18 to 24 inches away from a computer monitor. This new media sensibility remains to be fully explored, but at least three important concepts emerge that point the way to the use of immersive, interactive multimedia in the storydwellings of the Networked Economy.

Storydwellings ask and try to answer these questions: How do we create an environment in which our customers and other stakeholders play with stories that ultimately reflect and validate their social identity? How can we harness the principles that underlie digital storytelling of a non-linear nature, where users drive the narrative as opposed to an author who prescribes a linear story line? How do we transform clickstream data into meaningful, predictive profiles of customers, especially those in our share-determining market sectors?

Storydwellings exploit clickable media objects (one of the products of the smart media factory discussed earlier in this book, and also discussed in our treatment of firebrand "heat" in Chapter 4), which characterize a fundamentally new relationship between the consumer and a media-based experience. Like channel surfing TV, the screenager assumes *a priori* the right to act upon media as an object (as opposed to their parents who passively allow media to wash over them in the form of movies, plays, TV, etc.). In a storydwelling, clickable media objects provide all manner of interactive experiences. They work as navigation devices in the user interface, mouse-over animations or audio sound bites, re-mixable audio and music sound tracks, and Post-It™-style overlays of visitor comments, for example.

A storydwelling provides the raw materials for a metathematic construction, an entertainment experience pieced together by the user from multiple media sources. The TV channel surfer constructs a meta-program out of pieces from the three to five linear TV programs that she surfs among. Likewise, the storydwelling visitor assembles a customized entertainment experience on the dashboard-like Web browser, mixing the storydwelling's user interface and clickable media objects with a streaming audio soundtrack provided by a music CD or MP3 tracks, using a floating tool bar to control the audio sources. The resulting multilayered media construction represents a collaboration between visitor and the resources of the storydwelling; lacking this collaboration, with its endless possibilities for novelty and surprise, the storydwelling will fail to sustain ongoing interest and customer traffic.

Storydwellings, therefore, produce an experience that we call *intermediacy*—interactive, immediate, intimate experience that ultimately models, reflects, and feeds back the social identity, desires, and fears of the user. Careful analysis of TV channel surfers and the snippets of programs that they consume can reveal deep-seated aspirations, values, and beliefs—primary factors that motivate behavior. Likewise, analysis of content consumption by storydwelling visitors—through close study of their clickstream data—lets storydwelling publishers understand how customers use and respond to the media assets in their deep gravity well supersites, and how to better serve them with new experiences and stories on return visits.

Together, these three elements will let storydwellings become an important new entertainment medium. The storydwelling will complement existing entertainment media (movies, music, TV, etc.), but require entirely new artistic strategies able to exploit the Web's native strengths. Successful film, TV, and theatrical talents will fail to capture the spirit of the storydwelling. A new generation of artists and producers will emerge from within the screenager cohort to bring storydwellings to their full creative and commercial potential.

Because storydwellings will find their natural constituencies among minors (who will eventually become adults), brand managers will have to modify Web-integrated marketing techniques to protect the anonymity and privacy of these young customers. Because their audience includes the share-determining market sectors for so many brand firms, storydwellings will often serve as promotional adjuncts to a brand firm's knowledge refinery, dream factory, or satisfaction theater.

Brandstanding

We suggest that every knowledge worker of the Networked Economy, ranging all the way from CEO to sales clerk, can, should, and must have a personal Web site, what we call a "brandstanding." This neologism's echoes of grandstanding (showing off in front of a crowd) reflect the fundamental task of a brandstanding: to get lucrative engagements, maintain relationships with members of a global trust network and communities of practice or concern, and build passive, make-money-while-you-sleep revenue streams derived from the purchase or licensing of intellectual work products.

As a scaled-down, inexpensively produced deep gravity well supersite, the brandstanding showcases the capabilities of a knowledge worker in a variety of contexts. To illustrate this concept, we direct the reader to www.MichaelMoon.com.

Every knowledge worker will have a set of stakeholders with whom the knowledge worker must build and maintain a personal brand. My (Michael Moon's) stakeholders include:

- ► Readers of this book

- ► People who have attended one of my seminars

- ► Members of the press seeking interviews, quotes, and background information for their journalistic endeavors

- ► Current clients with paid subscriptions for ongoing research publications and advice

- ► Prospective clients investigating the value of such subscriptions or engagements

- ► Technology providers and vendors who want to educate me about their offerings so that I might mention them in a seminar, article, or book

- ► Business acquaintances exploring collaboration and networking opportunities

- ► Affiliates with whom I share documents, databases, and spreadsheets

- ► Curious visitors who have landed at MichaelMoon.com as a result of a link from a search engine, portal, or casual reference

- ► Family and friends who want to know what's happening with their beloved son, brother, or friend

Following the deep gravity well supersite model that we discussed in Chapter 4, the MichaelMoon.com home page organizes its resources to answer the essential questions most often posed by each stakeholder group. On the left side of the home page, each of the stakeholder navigation buttons triggers a pre-programmed quick search of the site's editorial database, and links to a search results page that contains a list of essential questions. Each links to an article that answers the question.

For members of the press, the questions cover the kind of topical news and background that journalists most often seek, including a *curricula vitae* that details career accomplishments, publications, presentations, and client engagements. Prospective clients receive a description of the kinds of clients with whom I work best, the types of problems which I am best equipped to solve (highlighting my distinctive capabilities), an explanation of my work methodology, parameters for engagements, details of subscription offerings, pro forma proposals, and testimonials from satisfied clients and industry luminaries. Family and friends find recent photographs, a family newsletter, my current relationship status, books, movies, plays, concerts, and other events I've found interesting (or not), and other personal news. For my new friends who want a better fix on me, I will provide a brief autobiography that highlights my greatest influences (books, mentors, and pivotal experiences).

As a knowledge worker, I ask myself almost every day: How can I productize what I know? How can I turn my insights, industry contacts, and work products (with confidential data removed) into products that I can sell while I'm sleeping?

The emergence of downloadable epublications, pioneered by MightyWords, iUniverse, Online Originals, Softbook, and the availability of modular ecommerce functions (credit card transaction processing, logistics fulfillment, etc.) that you can easily plug into a brandstanding Web site, let me sell monographs, white papers, and other nuggets of knowledge that answer the essential questions featured in my site.

All of this may sound ambitious, and expensive, but I have been able to publish this site with an inexpensive publishing platform, eWordsmith, that I rent from my Internet service provider, ServerSmiths.com of San Anselmo, California, for approximately $350 a month. Any of my staff can log on to this editorial system through a

Web browser, quickly navigate to the right online template, then cut-and-paste text and graphics of the material that we want published. eWordsmith includes workflow routing and approval tools that let me review and approve newly created text from any browser world-wide. A timed release mechanism lets me queue up articles to be published at pre-established intervals—a big plus that lets me travel for weeks on end without worrying about refreshing the site. The system has a listserv capability that lets me automatically notify my e-mail correspondents of cool new stuff to download at the site. An add-on (at extra cost) subscription management tool lets me sell up to nine different subscriptions at varying price points.

This approach provides a basic template for other knowledge workers, who may range from doctors, lawyers, accountants, book-keepers, graphic designers, waiters, restaurant managers, sales and customer services representatives—individuals with vested stake-holders who can and will help the knowledge worker get new engagements, build awareness and competence among trust net-works and communities of practice and concern, and, potentially, create passive revenue streams from the sale or licensed use of knowledge assets.

While we have slanted this brandstanding example for the solo practitioner, every CEO, CFO, and other member of the executive team can, should, and must have her own brandstanding site to tell stories to customers, investors, trade partners, and staff. In the spirit of firebranding the enterprise, every employee who has a relation-ship with customers or other stakeholders should also have a brand-standing site, underscoring the need for a corporate publishing platform and policies and practices for the creation and approval of suitable material for brandstanding sites within the firm's deep gravity well supersite.

Conclusion

In this chapter, we have offered a set of templates aimed to help you think about how to develop a deep gravity well supersite for your firm or operation. In the future, we intend to develop these templates into fuller treatments and make them available as download-able monographs, or as a future volume in the Firebranding book series. Visit Firebrands.com for the latest developments.

Chapter 7

Starting and Stoking the Fire: Acceleration Ramp for Launching a Firebrand

In this chapter, we outline the basics steps a business can take to plan and execute a successful firebranding strategy. We also suggest some go-to solution resources that firms can use to jump-start a firebranding program.

No One Escapes

If you have read this far, you have begun to realize the magnitude, scope, and enormity of the task of building a brand and competing in the Networked Economy. We've also shown that this revolution remains one of business designs—how your company finds and serves customers and captures value in return.

We've outlined a general course of action that will take most firms several years, if not a decade, to implement. Many firms who undertake this task will fail, for a variety of reasons, including bad timing, poor execution skills, the wrong business or technical decisions, the brilliance of an upstart competitor, a confluence of industry factors, and other unforeseen discontinuities.

This should in no way discourage you or freeze you in your tracks. The answer to the question of whether you will fail or not remains clear: you will fail. Peter Drucker makes the powerful case, in his book, *Innovation and Entrepreneurship: Practice and Principles* (Harperbusiness, 1993), that the successful firm emerges from the accidental success that the firm discovers, and exploits, while in the process of failing.

Success in the Networked Economy means attempting to do things that carry a high likelihood of failure, with the aim of discovering, or stimulating, an unintended consequence—an accidental success that your company is prepared to systematically exploit.

This means that the prescriptive firebranding action plan that we outline in this chapter will fail. Count on it. Nevertheless, this plan represents, in our assessment, your best chance of discovering what will work.

This also means that management must execute these tasks wholeheartedly, without holding back, and yet remain ever-ready to change the business model, based on new intelligence or feedback from the market. This will require the ability to distinguish between a singular effect that leads nowhere and a genuine opportunity.

Success also depends on a fundamental shift. Previously, firms organized to find and serve customers through various strategies conceived within the constraints of a relatively static business model. The Networked Economy often demands a radical transformation of the business model itself, including fundamental changes in core business practices, the need for, or obsolescence of particular IT infrastructures, and significant revisions of the skills portfolio of knowledge workers and other personnel.

While this shift of unprecedented magnitude continues, business owners and executives will need massive infusions of new knowledge into their businesses. Historically, the two most successful infusion techniques include buying it or renting it—mergers and acquisitions or outsourcing. In both cases, deep understanding of the industry, business designs, core business processes, and IT infrastructure will serve as the essential co-factors for successful knowledge infusions.

Fortunately, or unfortunately (depending on your point of view), this will entail the use of a variety of consultants who serve as the refineries and repositories of this new knowledge. The best consultants will approach their engagements with the idea of acting as *pro tem* members of the client firm's Board of Directors, where compensation derives from long-term results rather than up-front fees paid irrespective of results.

With these caveats in mind, we outline the basic steps of a firebranding action plan.

Acceleration Ramp for Launching a Firebrand

In workshops that we have conducted for new dot.com and existing companies, we have developed a step-by-step method to guide managers through the process of launching a firebrand. This "acceleration ramp" action plan distills what we've learned in our work with these clients.

For new dot.com start-ups, we can generally think through the firebranding process and develop an operations plan in two or three days of intensive workshop exercises and discussions. This process takes considerably longer for the more complex task of launching a firebrand within an established company with existing markets, distribution channels, customers, internal practices, corporate culture, and IT infrastructure.

Because the dot.com start-up does not carry this sort of baggage, the planning process takes considerably less time. But, start-ups have little or no historical data or feedback from real customers. This forces the start-up firm to rapidly form and test basic business assumptions and offerings, then quickly revise them as necessary to move forward successfully.

We've outlined the general steps that companies must follow, with specific observations for start-ups and existing firms at each point along the way.

1. Read this Book

Have the entire executive team read this book, underlining and otherwise marking it up and discussing it, as a necessary precursor to building consensus and alignment. As each person reads and responds to the book, the CEO should encourage a group process of annotation and discussion that leads to consensus about how to put these principles to work in the organization. Take as your model the reading clubs that have sprung up across the U.S. in recent years. Set up a calendar of discussion group meetings and assign a leader for each session. The leader should prepare notes and questions to guide the discussion, with the intent to create a shared understanding of firebranding principles and how they relate to the company. We highly recommend that the group document each session with notes and diagrams on an easel pad or white board (with notes transcribed). Visit Firebrands.com for other tools to facilitate this sort of discussion.

2. Establish the Branding Authority

A consensus should emerge as to who will stand as the chief branding officer. For dot.com start-ups, and ideally for existing firms, this responsibility will fall to the CEO who "gets it"—that branding directly correlates to the fiduciary responsibility of building shareholder confidence, company valuation, and the trust of customers and trade partners. For existing firms, if the CEO does not take this role, a member of the executive team must emerge, through consensus, as brand tsar.

3. Mandate Execution of a Firebranding Program

For both start-ups and existing firms, the CEO has to say, "Come hell or high water, we must execute a firebranding program," and take personal responsibility for it. The CEO must clearly command that firebranding move forward with the full backing of the executive committee and all other aspects of the firm, even in cases where a brand tsar wields the branding authority.

Make It a Game Worth Playing

Firebranding succeeds when each individual contributor understands and accepts a role that allows them to participate fully in the process. This means making it a game with clearly defined goals, ways of measuring progress against those goals, positive and negative consequences, and guidelines for what to do when things go wrong, or right. Jack Carse, in his book *Infinite Games* (Free Press, 1986), and many other management consultants advocate this approach. Firebranding requires the passionate engagement of the whole branding team.

4. Conduct a Brand Audit

Here, established firms use their advantage of having existing customers and the knowledge of years, or decades, of experience competing in markets. For the dot.com start-up the brand audit combines elements of hypothesizing and simulation, derived from the collective knowledge of its founders and trade partners, augmented by ongoing, quick-cycle research (focus groups, interactive surveys, e-mail discussion groups, etc.) of the customers and markets they wish to target.

Define the Company

Here, the branding team seeks to align its own personal motivations with the firebranding goals, to understand how the company finds and serves customers, and to identify emerging opportunities and competitive challenges.

Establish the Company/Brand Ego

Psychologists and relationship counselors generally agree that in order for an individual to have successful relationships she must have a well-developed and healthy ego—a sense of self, right and wrong, direction in life, and the ability to listen, understand, and cooperate with others. Companies must have the same. In our workshops, we ask each member of the branding team and executive committee to share the personal motivations, passions, and goals that they see expressed through their role in the firm's business activities and serving the firm's customers.

The company/brand ego emerges as the branding team listens to these declarations and as the branding authority weaves these passions and motivations into a whole: think of it as a chorus of voices that blend into a rich chord. Consider using group techniques that might include producing a group painting, or an artist's rendition of the way that each individual member's vision merges into a whole.

In all cases, the branding authority must harness the psychic energies of the branding team. Lacking this, specific firebranding plans and projects will fall flat because they fail to express the individual and collective passions of the branding team.

Explain and Diagram the Business Design

The CEO of a firm has many responsibilities. Perhaps the most important entails explaining the business design to customers, investors, trade partners, and employees. Use well-drawn charts and illustrations to depict the structure of the industry, the company's position in it, the kinds of customers it serves, how the firm's products or services tangibly enhance the customer, how the firm finds and serves these customers, how many more customers exist in the market, and how the firm plans to win their loyalty. The CEO must call attention to emerging categories and competitive threats.

EMERGING CATEGORIES

Identify any new categories of potential satisfaction that have begun to emerge in your customer's brandspace, reflecting the fruitful application of new technologies, law, government policy, social innovation, or new knowledge. This will require a healthy diet of external research efforts, analyst reports, consultant briefings, and extensive customer interaction to understand how they see the market and its new developments.

COMPETITIVE THREATS

Identify new or slightly improved business designs (whether used by a competitor or not) that pose the greatest challenge to your business design, emphasizing new satisfactions or new value-capture mechanisms. Adrian J. Slywotzky and David J. Morrison, in their book *Profit Patterns* (Times Books, 1999), provide a tool kit for thinking through how a business design can withstand competitive challenges.

Define the Customer

Here, the branding team creates a rich profile of the customer and what it means to the customer to have a relationship with the company and its brands.

Principle Satisfaction

Identify the principle satisfaction that customers buy when they buy into your category and buy your brand. Define this satisfaction in the customer's own language, using their key words and phrases as well as the mental maps by which customers organize their brand-space. This requires research.

Demographic Customer Success Profile

Delineate the demographic or economic (empirically based) factors that characterize your most successful, profitable, and strategic customer groups. Research should produce hard data profiles of your best and most profitable customers as well as those customers in the most important area, your share-determining market sector.

Share-Determining Market Sector

Identify the single group of customers that will account for tomorrow's market share in your brand's market category. The firm must target this group as a top priority. Use research to quantify how many of these customers exist, where they come from, and what research metrics most accurately track this all-important segment. These metrics should guide continuous, ongoing firebranding programs to create relationships with these customers as they move into the market.

Loyalty Lock-In

Use research to characterize the necessarily delicate balance of loyalty rewards and switching costs for customers of your brand. Conjoint analysis and trade-off studies will help you understand the sensitivities of how much and what kind of lock-in customers will accept in exchange for what kinds of products and services.

Flesh out the Firebrand Platform

A brand audit must assess the company's ability to execute a firebranding program. Examine in detail the necessary corporate IT infrastructure and partnerships.

Platform Architecture

Using the Firebrand Platform (Figure 4-2 in Chapter 4) as a basic template, your plan must spell out the particular eService functions that will add the most value to your targeted customer as well as a deployment timetable that sequences when to integrate important but secondary eServices. The audit should yield a laundry list of "cool new functions" that the firebranding team might add to its platform. Use research to track the deployment of similar features in "bellwether brands," 100 cool sites suggested by your firebranding team as models to study and understand.

IT and eService Road Map

Using the n-tier computing model (Figure 5-26, Chapter 5) and the Seven Best Practices of Firebranding road map (Chapter 5) as a template, devise an integration plan for current and planned IT infrastructure necessary to support internal business practices and the eServices that you will offer to customers. This will require extensive consultation with the firm's chief information officer and will likely require the engagement of several consulting firms with specialized expertise in the various aspects of this large and complex arena.

eMediaspace Partners

With whom must you form partnerships to build your Firebrand Platform and deploy your firebrand in eMediaspace? Identify potential partners within your supply and distribution value chains, marketing affiliates, special interest and trade magazines, communities of practice and concern, industry associations, and other relevant organizations or individuals. Consider redefining traditional supplier relationships into longer term, more closely co-destined partnerships where the business process of the two parties becomes more integrated and interactive.

Sketch the Brand Story

Your brand audit should define what kinds of stories you have told as well as what kinds of stories customers want to hear. This portion of the brand audit will reveal hilarious ("I have to laugh because otherwise I'll cry") missteps, mistakes, and blunders as well as successes and opportunities that you have missed, failed to exploit, or, happily, been able to maximize.

Brand Positioning

Work hard to identify the single idea that satisfied customers most often associate with the buying and using experience of your brand. In the case of a start-up, use a full complement of research techniques to understand the positioning hierarchy of the targeted market category, distinguishing the most desirable positionings still unclaimed. The law of firebranding dictates that a brand will have one and only one *pivotal satisfaction*. The branding team must set out on a heroic quest to find that one pivotal satisfaction; they will find it on the tips of customers' tongues. Its simplicity may make it difficult to recognize.

Execution

A brand audit must assess how consistently each element of the branding process uses each element of the marketing and customer communications program. Research must provide customers validation of each significant element of the intended brand positioning.

Strategic Positioning

Identify the market category, either existing and known today, or to be newly invented by you, in which the branding team can assert with authority and credibility that the firm has the number one position. This will require the collaboration of three groups: the branding team, its creative partners (advertising agency or brand consultancy), and market research.

Outline the Team's Processes and Programs for the Firebrand Launch

The brand audit should validate the processes and practices that the branding team will use to launch its firebrand.

Create a Firebranding Operations Plan

Seasoned business managers will recognize this as the basic blueprint they must have in place for launching any major initiative. It spells out in terms of a timeline and expenditures, the tasks, costs, milestones, and resources needed to execute the firebranding strategy. It states a set of operating assumptions (such as how long and how much it will cost to find a new customer for a product or service) as well as how to react to an assumption that proves incorrect. This operations plan also analyzes

272 Firebrands: Building Brand Loyalty in the Internet Age

anticipated benefits and quantifies a return on investment. To the generic operations plan template we add the following elements.

T.I.G.E.R. Units by Key Area

The plan spells out the mission and charter for each T.I.G.E.R. unit, specifying concrete goals, timelines, and management expectations for success.

Brandwidth Benchmarks of Branding Cycletime

Senior executives must benchmark how quickly the firm commercializes R&D. Other benchmarks include: How quickly does the firm typically bring a relevant offering to market? Achieve a preemptive positioning in its market? Create a community of practice around the offering? These benchmarks quantify the time and resources consumed in the value-creation and brand storytelling processes—important data when negotiating mergers and acquisitions and other strategic alliances. Management can also use historical benchmark data to motivate teams responsible for new firebranding initiatives.

5. Convene a Firebranding Summit

For dot.com start-ups, the brand audit or workshop serves as the summit. All the key players sit in the same room and reach consensus about the plan that will move the company forward.

For established companies, the summit entails a two-day, off-site meeting that includes top- and mid-level executives from all areas of the firm, as well as representatives from key eMediaspace partner organizations. The summit represents corporate culture-building theater at its best, calling attention through symbol and ritual, and telegraphing to all attendees the vital importance of branding and the new firebranding strategy.

Restate Corporate Mission

Your firm will need to re-think its corporate mission to account for the principles of firebranding (interactions with customers and stakeholders in trusted relationships with the firm and its brand), framing an intent to serve customers beyond mere gratification of a need. The mission must articulate a higher moral purpose to which the firm and its customers aspire—the fruits of a successful, long-term, interactive relationship, how society benefits as a function of this relationship. While cynicism and irony can undermine this altruistic statement, companies that lack a higher calling will compete at a disadvantage in markets now controlled by communities of practice and concern (customers interacting with other customers).

Inaugurate the Firebranding Strategy

The CEO or brand tsar must emphasize that firebranding will not fade as yet another management fad *du jour*. Instead, firebranding can, must, and will become a core practice of the firm. At the summit, senior executives must work hard to assimilate the firebranding action framework into the corporate culture.

Present the Firebranding Operations Plan

The chief executive officer (or brand tsar) spells out the firm's firebranding operations plan. Each key executive then presents a tactical plan for implementing his or her part of the whole integrated program.

Assign Tasks for Quarterly Brand Management Reviews

Using the Firebrand Planning Process (Figure 5-4, Chapter 5), the CEO or brand tsar details a systematic plan for conducting brand audits and analysis of the branding process on a quarterly basis. We cannot overstate the importance of task-based training programs for front-line brand managers, emphasizing shared application software templates and tools.

Go-To Brands

In our ongoing research, we maintain a growing list of vendors and service providers who can help you build your firebrand. You'll find this directory at Firebrands.com. In the spirit of community of practice for firebranding, we encourage you to help us help you by e-mailing to us the name and contact information for vendors that you use or plan to use in the following categories.

Categories of Service and Technology Providers

The following categories serve as a preliminary list that we will continue to expand and subdivide as we learn more about technologies for firebranding.

Strategic Brand Consultancies

These firms provide strategic guidance and implementation of global branding architectures.

iCorp IT Infrastructure

These computer, software, and service companies provide the basic IT building blocks for an n-tier client-server computing framework.

eCommerce Platforms

Solutions of this category build on an integrated suite of software applications and other essential building blocks for a comprehensive and usually industry-specific solution for eCommerce.

Deep Gravity Well Supersite Solutions

These computer, software, and service companies provide a broad array of solutions for building and maintaining large, complex Web sites.

eServices

These firms provide tools and hosted applications, such as HR or expense reporting, that enhance knowledge worker productivity within the firm and among customers and other stakeholders.

Digital Asset Management

This category represents a broad range of software applications and outsourced services that help media creator and producers find, retrieve, and route their work products (digital media files), reducing costs and cycletime while improving quality and inter-company collaboration.

Net-Integrated Communications Solutions

These vendors provide products or services that enable a firebrand to harness e-mail and other messaging technologies.

Integrated Projects Management Solutions
These firms provide tools, training, and consultation for building great teams and systems to support collaboration and workflow automation.

Web-Integrated Database Marketing and Sales
These firms provide a wide array of tools, marketing databases, training, and support services.

Globalization Services
These firms provide tools and services for localization, distance learning, and international logistics fulfillment.

Research and Benchmarking Services
These firms provide tools or client programs that gather qualitative and quantitative research data necessary for a brand audit and ongoing measurement of a firebranding program.

Interactive Investor Relations
These firms provide tools and service programs for developing and posting SEC-compliant documents and investor services.

Business of One Tools
This category includes the essential tools and practices that solo contractors and practitioners need to survive and thrive in the Networked Economy.

The Firebranding Library
This contains an annotated reading list of books, magazines, journals, articles, monographs, and Web sites related to firebranding principles and practices, the Networked Economy, information theory and engineering, management, and database marketing.

Firebrands.com
In this book, we have attempted to provide a comprehensive overview of a complex, richly nuanced subject: brands, and how technology and the Networked Economy transform brands into firebrands.

Perhaps no other area in commerce or technology innovates as rapidly as this field. By the time this book has reached you, portions may have become obsolete.

To address this, we have created Firebrands.com as a way of maintaining an evergreen presentation of this and related subjects. In addition, we offer free and paid reports and other resources designed to help you create and implement a successful firebranding strategy.

Space constraints of this book sometimes forced us to treat only briefly a subject or issue which in itself could fill an entire book. For those topics that we believe especially important, we plan to develop a series of monographs that treat in more depth and detail a core idea or prescriptive action plan.

Chapter 8

Futureproofing Your Firebrand

How can executives ensure that their firebranding efforts stay on track, adjusting to the unpredictable discontinuities and disruptions that will certainly punctuate the development of the Networked Economy over the next few years? In this concluding chapter, we introduce the "hype curve" as a way to help filter and parse the essential developments that lie behind business and trade press headlines. We offer concrete but generally applicable advice to guide strategic and tactical decisions and help "futureproof" your firebranding efforts. Finally, we introduce an overarching law of firebrands and put firebrands in the larger context of culture and the new brand eState.

Behind the Hype Curve

Gartner Group, a prominent research firm that tracks information technology developments, uses a model that they call the "hype curve" to explain how companies adopt new technologies and how the business and trade press, ever on the look-out for hot, new, disruptive technologies, will tend to over-hype developments long before they prove their worth and move into the mainstream. The hype curve reminds us of a similar model introduced 20 years ago by Brian Vanderhorst, which explained how underground culture and trends become fads, and through social contagion become accepted and broadly disseminated through popular culture. For more on the subject of social contagion, we highly recommend a recent book, *The Tipping Point* by Malcolm Gladwell (Little, Brown and Company, 2000). In future articles at Firebrands.com, we plan to discuss more fully how this phenomenon helps shape the development of communities of practice or concern in the Networked Economy.

Figure 8-1 illustrates how the availability of a new technology initially triggers trial and error experimentation by *early adopters*. Next, a wave of *progressive adopters* learn about the development through a network of esoteric conferences, technical journals, and word of mouth. They transform the hard-won insights of the early adopters into pragmatic, reliable, broadly supported solutions.

Contagion spreads when a prominent market research firm gives a name to this new phenomenon, trumpeting a new market category and the huge future potential market that lies just ahead. Recent examples include data warehousing, ERP (enterprise resource planning), CRM (customer relationship management), and media asset management. The newly named market category reaches critical mass when forecasts show annual vendor revenues reaching $1 billion within a three-year horizon. Trade and business magazines, smelling blood in the water (source of new advertising revenues), begin to dedicate ever-increasing amounts of editorial coverage to the new category. This triggers the full bandwagon effect.

Vendors leverage the buzzwords and editorial hype, focusing their promotional material to add fuel to the bandwagon. *Bandwagon adopters*, feeling that they must quickly catch up and adopt the next "new, new thing," begin to implement solutions based on the new technology. They discover shortcomings, lacunae, and other problems inherent in an incomplete solution, and thus enter the *trough of disillusionment*.

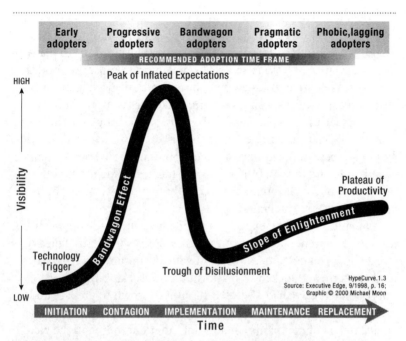

| Early adopters | Progressive adopters | Bandwagon adopters | Pragmatic adopters | Phobic,lagging adopters |

RECOMMENDED ADOPTION TIME FRAME

HIGH

Peak of Inflated Expectations

Visibility

Bandwagon Effect

Plateau of Productivity

Slope of Enlightenment

Technology Trigger

Trough of Disillusionment

LOW

HypeCurve.1.3
Source: Executive Edge, 9/1998, p. 16;
Graphic © 2000 Michael Moon

INITIATION   CONTAGION   IMPLEMENTATION   MAINTENANCE   REPLACEMENT

Time

Figure 8-1 Market research firms and business and trade publications often over-hype a new technology years before it proves its worth

At this point, a general consensus begins to emerge regarding the net positive benefit of implementation and the pain associated with fully-implemented solutions. These real-world, fact-based assessments illuminate the *slope of enlightenment*, attracting *pragmatic adopters* who seek realistic, incremental improvements in productivity and profit gains. By the time solutions based on the new technology reach a *plateau of productivity*, phobic, *lagging adopters* jump on board, just as these soon-to-be obsolete systems begin to face competition from new solutions based on new technologies.

Where does firebranding fall on the hype curve? Many elements of firebranding have moved well along the curve and now travel the slope of enlightenment, including many elements of net-integrated communications, integrated projects management, and Web-integrated database marketing. Still others have only recently hit the *peak of inflated expectations*. These include media asset management, database-driven publishing, and XML. We encourage the reader to visit Firebrands.com for an ongoing update of firebranding technologies and their current position on the hype curve.

The integrated approach to firebranding that we describe in this book remains in the early adopter and progressive adopter phases. Major trade and business press publications will continue to play up the importance of brands and clicks-and-mortar eBusiness models.

When Wall Street finds a way to put more realistic valuations on dot.com companies—using something like the law of firebrands we introduce later in this chapter—full contagion will erupt and the bandwagon will lead the parade. The popular consensus will emphasize building a base of opted-in customers, communities led by C-captains, acquisition and lock-in of platform partners, and the internal transformation of organizations led by tightly-focused T.I.G.E.R. units and eService entrepreneurs.

When this happens, expect major business and trade publications to criticize and berate companies and executives who have failed to create opted-in customers, trust networks, communities of practice and concern, and locked-in platform partners. Happily, readers of this book will have had 12- to 18-months in which to prepare and not only avoid a scolding but also to bask in the limelight of praise, as exemplars of companies that "got it" about branding in the Networked Economy.

Essential Questions to Ask as You Move Forward

To guide firebranding efforts moving forward, executives should ask themselves the following questions.

Among New Customers, What Satisfactions Did They Actually Buy?

This will require continuous, ongoing quantitative and qualitative research and massive inputs from customers, prospects, and trade partners via surveys, e-mail, online discussions, and face-to-face interviews. This will require a special kind of listening skill attuned to the sometimes emotional expressions of social identity hidden in customer comments. Brand managers will have to work hard to discern meaningful shifts in customer desires and expectations, as well as alternate ways of fulfilling the same.

In Which Categories Can We Create an Unassailable Positioning as the Number One Brand?

Al and Laura Ries, in their most recent book, *The 11 Immutable Laws of Internet Branding* (HarperBusiness, 2000), argue that Internet markets naturally gravitate towards a winner-take-all monopoly brand position. Unlike physical markets that need and reward a number two or number three brand, Internet markets punish all except the number one brand. Brand managers must create a new category in which they can, with authenticity and legitimacy, assert a number one brand positioning. They cannot afford the luxury of competing directly with another brand. Bear in mind that a *new* satisfaction often results from a great story told well. A new satisfaction, if sufficiently broad-based, can and will create its own market categories, as well as the opportunity to reposition the firm as the number one vendor in this category.

In the Share-Determining Sectors of Our Key Markets, Have Our Brand's Positioning and Esteem Grown or Diminished?

All brands that continue to thrive do so by remaining relevant to successive generations of customers. As we discussed previously, a share-determining market sector characterizes a small and generally overlooked portion of a larger market. Brand managers must not only identify this sector but also develop a special set of diagnostic tools and models to understand this segment better than any other. Dedicate a T.I.G.E.R. unit to this task, with a special focus on activities of brash new competitors and how they use new business models to bring new satisfactions to customers in this sector, as well as how they capture value in new or ingenious ways.

What Classic, Romantic, or Epic Story Gathers and Binds Customers and Stakeholders to a Trusted Relationship with Our Brand?

In the Networked Economy, and especially among communities of practice or concern, great storytelling remains paramount to a brand's success. More than ever, businesses need the range of artistic skills and strategies from the world of arts and letters. Track the new artistic trends that emerge from urban inner city subcultures and college campuses. Study the stories that define these communities and the trust networks that bind them. Remember, you sell more than mere products or services; your value-add, when transformed by customers into satisfactions, becomes a lens, a way of seeing, relating, and shaping the world of your customer. Brand stories give meaning and purpose to the purchase and consumption of products and services.

When Encountering a New Technology, Ask How Can This New Technology Enhance or Denigrate Our Brand Storytelling Effort?

Here, you must have T.I.G.E.R. units (small, tightly focused teams) dedicated to tracking and analyzing specific areas of the technology front. They must report regularly on key technology developments, the status of their early adopter implementations, and their fire-branding potential for the firm. Create a prominent public display (i.e., a wall board) of new technologies currently under investigation as well as the status of each with regard to their firebranding potential, and conduct lively intranet discussions about them. Management must work extra hard to prevent the hoarding of intelligence about new technologies, and instead should let it circulate widely within the company to stimulate new ideas.

How Can We Improve Our Branding Metrics to Better Understand Our Brand's Equity and Storytelling Effectiveness?

The three metrics discussed in this book—cycle-time, revenue and profit per database record, and brandwidth—serve as starting points. Your measurement of branding effectiveness must track the relative levels of satisfaction and referral potential of customers and other stakeholders. Management should make development of metrics derived from clickstream and other activity analyses a key priority and subject to review each quarter, as part of the brand management review. Metrics must drive and shape the feedback process. Every brand manager must master the art and science of "listening with data." They must use it to close the loop by measuring storytelling effectiveness and by quantifying variables related to brand use and satisfaction.

How Do We More Fully Incorporate Trusted Stakeholders into Our Increasingly Real-Time Value-Creation (Business) Process?

The answer to this question relies on two aspects of your eBusiness model: the agility and robustness of your IT infrastructure and the creativity of business development executives as expressed in a deal structure for trade and platform partners. We emphasize again the importance of object middleware as the essential "glue" and integration framework for an IT infrastructure. Without it, a company in the Networked Economy will encounter disastrous delays and SNAFUs while trying to integrate new technologies, eServices, and new stakeholders (especially platform partners). Many businesses will fail because they make the wrong choice in middleware.

Each deal structure must provide a framework for an ongoing, self-correcting, fair exchange of value among partners. Remember, most deals fall apart for two reasons. One, they do not work tactically from the bottom up. Two, their rigidity makes them incapable of adapting to change in business conditions. Make sure that frontline sales or field staff understand how these deals produce results. Working their input into the deal structure can help ensure that it will accommodate change, and garner their active support.

For a Specific Customer Set, Do We Have the Right Business Design, and How Do We Know We Do?

Management must develop a visual mapping language or "algebra" for depicting a variety of business models—who's the customer, what satisfactions do they buy, how is the marketplace organized, how does our business process link to the market and customers? The answers to these questions will change. Management must convene regularly scheduled meetings dedicated to understanding recent changes and to visualizing various future scenarios—new technologies, new competitors, new customer requirements—and how the firm might adapt in each new scenario. This iterative scenario-design process will yield a collection of trademaps and fluency in ways to quickly model, perceive, and respond to discontinuities and new opportunities.

The First Law of Firebrands

Economists now generally agree on the value of networks as expressed in Metcalfe's Law: The value of a network squares with each doubling of the number of its users—what they also call *network effects*. They cite fax machines, telephones, PCs connected to networks, etc., as examples of how doubling the number of users significantly increases the overall value of a network.

We apply this principle to firebrands, stating it formally as the first law of firebrands: The **economic value** of a brand in the Networked Economy squares with each doubling of the number of *opted-in customers and other stakeholders* (where opted-in connotes a trusted sharing of personal and confidential information) and cubes with each doubling of the number of *C-captains* who lead a community of practice or concern associated with the brand, *platform partners* who run their businesses or practices as an extension of the brand's eBusiness platform, and internal *eService entrepreneurs* who bring a new eService satisfaction to the brand's customers or key stakeholders. In each case they create or amplify a satisfaction associated with the brand.

This means that a firm pursuing a firebranding strategy must form the single-minded intent of creating opted-in customers and supporting C-captions, platform partners, and eService entrepreneurs. Taken to its logical conclusion, firebranding supplants company activities now grouped under marketing, sales, and service. Intermediaries, whether friendly or adverse to the brand, will play an important and eventually dominant role in the way customers buy a particular product or service and whether or not they choose to opt-in to some form of loyalty mechanism. This alone will force a fundamental reassessment of how a company finds and serves customer, and will call for a completely new set of tools, practices, and business models explicitly designed to build communities and trust networks.

To capture and earn the trust of customers and their communities of practice and concern in the Networked Economy, however, companies must do more than offer great products or services. To understand this final frontier of firebranding, we must not look at brands as tools of commerce. Instead, we must examine brands as a mechanism of culture.

Brands as a Mechanism of Culture

A mechanism of culture defines and passes on, from one generation to the next, a set of behavioral norms, perceptions, and taboos. Family, religion, politics, music, and the rest of the arts all serve this function. The Greek philosopher, Aristotle, defined humans as essentially a social and economic entity, meaning that we express our essential nature in a desire to organize in a variety of social systems and that we have a deep impulse to organize our collective affairs in terms of a rule of law that ensures justice and civil peace. Brands and their use in capitalist, market-based societies also speak to the essential nature of the Aristotelian human being. This carries profound, far-reaching implications, which we have barely touched upon in this book. We look forward to developing this argument in a future book with the working title, *The Brand eState.* Visit www.Firebrands.com for progress reports on this project.

How do brands work as a mechanism of culture? We have examined how many of our popular, beloved brands (Coke, Levi's, etc.) have become currencies of emotion and caring shared among family, friends, colleagues, and strangers. We've also discussed the way each person organizes a constellation of brands in what we call a personal brandspace. While it still shocks and dismays high culture arbiters, most of us relate to the world through the lens of brands and their consumption—look no further than the way we choose our clothes, automobiles, schools, neighborhoods, and other lifestyle attributes.

This notwithstanding, a survey of popular attitudes, and in particular the market behaviors of young adults in North America and other developed countries, clearly reveals a pervasive dissatisfaction with the mere pursuit of material wealth, leisure, and consumption. Perhaps more than any other generation that has preceded it, today's young adults want more, not only from life but from the institutions, including economic institutions, that define life.

This means that brands must do more than merely sell products or services. To stay crisp and relevant, brands of the twenty-first century must win the hearts and loyalties of customers and their trust networks. They must do this in an increasingly media-saturated environment under the gaze of many cynical young adults and teenagers that now constitute the share-determining market sectors for many brands.

Broad corporate initiatives such as diversity, corporate charity and giving, and sponsorship of social causes represent early attempts to bring new psychic and emotional satisfactions to customers and stakeholders. But, customer research shows that companies must pursue these altruistic, enlightened self-interests in a more congruent and authentic manner. These activities must express core values of the firms instead of paying lip service to faddish, politically correct concepts.

Even more important, your C-captains and their communities must not only believe in the brand, but must also advocate these brands as engines of social justice.

We believe that the most profitable firms of the twenty-first century will earn the respect and loyalty of customers and other stakeholders by serving causes higher and more noble than profit as an end in itself. These companies will be able to say, "We make higher levels of profit because we do two things right. We deliver a unique and desired satisfaction, and we do so to serve the higher aims of our customers and the greater common good."

This highlights the second law of firebrands: *the active participation of communities of concern or practice, and the advocacy and evangelism of brands by C-captains and platform partners, must serve a higher common good than merely making profits for the firm.* Customers and other stakeholders increasingly see their purchase and use of a brand as a political act with immediate, worldwide repercussions and judge the impact in partnership with a global network of trusted peers, associates, and other arbiters.

The New Brand eState

In the first chapter of this book, we introduced the notion of the brand eState, a new social class of activist customers and stakeholders who use their buying power to reward companies that deliver satisfactions (products or services easily transformed by customers into solutions) that meet or exceed customer requirements and expectations for quality and value. The experience of satisfaction reflects both the utilitarian aspect of a product or service and the entertainment or storytelling experience that shapes and frames the buying and using experience. Increasingly, this story will include, whether companies intend it or not, the brand producer firm's behavior as a corporate citizen of the world, as well as its demonstrated willingness to listen to customers and respond in thoughtful, if not inspirational (outside the box) ways.

Brands ignite to become firebrands when they harness the activism of communities of practice or concern as well as the self-service satisfactions that derive from eSupply. Rather than resisting this activism, we recommend that brand managers encourage it. This will require heavy investments in technical infrastructure and practices that we've outlined as the seven best practices of firebranding.

Rote replication of these practices will not ensure success, however. You must have the right business design and execute it quickly. More importantly, you must create partnerships with customers and other stakeholders based on trust, reciprocity, and an ongoing, self-correcting exchange of value. While this sounds great and may strike the reader as self-evident, we know that this will require a wholesale transformation of the enterprise, its core processes, and its culture.

To the casual observer, the successful firebranding team may closely resemble the great marketing and brand management teams of the twentieth century, but the experienced eye will see something radically different.

The successful firebranding team of the twenty-first century will create value, bring relevant offerings to market, serve and satisfy customers, and ultimately earn a profit for fundamentally different reasons. They will do the right thing because it's the right thing to do, not because it will bring higher profits or increased market share. Activist communities of practice and concern will sniff out the inauthentic rats and poseurs and swiftly punish them, not only in the marketplace of ideas, but also in the marketplace for products and services. We cannot overstate the power, intelligence, and near-omniscience of the global communities of practice and concern that will define your brand in the twenty-first century. Alas, most brand managers (with the possible exceptions of the readers of this book) will find themselves blindsided by roaring dissent, outrage, and criticism for not "getting it," just as the World Trade Organization did in Seattle in 1999.

In practical terms this means that brand managers must themselves undergo a near-spiritual transformation: they must trust that customers will see true and authentic value in their offerings and willingly engage in a fair exchange of value. This means that brand managers must willingly and knowingly surrender the tools of coercion, manipulation, and deception. They must trust, often in situations where no evidence or history supports that trust. This in no way abrogates the need to earn a profit, rather it argues for a different strategy for earning a profit. Customers will gladly grant a producer profit if they see the profit as the fruit of a fair exchange, and will do so in the larger context of supporting a company that serves the higher and more noble aims of society. Aristotle and the early Christians must take great pleasure in seeing their core ideas thus expressed as a foundational economic principle that, soon, no company or individual can afford to transgress.

Glossary

AFFINITY ALIGNMENT

Describes the two dimensions by which individuals assess a variety of different kinds of relationships.

AFFINITY ALIGNMENT MODEL

A conceptual roadmap that describes how a vendor will partner or compete with the various types of intermediaries in eMediaspace—business entities and individuals who influence customer purchases and loyalty.

BADGES OF BELONGING

Brands that signify membership in a peer group, social class, or kenship.

BANDWAGON ADOPTERS

Mainstream customers who adopt solutions in the heat of market hype, generally following in the footsteps of progressive adopters.

BETA TEST PILOTS ASSOCIATION

A trademark of Michael Moon, describing a market research panel composed of individuals who agree to test, review, and critique products, services, and brand resources.

BLEEDING EDGE PIONEERS

Experimenters and early adopters of new technology who often tolerate incomplete technical solutions while pursuing competitive advantage.

BRAND BUREAUCRACY

Devolution of the branding authority to a near-clerical task of applying slogans to mature products and services.

BRAND ESTATE

The community of 12 stakeholder groups with whom a brand-producing firm relates; the "e" emphasizes the particular importance of opted-in customers, community captains, platform partners, and eService entrepreneurs in how a firm builds its brands.

BRAND EXPRESSION MODEL

A conceptual roadmap that describes how a firm and its strategic partners (e.g., brand consultancy, ad agency) use its brand storytelling model; the brand story's type and manner of telling.

BRAND MANAGER

The individual who has principal responsibility for the brand-building process of a particular brand, which may include all activities from research and development through post-sales service and training.

BRAND RESOURCE

Any reusable physical or digital product or service that touches the buying and using experience of customers; notably, reusable media and information assets used for branding.

BRAND RESOURCE REPOSITORY

A centralized database of media information and knowledge assets used in the branding process.

BRAND STEWARD

Usually a highly regarded mid-level marketing executive who has influence but no control over the way other marketing managers spend branding dollars. This generally results in branding by committee, a recipe for muddled, fuzzy positioning, impotent branding, and loss of market share.

BRAND STORYTELLING

The process of sellers communicating with customers over a satisfaction lifecycle, moving customers through five stages: awareness, involvement, trial, commitment, and referral.

BRAND STORYTELLING MODEL

A conceptual roadmap that describes how a firm builds its strategic position, and how it specifically "deputizes" C-captains, platform entrepreneurs, and eService entrepreneurs to propagate the brand throughout the market.

BRAND TSAR

In companies where the CEO does not exercise branding authority, the brand tsar is the one executive chosen to assert enterprise-wide control of the branding process.

BRANDING AUDIT PROCESS

Quarterly activity of a brand management team that entails fact-based assessments of the current state of the brand, key customer segments, and competitors and their brands.

BRANDING AUTHORITY

The person or group charged with the responsibility for managing the branding process.

BRANDING FRANCHISE

The concerted work of three or more successful brand identities. McDonald's, Disney, and Microsoft have all established branding franchises.

BRANDING INTENT MODEL

A conceptual roadmap that describes how a vendor extends its internal corporate culture to external, customer-focused branding activities.

BRANDING THEATER

The ultimate evolution of brand expression; coordinates a cast of skillful actors with a great script, to the shocking delight of customers.

BRANDSPACE

The physical or electronic area through which brand messages flow from seller to buyer, and through which feedback about the buying and using experience flows from buyer back to seller.

BRANDSPACE MODEL

A conceptual roadmap that describes how a brand successfully positions itself or its offering in the minds and hearts of customers; strategies and tactics for repositioning competitors.

BRANDSTANDING WEB SITE

A Web site dedicated to promoting solo practitioners, contractors, and consultants.

BRANDWIDTH

A type of cycletime metric that measures how quickly the brand message becomes adopted by target market customers and other stakeholders; the capacity to create a brand.

BRICKS-AND-MORTAR FIRM

Traditional businesses with physical plants and points of market presence, such as a retail outlet, printed catalog, or salesperson in a client's office.

BROADBAND NETWORK

A next-generation high speed network service that will deliver rich media brand storytelling to customers and other stakeholders.

BUSINESS DESIGN

A conceptual roadmap that a vendor uses to describe its primary customers, the satisfaction that they purchase, the nature and conditions of a marketspace, how the vendor transforms its resources into products or services, and how customers transform those products or services into satisfactions.

BUSINESS MODEL

A conceptual roadmap and a more focused tactical subset of the firm's business design; how the firm captures value in the form of revenue, profit, discretionary funds of a customer, and market capitalization; how a firm drives its brand into a commanding, unassailable position in the market.

C-CAPTAIN

Short for community-captain; an individual who pulls together and leads an online community of practice or concern; the person that moderates online discussion groups and enforces consensually agreed rules and etiquette.

CIRCLE OF 12

A model describing the major stakeholder groups of a brand-producing firm.

CLICKS-AND-MORTAR EBUSINESS MODELS

Hybrid of traditional and online businesses, with strong online and flesh world points of market presence.

COMMUNITIES OF PRACTICE AND/OR CONCERN

A group of people dedicated to advancing a set of practices or who share a common concern; they often coalesce around a brand, led by a C-captain.

COMMUNITY STICKY NOTES

Graffiti-like comments appended to a brand Web site, using specialized software.

CONTAGION

Term used to describe how fads and trends quickly spread, creating a social phenomenon.

CORPORATE LIFECYCLE

The stages of growth, development, and maturation of a corporation, characterized by the distribution of authority and responsibility for branding.

CRISP MESSAGE

The message that succinctly communicates to a target customer a brand's satisfactions; based on a hard data success model that describes the target customers.

CULTURAL ICONS

As a mechanism of culture, the cultural icon transmits a set of values, perceptions, and behaviors to current and future generations; brands that transcend mere commercial activity.

CURRENCY OF AFFECTION

Branded product or service used to express affection, caring, and status among family, friends, or colleagues.

CYCLETIME

The amount of time required to complete a business process, successfully deliver an eService to the satisfaction of a customer or other stakeholder, or time elapsed before customers adopt the brand story that anchors and explains the buying and using experience of a product or service.

DEEP GRAVITY WELL SUPERSITE

Metaphor to describe a strategy for a branded Web site, emphasizing a series of progressively intimate interactions between the brand-producer, customers, and other stakeholders.

DEMAND CREATION

Second stage of the value creation process, including the activities of building awareness, trial, and preference for a brand, usually among first-time buyers.

DEMOGRAPHIC SUCCESS MODEL

A data set derived from customer and market analysis that highlights the overlap of three customer sectors: most satisfied, most profitable, and most strategic (those most responsible for future market share).

DIGITAL ASSET MANAGEMENT

A set of practices for managing the creation and reuse of electronic files used in the value creation or brand storytelling process.

DOMINANT MECHANISM

Part of the value capture aspect of a business design; represents the way the business gets paid and how buyers perceive all currencies of exchange as fair and equitable.

eMEDIASPACE

The convergence of markets, media, and points of market presence framed by the online world (a.k.a. cyberspace), where brand storytelling and transactions occur simultaneously.

ENTITY RELATIONSHIP DIAGRAM (ERD)

A technical specification and road map that describes what types of data the firm must collect, and how to join relational database tables (two or more types of data) to create high level business intelligence.

EPIPHANY IN A SATISFACTION LIFECYCLE

Pivotal moment of truth in a stakeholder's progress through each of five stages in the satisfaction lifecycle.

ePOP

Electronic point of purchase, including signage, merchandising, and presentations electronically displayed in a retail location.

eSERVICE ROAD MAP

A plan specifying progressive deployment of eServices over time by a brand producer; usually reflects the testing and validation of a specific customer or stakeholder group.

eSUPPLY

A combination of digital assets and eServices that fulfill self-service customer satisfactions 24/7.

FIREBRAND

A brand that has ignited in the hearts and minds of customers through their interactions with the brand-producing firm and other customers.

FIREBRAND HEAT

Multimedia assets added to the brand storytelling process sparking closer customer involvement.

FIREBRAND MODEL

A conceptual roadmap that describes how a firm builds trusted relationships with customers and other stakeholders; strategies and tactics for successfully deploying eServices.

"GET IT" SOLUTION SHOWCASES

Regularly scheduled showcase of promising new technical applications or solutions, hosted by a brand-producing firm for its employees and supply chain partners.

GO-TO BRANDS

Products or services preferred by customers; their first choices.

ICORP

Interactive corporation; an organization that has effective interactive relationships with customers, investors, trade partners and staff; an organization that delivers online interactive services based on an n-tier computing infrastructure.

INTEGRATED PROJECTS MANAGEMENT

Firebranding Best Practice #3, characterizing an advanced form of project management where each individual contributor has a total, inclusive view of the entire project and all its elements, usually accessed through a Web browser.

INTERACTIVE BID PROCUREMENT

An eService that allows a purchasing or procurement manager to quickly source solutions or providers from a global supply network.

INTERMEDIARIES

Individuals or groups that influence the buyer-seller relationship, usually aligning with the interests of the buyer.

KNOWLEDGE REFINERY

A specialized Web site optimized to enhance the productivity of knowledge workers, usually front-line professional service providers, field sales staff, or self-service clients; a Web site optimized for delivering answers to the essential questions of knowledge workers and brand eService users.

KNOWLEDGE WORKER

First coined by management guru Peter Drucker, describes workers whose primary work product consists of information, generally answers to questions of other knowledge workers or customers.

LOCKED-IN PLATFORM PARTNERS

Third- or fourth-parties who have set up permanent operations on a brand producer's Web site, thus becoming "locked-in" to that platform.

LOYALTY LOCK-IN

A structure in which brand users trade higher levels of personal services for higher switching costs.

MARKET CATEGORY MODEL

A market or portion of a market that a vendor has targeted to dominate.

MARKETSPACE

Describes a wired marketplace where online and interactive communications influence buyer and seller activities.

MIDDLEWARE PLATFORM

An integrated suite of software applications that enable rapid integration of new capabilities to the basic computing infrastructure of the brand-producing firm; the software "glue" for applications not originally designed for n-tier computing.

MONOGRAPH

An essay, of any length, devoted to one topic.

NAMING CONVENTION

Strategy by which a brand manager develops and assigns names to a product or service, all its ingredients, or the company itself, with the aim of associating the company and its offering(s) with the principle satisfaction that each brand characterizes.

NETWORKED ECONOMY

The fifth era of economic history characterized by the central role of trust networks and how they now organize work and productivity.

N-TIER APPLICATIONS

Current state-of-the-art architecture for enterprise computing that has been optimized for the Internet, permitting applications and systems to interoperate throughout a supply chain, and enabling customers and other stakeholders to interact with core business processes of the brand-producing firm.

OFFER-MARKET DEVELOPMENT

The first stage of the value creation process, describing how a company begins to commercialize its core competencies and intellectual property.

OPTED-IN CUSTOMER

A customer who agrees in advance to receive messages and other forms of brand communication; often enrolls through a subscription-like service offered by the brand producer.

ORPHAN BRANDS

Products or services about which the consumer has heard but with which the consumer has no direct experience; a brand a customer might use, if motivated by curiosity.

"OUT-THERE" BRANDS

Products or services that the consumer has tried but does not feel inspired to try again.

PRE-EMPTIVE POSITIONING

Exit point of the offer-market development stage of the value creation process; occurs when a brand manager brings a new satisfaction to market and it reshuffles the hierarchy of desired or expected satisfactions within the customer's brandspace.

PREFERENDA

The types of information, experience, and interactions that individuals might prefer out of the choices available to them.

PREFERENDA MODEL

A conceptual roadmap that describes how a vendor will fulfill customer preferences for pacing and structure of information consumption; for stories of a classic, romantic, or epic motif with a romantic, tragic, comedic, or satirical plot; and for self-service facilities.

PROGRESSIVE ADOPTERS

A customer who follows in the footsteps of early adopters; also known as a fast follower, rarely innovative but quickly emulates the innovators in a field.

PSYCHOGRAPHIC DATA

A type of survey data that tracks opinion, awareness, and beliefs of a research subject; generally correlates to the process of rationalizing the impulse to buy.

REAL-TIME RESOURCE ALLOCATION

An advanced application of integrated projects management that enables a company to marshal its personnel and resources immediately following a customer request or purchase.

RIOT

Returned investment of time.

ROI

Return on investment.

SALES CONVERSION

Third stage of the value creation process, when customers actually buy a branded product or service.

SATISFACTION

What customers buy; generally, a combination of a desire and expectation, as fulfilled through a branded product or service.

SATISFACTION FULFILLMENT

Fourth stage of the value creation process, when buyers and sellers collaborate to realize the full value of the branded product or service.

SATISFACTION LIFECYCLE

A five-stage process that describes the buying, using, and disposing experience of customers, highlighting the essential questions that sellers must help buyers answer along the way; the five stages, from buyer/seller perspectives, include lost in the fog/market creation; decision-making/sales cycle; learning curve/post-sales support; optimization/account management; evangelism/strategic partnering.

SATISFACTION THEATER

Integrated retail, combining the best of traditional retail merchandising and online eTailing.

SCREENAGERS

Term coined in 1994 by Dave Pola in *Morph's Outpost on the Digital Frontier* to describe teenagers with hundreds or thousands of hours of video game and computer experience; individuals who relate to interactive technology as an extension of their social identity.

SHARE DETERMINING MARKET SECTOR

The small, generally overlooked portion of a larger market that nonetheless determines a brand's future share of market; the next generation of customers.

SHARED WHITEBOARD

A specialized software application, accessed through a Web browser or other client, that enables two or more individuals to discuss and illustrate a project.

SMART MEDIA FACTORY

A group of workers and processes that create and use smart media assets (digital media files explicitly designed for systematic reuse and re-expression across multiple media).

SONIFICATION

The act of adding sound to the online user experience, adding a sensual or emotional dimension to the featured brand.

SOURCING

A type of customer behavior. Customers in the *sourcing* mode seek long-term supply contracts; a steady flow of consistently high-quality products and services from a handful of providers.

STAKEHOLDERS

Individuals, groups, and companies that have an emotional or economic stake in the health, well-being, and success of a brand and the brand-producing firm.

STORYDWELLING

A particular kind of Web site optimized for entertainment purposes, combining the best features of interactive multimedia CD-ROMs and multi-user games with traditional elements of broadcast and live performance entertainment.

STRATEGIC ATTRACTORS

Elements that the deep gravity well supersite uses to induce a stakeholder to form progressively more intimate, trusted relationships and to reward their contributions. They include a fun user-interface, personalized information, results on demand, community and kenship, and take on a special form at each layer.

STRATEGIC DATA MODEL

The overall specification of data to collect (a family of ERDs) and their instantiation in a particular software application; the master plan for integrating uniform sets of data from multiple production data systems or databases.

STRATEGIC POSITIONING MODEL

A conceptual map describing how a vendor will associate one benefit with one brand and drive this association to one customer segment, dominating one medium or branding channel.

SWITCHABLE BRANDS

Products or services which customers have some familiarity with but feel no allegiance to; alternate or substitute choices when a consumer can't find the go-to brand.

SWITCHABLE CUSTOMERS

Customers who have not formed an emotional allegiance or loyalty to one particular brand in a category.

SWITCHING COSTS

Physical or perceived costs associated with changing from one digital brand to another.

TATTOO

A brand that becomes a stinging, indelible reminder of the dissatisfaction buyers now associate with it.

T.I.G.E.R. UNITS

Acronym for Teams Integrated Getting Excellent Results; a small, self-managing group of people with complementary skills, optimized for a particular result.

TRAINING MODEL

A conceptual roadmap that describes how a firm hires individuals particularly well suited for its internal corporate culture; how a firm trains, motivates, and rewards its workers for producing both explicit and implicit results.

TRUST NETWORKS

Central organizing principle for the Networked Economy, describing social groups that share personal information and advice.

TRUSTED INTERACTIONS

Describes a customer's sharing of personal or confidential information with a seller, with the expectation that the seller will only use it to better serve and satisfy the customer.

UNIFORM ISSUE-PROBLEM CHARACTERIZATION

A database application and user input form that enables an individual to quickly describe, using shared terminology and parameters, the precise nature of a problem or issue such that another knowledge worker can re-create it.

UNIT OF WORK

The primary output of a knowledge worker, usually an answer to another knowledge worker's question, formatted and presented in a specific way.

VALUE CAPTURE

The particular mechanisms and overall strategy used by a brand-producing firm to structure the transaction between buyer and seller.

VALUE CHAIN

A collection of business entities, each of whom contributes a product or service that makes up a finished good (or service) purchased and used by an end-use customer.

VALUE CREATION

A five-stage process that spans *offer-market development, demand creation, sales conversion, solution fulfillment,* and *strategic development.* Value creation thus integrates product development, marketing, sales, service, and training.

VALUE CREATION MODEL
A conceptual roadmap that describes how a firm sources and transforms raw materials, labor, knowledge, and capital into products or services that customers buy and subsequently transform into desired or expected satisfactions.

VALUE-FULFILLMENT MODEL
The element of the business design that describes how the customer transforms an offering into a satisfaction—either an economic or lifestyle return on investment in the brand.

VOCABULARY ATTRIBUTES DATABASE
An expanding database of vocabulary and attributes that define the brand and everything associated with the brand.

WEBINAR AMPHITHEATER
A suite of applications that enables real-time, online delivery of seminars and other special events, using streaming media and a specialized user interface.

WORKFLOW MODELING LANGUAGE
Equivalent to a programming language, a workflow modeling language allows a business-process architect and a team of workflow engineers to quickly create a system that maps to existing organizational structures.

WOW
A crisp, engaging story or pitch that frames the selling proposition as, at least in part, an entertainment experience. For instance, the sheer delight a prospect feels on imagining a VW Beetle parked in her driveway. The unexpected pleasure of design, the anticipated compliments of friends and passers-by: it all adds up to "Wow!"

XML
Emerging technical standard that specifies how two or more systems can share data through the Web or specialized middleware applications.

ZERO GRAVITY
Effect produced on a business process fueled by eSupply.

Index

References to figures are in italics.